Death by Domestic Violence

Death by Domestic Violence

Preventing the Murders and Murder-Suicides

Katherine van Wormer and Albert R. Roberts

Social and Psychological Issues: Challenges and Solutions
Albert R. Roberts, Series Editor

Westport, Connecticut
London

Library of Congress Cataloging-in-Publication Data

van Wormer, Katherine S.
   Death by domestic violence : preventing the murders and murder-suicides /
   Katherine van Wormer and Albert R. Roberts.
      p. cm. — (Social and psychological issues : challenges and solutions,
   ISSN 1941-7985)
   Includes bibliographical references and index.
   ISBN 978-0-313-35489-2 (alk. paper)
   1. Family violence—Prevention. 2. Homicide. I. Roberts, Albert R. II. Title.
   HV6626.V36 2009
   364.4'0457—dc22   2008033665

British Library Cataloguing in Publication Data is available.

Library of Congress Catalog Card Number: 2008033665
ISBN: 978-0-313-35489-2
ISSN: 1941-7985

First published in 2009

Praeger Publishers, 88 Post Road West, Westport, CT 06881
An imprint of Greenwood Publishing Group, Inc.
www.praeger.com

Printed in the United States of America

The paper used in this book complies with the
Permanent Paper Standard issued by the National
Information Standards Organization (Z39.48–1984).

10 9 8 7 6 5 4 3 2 1

In loving memory of Albert R. Roberts, my co-author, who died of pancreatic cancer even as the final pages of this book were being written. Al enriched the fields of social work and criminal justice with his voluminous writings and the professional lives of so many through his warm, personal support. If you knew Al, you knew that the telephone was his medium: If you got one of those calls from Al Roberts, you would need to drop everything else to take it all in—so many plans and projects—and you might be on the phone, happily engrossed, all afternoon. Our last conversation was about this book on domestic homicide, about the magnitude of the topic and how this was not to be the usual textbook but something with a wider and different appeal. The conversation was uncharacteristically brief. But who could have known that this project, about which Al was so excited, would have been his last?

—Katherine van Wormer

Contents

Part III: Prevention   149

Preface

In the early 1980s, thanks to grassroots' organizing by the women's movement, domestic violence services and women's shelters began to be established across the United States. As a result, the partner homicide rates have been reduced considerably. Women now have an escape route from the battering, and they are far less likely to choose murder as a way out. Today, in the United States, over 1,000 women and over 300 men are killed annually by such violence. These figures used to be about 1,000 deaths for each gender. So yes, the domestic violence hot lines and women's shelters are saving the lives of men predominantly. This is one of many paradoxes related to the crime of domestic homicide. Others include the following:

- Because of the laws passed to protect the lives of women, many more women than before are being charged with assault and battery.
- Policies passed under the urging of feminist women's advocates who believe in women's agency have taken away women's choice.
- While government statistics based on police data consistently show that men are arrested for more serious acts of violence than women, media reports proclaim the opposite.
- Many battered women who have killed in self-defense are serving long prison terms.
- The moment a chronically battered and threatened woman takes action to escape is the moment of the greatest danger for her.
- In murder-suicide cases, committed almost exclusively by men, the predominant motive is often suicide.
- Having a gun for protection in a household greatly increases the risk of homicide to members of that household.

- Worldwide, these are the best of times for women (in terms of expanded opportunities and freedoms) and the worst of times (due to an insidious anti-feminist backlash).

Death by Domestic Violence: Preventing the Murders and the Murder-Suicides explores the above paradoxes. First we want to focus our attention on the "why." Our journey toward this path will take us into the interdisciplinary realms of psychology, sociology, and even biology. Our next consideration is the "what." This will bring us to look at the legislation and laws designed to protect victims and punish the perpetrators of domestic crime. The third consideration, Part III of this book, is the prevention aspect. How can such killings be prevented?

An investigation of this sort takes on a special urgency in light of threatened slashing of federal and state funding for victim assistance and domestic violence programming. It also takes on a special urgency as we hear in virtually every state of horrible incidents of mass shootings, whole family killings, and murder-suicides.

Because domestic violence and its extreme form, domestic homicide, are major public health problems, not only in the United States but throughout the world, a harm reduction model was chosen as the most appropriate formulation. Like the public health model, harm reduction emphasizes the importance of the collection and dissemination of information, the identification of persons at risk, a preventive rather than curative or after-the-fact approach, and program development. Harm reduction, in short, focuses on the prevention of injury and the saving of lives. It is our belief that murder in the family, like suicide, is highly preventable.

Harm reduction efforts are directed toward the total population perhaps beginning with the public schools, health care providers, and child welfare departments, and extending to victim assistance programs and the criminal justice system. Harm reduction includes primary prevention with a focus on educational campaigns and secondary prevention to target instances of violence at the structural and personal levels. Not only is greater funding needed to provide such programming but also a fearless and no-holds-barred approach, one that takes into account the impact of the anti-feminist rhetoric against women as well as the proliferation of ideological, one-size-fits-all explanations for family violence.

Perhaps in no other field are there more myths and misconceptions generated about a social problem and its eradication as is found in the field of domestic violence. Perhaps, as well, in no other field is the political pressure so strong to conform to a given belief system. Thus we hear, from the radical left, that the culture of the patriarchy is the sole cause of male-on-female domestic violence, and we hear from the media (influenced by a conservative agenda) that women are as violent as men. We hear both that drug and alcohol use is the cause of the violence, and conversely that substance abuse is just an excuse for bad behavior; we learn that women do not leave dangerous situations for practical reasons such as economics, and that women do not leave due to their own psychological state; that men conduct violence because of deep-seated psychological problems and, conversely, that violent men are just seeking power and control; and we are told that programs for batterers should confront men on their abuse of power, and that such programming should focus on the batterers' underlying sense of insecurity. Life is not either/or, however, and in most cases the truth is somewhere in between.

Unique to *Death by Domestic Violence* compared to other books in the field is

- the focus on risk factors for committing domestic homicide,
- the presentation of facts from scholarly literature and the U.S. Department of Justice in readable style for a popular market,
- the inclusion of moving personal narratives of the impact of victimization and how the abuse was overcome,
- an introduction of a harm reduction model for violence prevention and safety,
- discussion of restorative justice strategies for community control,
- introduction of a teen dating abuse assessment measure,
- attention to programming for the families left behind, to global domestic killings, murder-suicide, and the factor of substance abuse,
- attention to integrative treatment of substance abuse agencies and domestic violence services, and
- a presentation of rich, original data on domestic homicide and concerning battered women who were abused over varying periods of time.

Our goal in writing *Death by Domestic Violence* is twofold: to provide a readable resource on a compelling topic and to filter out from the research literature the latest findings on what works and what does not. As committed feminists, our interest in this field is personal and professional and has extended over several decades. Our priority is, first and foremost, on saving lives rather than on the promotion of any fixed political agenda. With this priority in mind, we explore the nature and types of family homicide (the killing of wives, killing of husbands, killing of children, or killing of women) and challenge the myths perpetrated by proponents of one school or the other. Our work, like that of other research in the field, has important implications for reshaping programming and rewriting laws to reduce the violence and save lives. To us, this is more than a goal; it is a mission.

Women and Families at Risk: An Overview

When former Police Sergeant Drew Peterson, aged 54, became the prime suspect in the disappearance of his fourth wife, Stacy Peterson, aged 23, the police began to wonder about the strange circumstances surrounding the death of wife number three who reportedly had drowned in a bathtub (Associated Press 2008a). So they reopened the investigation into her death, exhumed the body, and ruled her death to be a homicide. All this time, the search for the body of Stacy Peterson continued, while the suspect and his lawyer paraded around to the prime time talk shows to proclaim his innocence. Meanwhile, interviews with relatives and close friends of the women who were married to the police sergeant revealed a pattern of chronic physical and psychological abuse, possessiveness, and plans by the women to get a divorce from this man.

This high-profile case is reminiscent of an earlier wife-murder by a man also named Peterson. When Laci Peterson, who was eight months pregnant, suddenly disappeared, the search was highlighted daily in the press for months. When her body washed up on the shore, Scott Peterson was arrested and after a much-publicized trial was sentenced to death. The jury did not believe his alibi that he was fishing at the time (NBC News 2005).

We read of such glamorized cases in the news, watch the interviews with family members on cable TV, and listen to the commentary of legal experts. Missing in the reports is an analysis of the dynamics of domestic violence and domestic homicide, of the motives of the men to commit the crimes, or the suffering of the women trapped in the violence of such a marriage. Missing also in the news reports are attempts to relate what we learn from the highly publicized cases to femicide (the killing of one's wife or partner) in the local community. One exception occurred in the 1990s with the O.J. Simpson trial; the huge media attention gave visibility to the issue of domestic violence and brought the topics of battering, stalking, and partner murder into our national consciousness. The momentum was short-lived, however.

While we as a nation become distressed and obsess over the missing and murdered women we learn about on cable news shows, we often lose sight of more ordinary cases in our local communities. And even when we do attend to these cases, the focus is more on prosecution of the accused murderer than on prevention of such murders from occurring in the first place. Prevention starts with a focus on problems in the family and on unhealthy relationships that are associated with violence.

Death by Domestic Violence: Preventing the Murders and Murder-Suicides is written, as the title implies, as an effort in prevention and harm reduction. Our goal, by providing relevant ideas and information, is to help prevent situations of domestic violence from escalating into death. We are talking here not only of the death of the woman, but also, more rarely, the death of the man, and of the children.

A PUBLIC HEALTH PROBLEM

Intimate partner violence is a major public health problem throughout the world. Regardless of the social class, race, ethnicity, or religion, the dynamics are relatively the same. One partner uses threats and violence to control the other partner; the latter pulls away (or in some countries tries to assert her freedom); and the threats and violence escalate. This is the general male-on-female pattern; women who kill act out of different motives, often relating to the fear of being killed. Such fear can be a motivating factor in a woman's decision to kill her abuser. In either situation, whole families are terrorized by the violence.

In the United States and globally, a woman is more vulnerable to violence in her home than on the streets. In the United Kingdom, domestic violence costs the lives of more than two women every week (Home Office 2005), and in the United States, with a much larger population, estimates are that more than three women a day are killed by their intimate partners (Rennison 2003). In other countries where women have fewer rights, or no rights at all, the beatings and murders of wives and daughters are commonplace (see Chapter 7, "Domestic Homicide Worldwide").

Today, across the states, the within-family violence continues as it has throughout history, sometimes taking the form of murder, murder-suicide, and increasingly, shockingly, whole family murder. When such tragedy strikes close to home, our world is turned upside down. Our reaction is often summed up in two words—"If only." If only we had known. If only he could have gotten help or she could have managed to get away. If only we had done something. And therein lies the rub: The real tragedy is that such senseless killings could have been prevented.

Death by Domestic Violence explores the causes and consequences of such senseless killings. It is the seemingly senselessness of such acts that brings us to ponder the following questions: What are the profiles of battering men? Which violent men are most at risk of killing their victims? Are such abusers inherently more violent, more psychotic, or more drunk than men whose violence is less threatening? And how about women who kill? Are they just protecting themselves or are they acting out of rage perhaps because of their partner's behavior? And above all, how can such unnecessary deaths be prevented?

These are just a few of the burning questions that will be tackled in the chapters to follow. Our search for answers is informed by extensive data, some from official sources, but most in the form of personal interviews with intimate partners with a close connection to the crime—male prison inmates convicted of partner murder, or femicide; women serving time in prison for homicide of their husbands and/or partners; and women who survived murder attempts. The personal narratives that highlight this book are derived from both original sources from the authors and from qualitative research literature.

TYPES OF DOMESTIC HOMICIDE

The term *domestic homicide* refers to more than just killing between spouses or partners. And before going further, let us look at some of these terms as defined in the Oxford English Dictionary (Oxford University Press 2007). *Homicide* means, literally, the killing of a man; yet it is applied to both genders. We are of course familiar with *infanticide,* the killing of one's infant. Some other less familiar terms derived from Latin are *femicide,* the murder of a woman; *filicide,* the murder by a parent or stepparent of a child; *matricide,* the killing of one's mother; *patricide,* the killing of one's father; *fratricide,* the killing of one's sibling; and finally, *familicide,* the killing of one's family.

Sometimes following the murder of his partner, the man commits suicide. Each year about one-third of the thousand or so domestic murders of women are murder-suicides (Roehl, O'Sullivan, and Webster 2005). Until recently, cases of a parent wiping out his or her whole family were extremely rare. The year 2007 saw a spate of such cases, however, involving mainly fathers. In Alabama, one father threw his children off a bridge; in New Jersey, a man drowned his daughters, then hanged himself; and a California man shot his wife and two daughters in a parked car before turning the gun on himself (Goldman 2007). The most plausible explanation for the spate of cases of familicide is the fact of contagion bred from the media. One clue is that such familicides tend to occur in clusters (Goldman). As we know from the school shootings, when news of one such event is widely broadcast, copycat shootings are predictable outcomes. Suggestion, as social psychologists tell us, is a powerful force (Aronson 2007). When news images are presented over and over on TV, their impact is heightened.

Contagion may have played a role in a string of killings in Massachusetts. This New England state saw 39 domestic homicide casualties in one year—2007—alone (Underwood 2007). In every case, we can imagine that the families suffer the psychological devastation wreaked by the murders long after the headlines are forgotten. David Carney, for example, lost his beloved daughter (Cynthia), aged 41, and his 9-year-old granddaughter, both of whom were slain by their husband and father, respectively. The father (Benoit) then stabbed himself. As described in the *Boston Herald* (Underwood 2007, 4),

> Investigators found the pair dead with multiple stab wounds. Benoit, who was still on the phone with a police dispatcher when the cops arrived, had "substantial cuts and had lost a substantial amount of blood."
>
> Now, David Carney and Cynthia's eldest child, Joseph, are all that's left of a loving family torn apart by a killer in their midst.
>
> "My Grandson Joey turned 18 on the day of the murder. They wouldn't let me arrange the funeral because Joey was the next of kin. He had to arrange the funerals for his mother and sister," Carney said. "He has good days and bad days. We don't talk about it—it's too painful for us."
>
> Carney now spends time tending to Cynthia and little Sarah's graves in St. James Cemetery in Whitman.

When one's family members are so savagely murdered, the grieving rarely ever ends. (For a therapist's account of the pain of murder in the family, see Chapter 6, "Portraits of Life in the Aftermath of Domestic Homicide.") Let us look more closely at the various types of domestic homicide.

Men Who Kill Their Partners

The brief accounts above like other accounts drawn from media reports tell us little about the buildup of the violence, the dangers facing the victims before they were killed, or the everyday assaults that would have preceded the ultimate attack. So what is it like on a daily basis living with a potential killer?

In search of the answers, we can listen to the stories of potential murder victims who have gotten away. We can turn to insights offered by Kathryn Ann Farr (2002) in interviews with a sample of women, all of whom survived an attempted domestic homicide. Most typically, as described by these women and confirmed by Farr in police reports, the perpetrator drank heavily and/or used illicit drugs, was an alcoholic or drug addict, was a gun owner, and, if the victim had left him, was her stalker. One victim described the attacks as so terrifying that she was certain she was going to die.

To personalize this description of offender traits with one survivor's story, read the following chilling account of life with a potential murderer. This narrative was obtained in an interview (by K. van Wormer, October 6, 2007) with a survivor (who is also a volunteer) at a domestic advocacy organization. In the survivor's words,

> Steve would buy my clothes for me; he told me who I could talk to, what I could eat— the whole nine yards. When I put on makeup, he would approve and watch as

I put it on. If church was out at 12:00, I had to be home by 12:10. "You're screwing around," he would say. He made me do crazy things sexually or I'd be punished. I decided to leave; I left my kids. Then I started to self-medicate because I couldn't stand to live without my kids. So I returned. I drank until I was too drunk or too stoned to care when he beat me; I felt like I deserved it. He'd beat me for anything and everything; he beat me because the scrambled eggs were not the way he wanted. He never hit me on the face where it was visible. I tried to escape but couldn't get away. I tried to commit suicide—three or four times. I remember pointing the gun at my chin, and just when I was going to pull the trigger someone got the gun. I took pills and once slept for 24 hours.

The beatings went on and on. "If you tell," he said, "I will kill you." The last time I saw him he said, "Do you want to say good-bye now? Because I'm going to kill you." I grabbed my son and we ran. That was 2003; he's still looking for me.

Lack of employment, the escalation of violence, forced sex, substance abuse, access to a gun, a pending breakup: these are among the key ingredients leading up to domestic homicide in the United States (Adams 2007). The buildup to murder may be gradual, but to persons outside of the immediate family, the tragedy seems to have come about very suddenly. Bang, bang, and it is all over; the tell-tale yellow police tape is placed around the house. "They stayed to themselves," the neighbors say. Some lives are snuffed out, while the lives of those who remain behind may be damaged forever.

Virtually all such tragic male murder-suicide cases follow a breakup or the threat of a breakup and are of the "if I can't have you, no one can" variety. Patriarchal dominance, explosive violence, extreme possessiveness, jealousy, and a pathological fear of rejection by his wife or partner—these are among the key features of male-on-female domestic homicide (Harper and Voigt 2007). Substance abuse and job loss are other factors that figure in as well.

Men Who Kill the Whole Family

A string of whole-family murders or familicides have taken place recently in the Washington, DC, area. Consider the following cases that were highlighted in the *Washington Post* (Miroff 2008):

A man who killed his two young children and their mother in a Stafford County mobile home before taking his own life Monday had been high on cocaine and drinking whiskey for days, according to a woman who said she had spent the weekend with the man and was planning to move in with him next month....

The incident was the latest in a recent string of domestic slayings in the Washington region. In March, a Montgomery County man drowned his three children in a hotel room bathtub, and since last year, at least six other family murder-suicides have taken place....Jackson was a landscaper but was having trouble finding work lately....

"She wanted to move back with her family," (a neighbor) said, adding that there had been no indication of trouble at the couple's home Monday....(Jackson's mistress) said however, that Jackson had a knife and two handguns, telling her he had a concealed weapons permit. She also said Jackson bought a large bottle of whiskey and drank heavily from it over the weekend.

Fathers who kill their children sometimes are seeking revenge on their wives by taking away what is most precious to them. J. Marbella (2008) describes just such a case that took place in Baltimore when a man who had been engaged in a custody battle with his wife drowned the three children in a bathtub. Other fathers are driven to child murder by feelings that they have failed to adequately provide for or been unable to properly take care of their families. This may be what happened recently in Iowa City (Associated Press 2008b):

> An embattled former bank executive committed suicide by crashing his van after killing his wife and making failed attempts to asphyxiate their four children in a garage, then slaying them individually, authorities said Tuesday.
>
> Steven Sueppel, who had been charged with embezzlement, was missing after his family's bodies were discovered Monday morning. His van was found wrecked and ablaze on Interstate 80 about nine miles away, and police said they used dental records to identify the burned body inside as Sueppel's...
>
> Court records show that Steven Sueppel, 42, was indicted last month on charges of stealing about $560,000 from Hills Bank and Trust in Johnson County, where he was vice president and controller.

The motive here is hard to figure. But a similar case from Austria offers some clues. One difference in this case is that the killer did not commit suicide and simply turned himself in to the police (CNN 2008):

> The man walked into a Vienna police station early Wednesday and told authorities he had killed his wife and 7-year-old daughter early Tuesday, police spokesman Michael Braunsperger said.
>
> The man, a self-employed public relations consultant according to The Associated Press, said he had also murdered both his parents and his father-in-law in the cities of Ansfelden and Linz, respectively, the spokesman said.
>
> Police found the five victims, who had all been killed with an ax, Braunsperger said. The man said his motive was "financial difficulties." "He said he'd been speculating on the financial markets and had lost everything, so he...wanted to spare his family the shame," Braunsperger said.

The explanation for the motive in the Austrian case helps shed light on what compelled the man in Iowa, in similar financial straits, to take the lives of his family. Collectively these case illustrations were chosen from the media because they represent several of the major themes of domestic homicide that are the subject for later pages of this book. Among these themes are gender differences in this form of violence; the role of stress and psychological problems in the shaping of a deadly plan; the risks of escape to many battering victims; the way children become casualties in domestic battles; and, finally, the enduring tragedy to the family members who survived. When crimes of this magnitude take place, the whole community is shaken. "If only we had known," is the common refrain. Even readers of media accounts suffer at least temporarily as they grasp the reality of the torture that the victims endured. They cry out for the children who were killed.

Women Who Kill Their Partners

When women kill their husbands and partners, the typical pattern is distinctly different. Women who are being beaten are often terrified of being seriously hurt, disfigured—teeth knocked out, jaw broken—and frequently of being killed. Death threats often accompany the beatings. The victim knows she may be killed from a beating that has gotten out of hand, or that her partner may be plotting and scheming to take her life or both their lives. Especially when the perpetrator is depressed and suicidal, a well-planned homicide-followed-by-suicide may be carried out. In all likelihood, the men typically do not see it coming and so are caught off guard. In the typical scenario, the woman kills her batterer in self-defense, out of fear that he will kill her. A recent article from Iowa entitled "Muscatine Woman Convicted of Killing Ex-Boyfriend" (Associated Press 2007) describes such a case:

> Cathryn Linn, 44, faces life in prison for first-degree murder. She was arrested Feb. 7 after authorities found Barry Blanchard, 42, shot to death in her home.
> Linn claimed she was physically abused by her ex-boyfriend. She testified Thursday that Blanchard was known as a tough guy and would tell her stories of killing people when he was in the military....
> "He was very adamant about letting me know if I messed up, I would be dead," Linn said.

Another possible scenario takes place when a woman who has been beaten one time too many takes a gun (usually his gun) and shoots him. We may assume that one of her motives is to put an end to the violence but it could be that her long-suppressed anger would come into play as well. Although the research literature rarely includes this motivation, van Wormer learned of at least a few revenge plots carried out by inmates at the Julia Tutwiler Correctional Institution in Wetumpka, Alabama. Guns and poison provided the means of getting even for past abuse.

Women Who Kill Their Children

In regard to filicide or parental murder, male-female differences are pronounced. Women who kill their children tend not to kill the spouse as well; men may or may not kill their wives and the children. Other gender differences are apparent as well. A typology of mothers who have killed their children is provided by McKee (2006). Mothers who kill their children are of five basic types:

abusive/neglectful, psychotic/suicidal, psychopathic, detached, and retaliatory. The abusive/neglectful mothers are often alcohol abusers and/or drug addicts. Detached mothers are defined as those who fail to bond with their newborn infants, and retaliatory mothers are those who kill to get revenge on someone. Actually, as McKee informs us, parents who kill their children for revenge are almost always fathers.

Mothers of the psychotic/suicidal type who take their children's lives are generally delusional, believing the children are possessed of the devil. They kill, in short, out of a delusional sense of altruism. Andrea Yates, who drowned her five small children, is a prime example of someone having such a psychotic breakdown. Mental illness also figures in the following news story from the *New York Times* (McFadden and Macropoulos 2008):

> Lashuan Harris, 24, who threw her three young sons to their deaths in San Francisco Bay...was declared insane by a judge one day after a California jury found her guilty of second-degree murder. The defense argued that she was schizophrenic, borderline mentally retarded and convinced that she was acting on orders from God when she threw the boys...into the water.

Another source of knowledge is of course the official data on the extent and frequency of domestic homicide. Thus we turn to social science to help us separate the myths from fact. In order to shape effective policies and treatment programming to prevent the murders and murder-suicides, we need to challenge the following myths about domestic homicide and replace them with accurate information.

Myth No. 1: Women Today Are as Violent as Men

Although women, like men, can be violent, around 85 percent of the victims of domestic violence, according to government arrest data, are female (Bureau of Justice Statistics [BJS] 2003). Claims by social scientists such as Donald Dutton (2007) and in the media that women engage in partner violence to the same degree as men are given little support in the national (or global) crime statistics. Reports showing women as violent in intimate relationships as men are based on self-reports in national surveys. To get the true picture, we need to look at the homicide deaths; homicide reports are the most reliable of the criminal justice data because they are taken the most seriously by legal authorities.

Turning to domestic homicide, according to the most recent BJS (2007a) report, here is the official breakdown for 2005: 329 males and 1,181 females were killed in that year by their intimate partners. Clearly men are much more likely to kill their partners than women are to kill theirs. The character of the homicide differs by gender as well (BJS 2007a). Whereas men are more apt to kill a stranger or be killed by a stranger, female homicides (whether the woman is the perpetrator or victim) generally involve intimates or other family members. Same-sex homicide is predominantly male; the gay male rate of killing is about 12 times the lesbian rate (Garcia, Soria, and Hurwitz 2007).

The claims that women assault men as much as men assault women (such as by Dutton 2007) fail to take into account women's physical vulnerabilities. Pregnant and recently pregnant women are extremely vulnerable. They are also at high risk of domestic violence at this time. Further, they are more likely to be victims of homicide (at the hands of their partners) than to die of any other cause. Homicide is a leading cause of traumatic death for pregnant and postpartum women in the United States, accounting for 31 percent of maternal injury deaths (Family Violence Prevention Fund 2008). Throughout the world, pregnancy is a period of high risk for both battering and homicide.

A sample of 105 women inmates who had been convicted of killing their partners with an equal sample of battered women from the community, found that virtually all of the women in prison had a history of being battered. Compared to the battered women who did not kill their partners, women in the prison sample were far more likely to have received death threats from their partners, threats that were specific as to time and place and method. Also in contrast to the comparison group, the majority of the women prisoners had a history of sexual abuse, a substance use problem, had attempted suicide, and had access to the batterers' guns.

Myth No. 2: There Has Been an Increase in Violent Crime, Especially for Women

This claim is widespread in media reports (see Chesney-Lind 2002; van Wormer and Bartollas 2007). The reason for the claim is that law enforcement much more often arrests females today than they did formerly for simple and aggravated assault. These are domestic violence situations (see Chapter 8, "Response of the U.S. Criminal Justice System"). So the changes are in the law, not in the actual rates of female-on-male violence. According to the most comprehensive data available (BJS 2007a), the rates for intimate homicide are down for women as well as men: Between 1975 and 2005, the number of intimate homicides for all race and gender groups declined—the number of black males killed by intimates dropped by 83 percent, white males killed by 61 percent, black females by 52 percent, and white females by 6 percent. View the charts below in Box 1.1.

Interestingly, in the early 1970s (not shown on these charts), before domestic partner shelters and other victim protection services were introduced, about as many women killed their intimate partners as male partners killed the women. There were well over a thousand homicides committed by each gender at this time. One could speculate that many of the women then as women today were shooting their husbands and partners because they felt trapped. Then when domestic violence hotlines and other services were introduced, the battered women had an alternative means of escape other than taking the life of the man.

Box 1.1   Homicide Trends in the U.S.: Intimate Homicide

There has been a decline in homicide of intimates, especially male victims.

Intimates are defined to include spouses, ex-spouses, boyfriends, and girlfriends.

- The number of men murdered by intimates dropped by 75% since 1976.
- The number of women killed by intimates was stable for nearly two decades. After 1993, the number declined reaching the lowest level recorded in 2004.

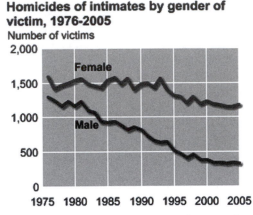

Homicides of intimates by gender of victim, 1976-2005

Number of victims

In general, the number of intimate victims in each race and gender group declined.

Between 1976 and 2005—

- the number of white females killed by intimates rose in the mid-1980s, then declined after 1993 reaching the lowest recorded in 2002; the number fluctuated slightly after 2002;
- the number of intimate homicides for all other race and gender groups declined over the period; the number of black males killed by intimates dropped by 83%, white males by 61%, black females by 52%, and white females by 6%.

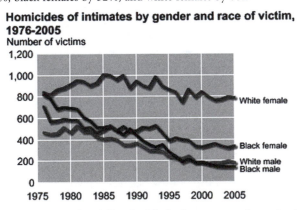

Homicides of intimates by gender and race of victim, 1976-2005

Number of victims

The intimate homicide rate has fallen for blacks in every gender and relationship category while the rate for whites has not declined for all categories.

The intimate homicide rate—

- for white girlfriends was higher in 2005 than it was in 1976;
- for white wives and ex-wives has declined but not as much as that for white husbands and ex-husbands;
- for black husbands and ex-husbands was 20 times greater in 1976 than it was in 2005;
- is higher for black girlfriends than any other group in 2005, although it has declined 66% since 1976.

Source: Bureau of Justice Statistics, *Homicide Trends in the U.S.: Intimate Homicide.* Washington, DC: U.S. Department of Justice, July 11, 2007, http://ojp.usdoj.gov/bjs/homicide/intimates.htm.

W. Wells and W. DeLeon-Granados (2004, 233) explain the striking decline in homicides committed by women in terms of "exposure reduction theory." Reduce the victim's exposure to violence and to the abusive man, this theory goes, and she will be spared from seeking a desperate way out. Unfortunately, though, since men's motives for killing their wives/partners are different, not for defense but for retaliation after a breakup, when the woman does escape, her life may still be at risk.

Myth No. 3: The Domestic Homicide Rate Cuts Evenly across All Social and Racial Groups

The Bureau of Justice Statistics does not provide a breakdown by class or income for victims of domestic homicide, but it does so for nonfatal domestic violence (BJS 2007b). Thus we learn from their charts that females in households that earned less than $7,500 per year had far higher rates of female victimization than did females in households at higher income levels. The higher the income, the lower the rates of domestic violence.

Domestic homicide, like domestic violence, does cut across all classes and races. Consider the case of the banker above who killed his whole family and then himself. Note, however, that he was in a financial and legal jam, having been fired for charges of embezzlement from his bank. Unemployment and poverty are two variables highly associated with intimate violence including homicide (see Ellison et al. 2007 and Garcia, Soria, and Hurwitz 2007). Studies of men in prison convicted of killing their girlfriends and wives and studies of a comparable group of female inmates indicate that economic problems were one factor in the tension in the relationship before the homicides took place. Since economic problems are more prominent among the lower classes, we can conclude that social class is one variable that should be considered in the study of intimate homicide.

As far as race is concerned, for unknown reasons the number of African American partners and spouses killed by women has declined significantly. In the past the rate of men so murdered was substantial. Despite the decline, the homicide rate for African Americans of both genders is still well above the white rate. The nonfatal victimization rate is quite high as well. According to our calculations from the BJS (2007b) data, the black male spouse victimization rate is four times the comparable white rate, and the boyfriend murder rate is seven times the comparable white rate. It should be noted also that white women are still being victimized at almost the same level as in previous years.

Myth No. 4: Domestic Homicide Followed by Suicide Is Extremely Rare

As mentioned above, about one-third of domestic homicides in the United States end in the suicide of the perpetrator. Murder-suicides occur at the rate of between one and two a day, three-fourths of which involve domestic partner situations (Violence Policy Center 2008).

For the study, the VPC used a national clipping service to collect every reported murder-suicide in the United States from January 1, 2007, to June 30, 2007. Currently there is no national tracking system for these incidents. Murder-suicide is overwhelmingly a male-on-female crime.

Research shows that the individual who is dangerously violent and also prone to depression is at most risk of killing his partner and himself. The risk is exacerbated when the female partner makes a move to break off the relationship (van Wormer and Bartollas 2007). Weapon availability, of course, figures in, boosting American murder-suicide rates far above that of their European and many Asian counterparts (VPC 2008). (Chapter 3 explores this phenomenon in detail.)

Myth No. 5: Guns in the Home Provide Protection from Violent Crime

Domestic violence homicides take place in all regions of the United States, and in the majority of these murders, the weapon used was a handgun. The national, non-profit Violence Policy Center (2007), located in Washington, DC, in 2006 prepared a state-by-state ranking based on the numbers of women who were murdered in the year 2005 and found that, overwhelmingly, the perpetrator was a husband, boyfriend, or other close relative—rather than a stranger. The study found that, during the period of the study, 1,713 (52 percent) women throughout the United States who were murdered by a man were killed with a firearm. The states with the highest per capita number of women who were killed by men in 2005 were (in order of prevalence) Nevada, Alaska, Louisiana, New Mexico, Mississippi, Arkansas, South Carolina, Alabama, Tennessee, and Oklahoma. These are also states, generally speaking, in which gun control is the most lax.

Myth No. 6: Use of Alcohol and Other Drugs Is Not a Significant Factor in Violence; Drinking and Drug Use Are Often Just Excuses for the Violence

It is true that some individuals who engage in bad behavior claim they were drunk or high on drugs as an excuse for their behavior. In his interviews with male inmates who had murdered their wives, David Adams (2007), for example, found that most of them claimed they had been drinking or using drugs.

To obtain more objective results, he interviewed 20 women who had narrowly escaped being murdered. Three-fourths of these survivors characterized their attackers as heavy substance abusers. Interestingly, they also noted that the men displayed irrational bouts of jealousy and that they had poor work records.

Other research confirms a relationship between substance use and intimate partner violence. Fals-Stewart, Leonard, and Birchler (2005) found that in men who drank, violence escalated on drinking days in proportion to the amount of alcohol consumed. Additionally, these researchers found that among men in a domestic violence intervention program who had a diagnosis of antisocial personality disorder, heavy drinking was strongly associated with severe intimate partner violence.

The substances most closely associated with aggression are the depressant, alcohol, and the stimulants, cocaine and methamphetamines (van Wormer and Davis 2008). If batterers who had substance abuse problems abstained from alcohol and other drug use, we could predict their rate of violence would decrease. Indeed, at least one study has found that male batterers who were receiving substance abuse treatment improved their behavior markedly as a result of the treatment. This was true even though the interventions did not directly focus on domestic violence (Stuart 2005). More research is needed on this point.

How about substance abuse in battered women? A recent study by Call and Nelsen (2007) of 30 mostly low-income women of color who were in treatment for substance abuse problems and who also reported partner abuse revealed a close association between the violence and the use of substances. Alcohol and other drugs were often drunk or used after being beaten because these substances "helped them deal with it or because substances 'kept them blind' to it" (341). A smaller group stated that they were physically abused because of their alcohol and other drug use. (See Chapters 2 and 4 for a closer examination of the link between substance use and battering.)

Myth No. 7: Female Victims Are Slow to Escape Because of an Attraction to Violent Men and Due to Poor Judgment in General

There is a great deal of misunderstanding of just how hard it is for a battered woman in a relationship with a seriously violent man to get away. The breakup or even the hint that the woman is leaving is enough to expose her to danger. "If you ever try to leave me, I'll kill you" is a common threat in such situations. Then there are emotional reactions to years of escalating violence that are associated with feelings of depression and helplessness. Some women experience traumatic bonding, a psychological response to being beaten and controlled by a seemingly all-powerful person. Kidnap victims sometimes fail to escape to safety when they can do so because of this psychological force (van Wormer 2007).

Other reasons that a battered woman finds it hard to make the break, as identified in the literature, are financial dependency, fear that she will be hunted down, and worry about the children's future and that she might lose custody in court (Roberts 2007). We also need to consider that a woman who lives with an abusive man is most likely socially isolated; therefore, her support system is weak. Her feeling of helplessness is compounded by the reality that she has nowhere to go.

Myth No. 8: Women Who Kill the Men Who Beat Them Rarely Are Punished for Their Crimes

In cases of female-on-male intimate partner homicide, the power imbalance between men and women comes into play. Therefore, women who kill, as Karlene Faith (1993) explains, generally do so when the man is in some way incapacitated—asleep or drunk, for example. A strategy that may make sense in terms of getting rid of the threat is not always the best strategy from a legal standpoint. Premeditation often comes into play in these cases, a fact that makes a claim of self-defense problematic. Moreover, it cannot be argued that the woman was in immediate danger. When the case comes to trial, invariably, the prosecutor will ask in cross examination, "Isn't it true that you could just have left or called for help?" Many women do serve long prison terms for murder and manslaughter in these situations, accordingly. (Learn details of the criminal justice response to domestic homicide in Chapter 8.)

Myth No. 9: Men Who Batter Cannot Change

All batterers are not alike. Adams (2007), in his extensive research on men who killed their partners, identified distinct personality types, as we will see in Chapter 2. An earlier study by Jacobson and Gottman (1998), which focused on working with battering men, described two types, the "pit bulls" and the "cobras." The former were highly sensitive men who were insecure and very possessive. The latter were roughly comparable to psychopaths or men with anti-social personalities. These men, like Adams's materially motivated killers who killed for money, and the career criminals, are the least likely to change. The more sensitive types, however, are often dissatisfied with their lives and behavior and so psychotherapy and group therapy (and sometimes religion) can help these men turn their lives and relationships around. Refer to Chapters 2 and 11 in this book for more specific information.

Myth No. 10: Batterer Education Programming Is Based on Empirically Validated Principles

As we review the history of how batterer educational interventions evolved from the auspices of paraprofessional trainings, as presented in Chapter 11, we will see that the programming is anything but scientifically based. Some aspects of the programming work rather well, and others are in need of change to bring the content in line with current research findings on the nature of violence.

Attention to empirically based findings regarding the science of enhancing motivation in involuntary clients is important as well. Under the circumstances, we need to seriously consider scholarly criticism, such as that provided by Canadian social psychologist Donald Dutton. Dutton writes from personal experience working with batterers and as a social scientist who has conducted research evaluations of batterer intervention programs. Although we do not accept his conclusion that women are as violent as men, a theme that is reiterated throughout his book, *Rethinking Domestic Violence,* Dutton's critical analysis of the dominant approach to the reeducation of battering men is compelling and is consistent with research findings from other sources.

Myth No. 11: Very Little Can Be Done to Prevent Battered Women from Being Murdered by Their Abusers

Domestic homicide is a major public health problem and can be prevented with safety measures taken to reduce the harm of family violence. Harm reduction measures currently used are arrest and prosecution of batterers, the issuing of protection restraining orders, and mandatory batterer education. Community educational initiatives are being widely instituted as well, such as teen dating violence prevention programs and male mentoring programs in the schools. Health professionals are using danger assessment tools to assess the level of risk of homicide for victims.

Although much improvement is needed in the system to ensure the safety of women, and especially more generous funding for domestic violence services across the nation, we know that many of the reforms instituted over the last few decades have proven beneficial. Some research shows, for example, that batterers who are middle class with well-paying jobs are deterred from further violence through an arrest. The findings are mixed on the effectiveness of current arrest policies in preventing homicide, but most critics concede that law enforcement officers and court officials are far more sensitive to crimes of family violence than they were in the past (Roberts 2002). The introduction of victim assistance programs and women's shelters have provided legal help and a refuge for families at risk. Shelters for men at risk of battering their wives would protect women even further. A form of inpatient treatment including substance abuse treatment could be provided for such men. Because of the close connection between domestic violence and substance abuse, cross-trainings of staff in substance abuse treatment and domestic violence services are presently underway.

Adams (2007) points out that most of the murderers he interviewed said they would not have killed their partner had they not had access to a gun. Women who kill would even be less likely to do so without access to such an equalizing weapon. Adams further recommends that the laws at the federal and state levels be tightened to effectively remove guns from the homes of known abusers. All safety plans include questions concerning access to such weapons.

Some of the new technologies are providing protection. Among them are cell phones preprogrammed to notify authorities of emergency situations, electronic monitoring that can track offenders and potential victims, and informational Web sites family members can access when feeling threatened. So in conclusion, yes, a great deal can be done to prevent domestic violence and, therefore, in effect, domestic homicide. (Chapters 2, 10, and 11 are most relevant to this discussion.)

Let us conclude this chapter with a chilling story from another place and time. Written by an 85-year-old southern storyteller from Louisiana, the essay about Elise Talmage says a lot about how the world has changed and yet, how some things have not changed at all.

ERMA
ELISE TALMAGE

Amite, Louisiana 1932
Elise, age 10

I heard Big Mama murmur aloud as if she had just been thinking to herself, "Why no one in this town would have condemned Erma. You couldn't have collected a jury that would have blamed the poor child."

This was what I overheard through the sneezing and coughing while we sat on the gallery, so I quickly dragged my feet to stop the swing which hung at the corner of the porch and squeaked. Not wanting to miss a word I leaned forward curious about Erma because sometimes I just couldn't get adults to talk.

We were all in our seats on the porch after having eaten our supper. Papa, my grandfather, was in the front straw rocker coughing and hacking with his asthma which was terrible. Then came Charles and Charlotte, my aunt and uncle, both peculiar who refused to be called Aunt and Uncle claiming they were too young though both were really middle aged. Charles cleared his throat constantly. Next came mother sneezing and blowing with hay fever. Big Mama sat near me coughing with the bronchitis she always had, and of course I was in the swing desperately trying to hear over the racket. In the twilight one couldn't even hear the crickets or the sleepy bird sounds on account of family allergies.

I had been curious for some time about the house next door, a small unpainted cottage mostly hidden from the road, which had an air of being ashamed of itself and trying to hide on its lot. One would think no one lived there but I knew someone did. This was where Maud Williams lived with a little girl the age of my little sister.

Maud was very beautiful with long fluffy dark hair piled on top in a knot, skin like a magnolia petal, and blue eyes. She walked past Papa's house every day going to and fro from town always under her parasol with her head held high as if daring anyone to gossip.

I was picking up her story in bits and pieces when the family talked in the evening on the gallery and sometimes Big Mama would tell me something when I kept nagging.

Maud's niece was named Erma and her mother had been Erma too. The first Erma had been a pretty blond girl who grew up with my mother. Daddy told me that she had married a local dentist while mother had married the Presbyterian minister's younger brother from New Orleans.

"It wasn't Wood's fault," Big Mama kept saying defensively of her brother. "He simply couldn't help her."

Erma had gone to Uncle Wood's law office displaying bruises, and Uncle Wood told her she had to leave her husband, then the law could help.

Erma had tried. She fled to her brother's house out of town but the dentist, Dr. Hyde, followed her there threatening to kill her brother if she didn't return. Later she fled to her family home on Duncan Avenue next to Papa's where her sister Maud lived.

They all heard the shot. Papa and Big Mama rushed over with other neighbors to find Dr. Hyde dead and poor Erma having killed him.

When the police arrived Erma asked to use the bathroom, and there she drank lye. Nothing could be done to help her, and Erma handed her baby to Maud.

One by one the coughing and sneezing on the gallery was hushed and the sound of the crickets and sleepy birds could be heard as the family began to re-gather under the stones at the end of Duncan Avenue; another Flora occupied the old home. She was one of three Flora's in the family all named after Big Mama and each other.

Last week I drove south to Amite again and strolled out on the gallery where the rockers still sit leaving the ghosts of the past inside waiting until after supper.

Walking north down Duncan Avenue I passed the Williams' old cottage. The second Erma lives there now, an old lady with a bullet hole in the wall and the bathroom where her mother collapsed. All was in shadow. I longed to knock but sister Flora said Erma doesn't like company. Perhaps she has company we can't see.

Unpublished story. Printed with permission of Elise Talmage who lives on a farm in Bowling Green, Kentucky.

CONCLUSION

This chapter has presented real stories from news and personal sources of death by domestic violence. Sometimes the killings were of one individual, the partner; in other situations described, the killings were of multiple members of the family. Domestic violence was the precipitant in the majority, and possibly, all of these tragedies. Every one of the deaths described in the case illustrations was preventable. And yet it would have seemed to those caught up in the situations—victim or perpetrator— that there was no way out. The overarching purpose of this book is to show that there is such a way.

Harm reduction, which derives from a public health model, is the guiding framework for this volume. Harm reduction is about preventing problems before they start and developing safety and treatment plans for persons who are at risk—risk of lashing out, or risk of being victimized. As presented in this book, harm reduction means zero tolerance for hitting, slapping, threatening with guns, and otherwise hurting people. On the positive side, in the belief that people can change, harm reduction promotes hope and help for the perpetrators of violence. Consistent with harm reduction principles is the offering of interventions and adequate social services to reduce victims' dependency on their abusers.

In sum, domestic violence as we have seen in this chapter is harmful, destructive of one's mental and physical health, and sometimes fatal. This overview has focused on cases in which domestic violence ends in the death of one of the parties, most often the woman. In cases of domestic homicide, the gender differences are pronounced. Hopefully, in drawing on facts and statistics from government sources, we have demolished some of the myths about domestic homicide. Next we come to an examination of the risks facing individuals in situations of domestic violence—the risks that the violence will escalate into murder.

REFERENCES

Adams, D. 2007. *Why do they kill? Men who murder their intimate partners.* Nashville, TN: Vanderbilt University Press.

Aronson, E. 2007. *The social animal.* New York: Worth.

Associated Press. 2007. Muscatine woman convicted of killing ex-boyfriend. *Waterloo Courier,* September 16.

Associated Press. 2008a. Peterson's third wife's death ruled a homicide. *Today,* February 22. MSNBC. http://today.msnbc.msn.com/id/23283569/ (accessed May 2008).

Associated Press. 2008b. Iowa man killed wife, four kids, then self. *USA Today,* March 26. http://www.usatoday.com/news/nation/2008-03-24-iowa-city_N.htm?csp=34 (accessed May 2008.

Bureau of Justice Statistics. 2003. *Intimate partner violence, 1993–2001.* Crime Data Brief (NCJ 197838), February. http://www.ojp.usdoj.gov/bjs/abstract/ipv01.htm.

Bureau of Justice Statistics (BJS). 2007a. *Homicide trends in the U.S.: Intimate homicide.* Washington, DC: U.S. Department of Justice, July. http://www.ojp.usdoj.gov/bjs/homicide/intimates.htm (accessed December 2007).

Bureau of Justice Statistics. 2007b. *Intimate partner violence in the U.S.: Victim characteristics.* Washington, DC: U.S. Department of Justice, December 19. http://www.ojp.usdoj.gov/bjs/intimate/victims.htm#gender (accessed May 2008).

Cable News Network (CNN). 2008. "Shamed" Austrian man kills family with ax. *CNN.com/europe,* May 14. http://beta.cnn.com/2008/WORLD/europe/05/14/austria.family/index.html (accessed May 2008).

Call, C., and J. Nelsen. 2007. Partner abuse and women's substance problems: From vulnerability to strength. *Affilia* 22:334–46.

Chesney-Lind, M. 2002. Criminalizing victimization: The unintended consequences of proarrest policies for girls and women. *Criminology and Public Policy* 2:81–90.

Dutton, D. 2007. *Rethinking domestic violence.* Vancouver, Canada: University of British Columbia Press.

Ellison, C., J. Trinitapoli, K. Anderson, and B. Johnson. 2007. Race/ethnicity, religious involvement, and domestic violence. *Violence Against Women* 13:1094–1112.

Faith, K. 1993. *Unruly women: The politics of confinement and resistance.* London: Press Gang Publications.

Fals-Stewart, W., K. Leonard, and G. Birchler. 2005. The occurrence of male-to-female intimate partner violence on days of men's drinking: The moderating effects of antisocial personality disorder. *Journal of Consulting and Clinical Psychology* 73, no. 2: 239–48.

Family Violence Prevention Fund. 2008. Domestic violence is a serious, widespread social problem in America: The facts. http://www.endabuse.org/resources/facts/ (accessed May 2008).

Farr, K.A. 2002. Battered women who were "being killed and survived it": Straight talk from survivors. *Violence and Victims* 17, no. 3: 267–82.

Garcia, L., C. Soria, and E. Hurwitz. 2007. Homicides and intimate partner violence: A literature review. *Trauma, Violence & Abuse* 8:370–83.

Goldman, R. 2007. Mothers and fathers who murder. *ABC News,* August 1. http://abcnews.go.com/US/story?id=3435710&page=1 (accessed May 2008).

Harper, D.W., and L. Voigt. 2007. Homicide followed by suicide.*Homicide Studies* 11, no. 4: 295–318.

Home Office. 2005. Domestic violence: National plan for domestic violence. London: Home Office. http://www.crimereduction.gov.uk/domesticviolence (accessed February 2007).

Jacobson, N.S., and J.M. Gottman. 1998. *When men batter women: New insights into ending abusive relationships.* New York: Simon & Schuster.

Marbella, J. 2008. Children casualties in divorce warfare. *Baltimore Sun,* April 1. www.baltimoresun.com. (accessed May 2008).

McFadden, R., and A. Macropoulos. 2008. Mother is held in Long Island slaying of three children. *New York Times,* February 25. www.nytimes.com/2008/02/25/nyregion/25slay.html?fta=y. (accessed May 2008).

McKee, G. 2006. *Why mothers kill: A forensic psychologist's casebook.* New York: Oxford University Press.

Miroff, N. 2008. Four dead in murder, suicide in Virginia. *Washington Post,* May 7. http://www.washingtonpost.com/wp-dyn/content/article/2008/05/06/AR2008050600936.html?nav=emailpage (accessed May 2008).

MSNBC. 2005. Scott Peterson sentenced to death. *NBC News,* March 17. http://www.msnbc.msn.com/id/7204523 (accessed May 2008).

Oxford University Press. 2007. *The shorter Oxford English dictionary, Sixth Edition.* New York: Oxford University Press.

Rennison, C.M. 2003. Intimate partner violence 1993–2001. Washington, DC: U.S. Department of Justice, Bureau of Justice Statistics.

Roberts, A.R. 2002. Myths, facts, and realities regarding battered women and their children: An overview. In *Handbook of domestic violence: Intervention strategies,* ed. A.R. Roberts, 3–22. New York: Oxford University Press.

Roberts, A.R. 2007. Domestic violence continuum, forensic assessment and crisis intervention. *Families in Society* 88, no. 1: 42–54.

Roehl, J., C. O'Sullivan, and D. Webster. 2005. Intimate partner violence risk assessment validation study, final report. Document #209732. Washington, DC: U.S. Department of Justice.

Stuart, G.L. 2005. Improving violence intervention outcomes by integrating alcohol treatment. *Journal of Interpersonal Violence* 20:388–93.

Underwood, M. 2007. Months later, Dad still reeling from losses. *Boston Herald,* September 3.

van Wormer, K. 2007. *Human behavior and the social environment, micro level.* New York: Oxford University Press.

van Wormer, K., and C. Bartollas. 2007. *Women and the criminal justice system.* Boston: Allyn & Bacon.

van Wormer, K., and D.R. Davis. 2008. *Addiction treatment: A strengths perspective.* Belmont, CA: Cengage.

Violence Policy Center (VPC). 2007. Nevada ranks No. 1 in rate of women murdered by men. Washington, DC: VPC, September 18. http://www.vpc.org/press/0709wmmw.htm. (accessed May 2008).

Violence Policy Center. 2008. *American roulette: Murder-suicide in the United States.* Washington, DC: VPC, http://www.vpc.org/studies/amroul2008.pdf (accessed July 2008).

Wells, W., and W. DeLeon-Granados. 2004. Intimate partner homicide decline: Disaggregated trends, theoretical explanations, and policy implications. *Criminal Justice Policy Review* 15, no. 2: 229–46.

Part I

The Psychology of
Life-Threatening Abuse

2

Risk Factors for Domestic Homicide

One of the foremost authorities on partner homicide, Donald Dutton, was a consultant of the prosecution team in the murder trial of O.J. Simpson. Simpson was charged in the brutal stabbing murder of his ex-wife, Nicole Brown Simpson, and her friend, Ronald Goldman. In *The Batterer: A Psychological Profile,* Dutton (1997, 3–4) described the defendant as having a Dr. Jekyll/Mr. Hyde type of personality. The public was shocked to learn of the dark side of their football hero. In Dutton's words,

> To his adoring fans, O.J. was a superhero, a legend...one of the greatest running backs in football history....Suddenly we all learned that our superhero was a wife batterer. The media played Nicole Brown Simpson's frantic 911 call to the LAPD. She was pleading for help, with O.J. ranting and cursing and breaking down the door in the background.

Another expert on domestic violence—Lenore Walker— also was involved as a consultant for the trial of O.J. Simpson, but on the opposing side. When Walker joined O.J. Simpson's defense team, feminists from across the world were shocked. Her role in the case was especially shocking to battered women's advocates because Walker was the pioneer of the women's shelter movement. She was author of the classic book, *The Battered Woman,* published in 1979, which helped a whole generation to understand the psychology of victimization terms such as "the battered woman syndrome," "learned helplessness," and "the cycle theory of violence," which were popularized through Walker's works. But here she was one and a half decades later involved in one of the most notorious murder trials in history working toward the defense of a known batterer!

So why did Lenore Walker step forward to the defense of an accused murderer who was on record for previously battering his wife? Walker was guided, as she later claimed, by the scientific evidence: "The battering was intermittent and did not escalate; when Nicole was on the phone begging for help, Simpson did not enter the room: there was no reported sexual abuse....Just because O.J. was a batterer...it didn't make him a killer," Walker lamely explained (2000, 149). Unfortunately, the key witnesses to the bloody scene are dead. We will revisit the case later in this chapter, and, using hindsight, consider whether Simpson's behavior and characteristics fit the profile of the dangerous batterer at risk of committing homicide.

Since the much publicized trial of O.J. Simpson, more research has been done in the area of partner and spousal homicide, and an instrument for risk assessment has been devised. Having a means of providing an objective risk assessment for battered and threatened women is essential because the victim who is being abused is too close to the situation to see it clearly: A normal response to an immediate situation of danger is often to shut out awareness of the danger as a survival defense mechanism (van Wormer 2007). Some women may be psychologically traumatized and told they "are crazy" or just imagining things when they express fear of their partner. Most others see no serious risk at all, even when their very lives and those of other family members are at stake.

The decision that a battered woman who has left her batterer makes is whether or not to return to live with the man who has abused her; this decision should always be regarded as potentially life threatening. By the same token, a woman's decision to make a break in the first place and call for help is clearly fraught with danger. Men who are victimized by their female partners or spouses have tough choices to make as well, but the dynamics of their situation may differ. Those men who are most in danger of domestic homicide at the hands of their wives are actually the battering men, and they are rarely aware of the dangers they face. Indeed, as we will see as we go on, the dynamics of homicide victimization for the male and for the female are generally different.

We begin with an overview of the literature on key predictive factors in domestic homicide. We then ponder the connection between domestic violence that is nonlethal and domestic violence that ends in homicide. Why do men kill their wives and partners, and why do women kill as well? To help answer this question, we consider the biological roots of aggression, explore the psychology of fatal battering, and look at social forces that might contribute to the murder of an intimate partner. Throughout the discussion, a contrast is drawn between male and female motivation for partner homicide, and risk factors for murder-suicide are differentiated from homicides that do not end in suicide. This chapter culminates in the presentation of the Danger Assessment Tool, an instrument devised by Jacqueline Campbell (2006) for intervention with battered women, but not before we consider the case history of a spousal murder-suicide that followed military service in the war zone in Iraq.

WHAT THE RESEARCH TELLS US

An overview of the literature on intimate partner homicide by Zahn (2003) pointed to several key risk factors of battered women—the frequency and severity of violent attacks, substance abuse problems, and possession of a gun—and what the motivation is for such homicidal acts.

Two earlier books on domestic homicide—*Homicide in Families* by Goetting (1995) and *Understanding Domestic Homicide* by Websdale (1999)—enlighten us on motivation for partner homicide and on gender differences in such motivation. For the man, the act of killing is typically offensive and preceded by escalating violence; for the woman the act is typically defensive, or committed out of self-preservation. Male-female differences are evidenced in the location of the homicides as well—women most often kill in the home; men commonly kill their partners outside of a shared dwelling (Kurst-Swanger and Petcosky 2003). Class factors figure in the equation as well. Whereas inner-city African Americans have high rates of domestic homicide committed by both genders, their middle class counterparts do not (Kurst-Swarger and Petcosky). Websdale and Goetting, similarly, describe the typical wife killer as an undereducated, unemployed father, and one who has an arrest record.

David Adams (2007) conducted in-depth interviews with 31 wife murderers who were confined in five U.S. prisons; in addition, he interviewed 20 female victims of attempted murder and 19 female victims of battering that did not seem to be life threatening. From the data gathered from interviews, media accounts, and official files, he classified the men into five basic types: jealous, substance abusing, materially motivated, suicidal, and career criminal. He found some overlap between types, especially between those who were jealous and substance abusing.

Jealousy also may figure in the high battering and homicide rates that occur during a woman's pregnancy and shortly after she has given birth. But material and other practical motives may be at work as well. More research into this matter could enlighten us here.

The question of child abuse in the backgrounds of the homicidal men is also something to consider. Interviews with the men and with victims who were almost killed revealed a pattern of highly abusive fathers punctuated by long periods of father absence. The father-son relationship was either nonexistent or consistently problematic; many of the fathers beat their wives in front of the children.

One major finding of Adams's interviews was that an escalation of violence preceded the near lethal attacks—from a honeymoon period in the early part of the marriage or cohabitation, to violence followed by an apology, to more severe violence for which the victim is blamed. This pattern which was revealed in interviews with women who were almost killed differs from the cycle of violence that is described by Walker (2000) and others in which violence was continually followed by a honeymoon period. But here we are talking about attempted homicide, so the pattern may be more linear.

Research on other forms of domestic homicide such as the killing of one's own parent shows that situations in which adolescents have suffered long-term abuse, are depressed, have easy access to guns, and have failed in efforts to get outside help are typical of the situations that have ended in parental murder (Kurst-Swarger and Petcosky). The infamous Menendez murder trials of the early 1990s, in which two brothers were convicted of killing their parents, involved defense claims of incest and terrorization.

The risk for sibling homicide is found in long-standing resentments, usually among brothers, and in a combination of external stressors, mental illness, and heavy alcohol use (Websdale). Whereas the perpetrators in these situations tend to be white, child homicide is disproportionately common in the black inner-city community (Goetting 1995). Growing up in violent homes is a theme that transcends most of these situations in which one family member kills another.

WHAT IS THE CONNECTION BETWEEN BATTERING AND HOMICIDE?

First let us consider *femicide,* or male-on-female homicide. What the literature shows, in short, is that spousal homicide and domestic violence are closely linked; these links have been consistent over time and space (across all countries examined) (Aldridge and Browne 2003). Confirmation in the research literature has come from family informants, police, and the murderers themselves. Estimates of the percentage of partner murder victims that have been first battered by their murderers or attempted murderers range from 25 percent in perpetrator reports to over 76 percent in reports by the victim informants: Clearly the former figures provided by the murderers themselves are underestimates.

There are no comparable estimates for female-on-male homicides. The literature on risk factors for women killing their husbands/partners overwhelmingly concludes that women do not kill through an escalation of violence against these men, but, rather, they kill as a reaction to their own victimization, generally out of self-defense. Self protection seems to be the primary motivation; however, one could speculate that the desire to end the abuse or to get back at the abuser would be an understandable human response to a situation of pain and terror. The fact that the introduction of domestic violence services is associated with a significant decline in the number of men who are now being killed by their wives and partners provides some indication of the motivation for many such killings— most likely, because when there was no women's shelter or other services for battered women, there was no other escape. In the past as the "burning bed" example makes clear, some women who were trapped resorted to drastic measures to get free.

Picture a continuum of violence that extends from minor hits and slaps at one end to extreme brutality and shooting, strangling, and choking to death at the other. Some theorists see a man's murder of his wife or partner as one end of a continuum of violence; others, however, view homicide as a form of behavior distinct from nonlethal domestic violence. Gelles (1991), for example, argues that homicide and infanticide may have a biological, even evolutionary basis unlike less severe forms of violence which can be explained by cultural and learning theories. As Aldridge and Browne (2003) indicate, however, the same kind of violent rage that causes serious injury can result in blows that are fatal. The triggering event is often the female's rejection of her partner. Koziol-McLain et al. (2006) concur with this perception of steadily escalating violence as the gateway to homicide. From this perspective, the most significant precipitating factor in femicide is prior domestic violence against the woman. Accordingly, a risk assessment of the danger facing a victim is not only desirable but also an essential part of any safety plan. One matter that should be addressed in any safety plan is whether or not the victim of battering is pregnant.

THE SHOCKING LINK BETWEEN PREGNANCY AND HOMICIDE

A year-long investigation by the *Washington Post* of national death records from 1990 to 2004 uncovered 1,367 deaths of pregnant women and new mothers (St. George 2004). Researchers, according to the news reports, were stunned at this discovery. According to the Centers for Disease Control (CDC) (Chang et al. 2005), the maternal homicide rate for African Americans was found to be seven times the white rate. For all pregnant women under age 20, partner homicide is the leading cause of death. Many of the women who were murdered did not have prenatal care. When the death rates of older women are included in the statistics, 44 percent of pregnant women who died were killed in car crashes and 31 percent by homicide. In the majority (57 percent) of the murder cases, firearms were used; stabbing and strangling were the next most commonly used methods of killing.

Although the CDC found homicide to be the second cause of death for pregnant women, there is some reason to believe it is their leading cause of death. At present there is no reliable system in place to track maternal homicides either on the state or federal levels. Two extremely comprehensive studies were undertaken, one in Maryland and the other in Massachusetts. These investigations clearly showed that the leading cause of maternal death for pregnant women in those states was domestic homicide (St. George 2004). In Maryland, which now keeps records on maternal homicides, more than 10 percent of all homicides among women ages 14 to 44 happen to pregnant or postpartum women.

Battering often precedes the killing of pregnant women. The causes of the attacks on these women, however, are not totally understood. Adams's (2007) research is helpful in this regard because he asked specifically about pregnancy in his interviews with both samples—the men in prison and the women victims of attempted murder. While all but one of the men denied beating women while they were pregnant, two-thirds of the women said they were beaten during this time. Two of the women had miscarriages as a result. The violence, however, did not escalate. We can get an indication of the motive for violence against pregnant women in the explanation given by one interviewee who said her husband had told her she was "not focused on him" (162). Another speculated that she was beaten because she stopped drinking with him during her pregnancies. The factor of jealousy that is so prominent in male-on-female homicide is evidenced here as well, but now the jealousy is over an unborn child or infant. As women lose interest in sex during this time, the men are likely to feel frustrated and neglected. Another explanation for the high rate of attacks on pregnant women is provided by Wilcox (2006) who suggests that a woman's increased vulnerability during this time makes her more susceptible to control by the man and to violence.

According to the CDC research, most of the young pregnant women who were murdered were of low socioeconomic status. This fact may indicate that economic arguments may come into play. One famous case that was fictionalized by Theodore Dreiser (1925) in one of the great American classics, *An American Tragedy,* concerned the drowning of a pregnant lower-class girlfriend by her ambitious lover who had a chance of being socially mobile through marriage to a prominent young woman. The 1951 film version, *A Place in the Sun,* starred Montgomery Cliff and Elizabeth Taylor.

Economic and convenience factors are evidenced in several of the homicides described in the *Washington Post* series on the murders of pregnant women. The facts in the following cases emerged from interviews with family members, prosecutors, and the police. The dead included a 23-year-old college student who was beaten to death by her lover, who was married, when she refused to end her pregnancy; a high school student who got pregnant by her manager at McDonald's and asked him for money for an abortion; a 29-year-old who was killed by her married lover; a 16-year-old whose boyfriend did not wish to pay child support and also feared charges of statutory rape if their relationship came to light; a 14-year-old who refused to move in with her boyfriend who had gotten her pregnant.

To understand more about what drives people to resort to such acts of horror and destruction, not just in pregnancy cases but in general, we need to consult a wide range of sources and examine theories from more than one discipline. Even if we are looking at only one type of domestic homicide such as wife murder or the killing of a child, no single explanation is sufficient in itself to explain every situation. Let us now examine this public health problem multidimensionally, starting with the most basic component—biology.

BIOLOGICAL THEORY
Biological Aspects of Aggression

Battering may be conceived of in terms of cultural, psychological, or, as is our concern here, biological causation. Evolutionists such as Wrangham and

Peterson (1996), authors of *Demonic Males: Apes and the Origins of Human Violence,* look to biology to explain patterns of dominance. Emphasizing male dominance, these authors study predatory violence including rape and murder among chimpanzees and other apes, our closest living relatives. They stress the need to study such violence as biological phenomena with meaning for us all. Their findings have important implications for the study of oppression in human society in revealing the degree to which aggressive behavior, if goal oriented and calculated, can be rewarding in providing a sense of power.

Battering, according to Wrangham and Peterson, is rare in nonhuman animals and occurs only in species where females have few allies for protection. In their provocative exploration of ape male-on-female battering in the wilderness, these biologists found that the key predictive factor in primate battering was vulnerability. Significantly, even in the primate animal kingdom, as the authors suggest, "The underlying issue looks to be domination or control" (146). Human battering, similarly, is about the coercion and intimidation that men impose on women in order to control them (Goetting 1999).

Using MRI technology, scientists are on the threshold of discoveries concerning biochemical processes associated with the impulsive, forceful activities and exploitative attitudes and blaming of victims characteristic of antisocial personality. In general, eight times as many men as women receive this label (American Psychiatric Association [APA] 2000).

Biological factors that play a role in human male aggression and violence are the male hormone testosterone and low levels of the neurotransmitter serotonin which is also associated with aggression as well as addiction. Research on prison inmates reveals that males and females with abnormally high levels of testosterone tended to have been convicted of violent crimes and to show high dominance and aggression toward other inmates (Dabbs and Dabbs 2000).

In a comparison of school performance and head injury histories of violent and nonviolent male prisoners, Leon-Carrion and Ramos (2003) found that what differentiated the two groups was a history of having a past untreated head injury.

Sociobiological theory is sometimes applied to the murder of infants and small children. Drawing on evolutionary concepts, theorists of this school hold that children who are not genetically related to the persons who are parenting them are exceptionally vulnerable (Kurst-Swanger and Petcosky 2003). Some credence is given to this argument in that stepfathers and boyfriends of the mother are known to be disproportionately involved in the deaths of unrelated offspring.

Aggression is also engendered in certain individuals when they are intoxicated. Although we recognize that persons who are feeling overwhelmed, for example, with anger, may turn to alcohol or other mood altering substances for relief, from a biological standpoint, we can still consider the impact of such chemicals on the erratic behavior that might be the end result.

Substance Abuse

The ingestion of chemical substances such as alcohol and other mood altering drugs is associated with changes in the brain. Some of the changes are long term and even permanent; others are of short-term duration until the effect of the intoxicants wears off. This fact has been confirmed in laboratory studies with both humans and nonhuman primates (Moeller and Dougherty 2001; van Wormer and Davis 2008). Men diagnosed with antisocial personality are especially prone to exhibit aggressive behavior when drunk. Therefore, it is appropriate to consider the role of substance use as a biological factor that might have a bearing first in regard to violence in general, and second, in regard to homicide. Key points related to physiology are the lowering of inhibitions on the part of potential victims as well as perpetrators of homicide and the clouded thinking associated with intoxication. The relationship between substance abuse and domestic homicide is explored more fully in Chapter 4.

Mental Disorders

Mental illness and traumatic brain injury are biologically based disorders that may be implicated in the killing of a family member. Such acts of extreme violence, such as those of Andrea Yates who drowned her five small children, may occur under a delusion that the devil was within the perpetrator. Brain damage, as from serious head injury, is sometimes associated with the type of seemingly uncontrollable rages that may result in murder. In her study of battering men, Marano (1993) links intrapsychic deficits—a hypersensitivity to abandonment, inability to control negative emotions, and poor impulse control—with biological deficits—low serotonin levels in the brain, high testosterone production, and brain damage from head injury. Scientists at the University of Iowa have identified rare cases in which injuries to the brain in infancy prevented people from learning normal moral behavior and from feeling guilt or remorse after hurting people (van Wormer 2007). Dutton (2007) explains predatory behavior in boys and men as resulting from exposure to psychological trauma early in life. Abnormalities in the prefrontal cortex have been found in murderers that probably are indicative of developmental trauma, not only from receiving violence directly but even from just witnessing domestic assaults.

A biological proclivity toward rage does not mean control is totally absent in most cases. Battering men in treatment often claim they totally lose control over their wives, usually in reaction to their wives' pestering, yet for many of them, their violence is selective and only inflicted on family members.

THE PSYCHOLOGY OF DOMESTIC HOMICIDE

The overlap between biologically based and psychological factors is considerable. For the sake of organization, we are considering personality traits and the dynamics of life-threatening attacks under this category of the psychology of domestic homicide.

Men Who Kill

Two relevant personality types are described in the literature of domestic homicide. The first is the personality disorder, antisocial personality. Men in this category lack normal emotions such as love, jealousy, or the ability to feel empathy or remorse. So when they kill, they do so not out of jealousy but because they want to get rid of the person or for financial gain. Aldridge and Browne (2003) refer to these murders as "instrumental killings." Adams (2007) includes such killers (7 out of the 31 interviewed) under the category "materially motivated." Such individuals do not necessarily have histories of physically abusive behavior. And, as reported when interviewed, emotional feelings for their partners or for any previous partners were lacking. They looked to the women in their lives for sex and material benefits.

Jacobson and Gottman (1998) monitored 140 couples in which the man had a history of violence. They attached electronic sensors to the heads of men who were prompted to discuss marital problems. The researchers were surprised to find that the ones they eventually labeled cobras, the most violent men who sounded and looked aggressive, were actually internally calm. So self-centered are such antisocial men, that once their partners were out of the way they tended to let go of the relationship. The danger of violence with cobras occurs during the initial separation whereas more typical types of batterers become more dangerous following separation due to their ambivalent feelings of love. The cobras, about 20 percent of the total of the most violent husbands, are sadistic, prone to death threats, and according to the researchers, belong in prison (Marano 1993). In comparisons of battering men who have committed homicide and offenders who have not, the homicide offenders are more likely to have personality disorders (Aldridge and Browne 2003). Because these men have a certain charisma, as Jacobson and Gottman note, their wives and girlfriends tend to find them hard to resist.

The second personality type of batterers that Jacobson and Gottman identified in their experiment, they called "pit bulls." These men were found to become internally aroused with heart rates that increased with their anger; they never let up. The wives of pit bulls often took the risk of arguing back. If the women ever left the relationship, such men tended to stalk them. In a later study, Jacobson coded the physiological response of violent couples (as reported in Aldridge and Browne 2003). The chief finding was that only male violence or threatening behavior induces fear in the recipient, a significant gender difference in response to such aggression.

In his classic work on violence, former prison psychiatrist James Gilligan (1997, 129) describes one man whom he saw as typical of wife murderers in general. This inmate, Walter T., had an image of himself as a dependent, helpless infant who expected his wife to nurture him so he would not die. When she threatened to leave him, therefore, he experienced it "as the equivalent of a death threat" and so he decided to kill her regardless of the consequences to himself.

One theme that dominates the criminal justice literature is the theme of jealousy and possessiveness. In his work with battering men, Dutton (2007, 167) found that fear of abandonment was common: "Assaultive males in our treatment groups talked about jealousy and abandonment a great deal in treatment even while trying to maintain a distanced 'cool' or dismissing tone about their emotional dependence on their wives." When responding to scenarios in which the woman wanted to spend time with her friends, violence-prone men reported themselves anxious and angry, even feeling humiliated. Similarly, research summarized by Marano (1993) shows that violent men in hypothetical jealousy-provoking situations consistently tend to misinterpret their wives' motives as intentionally hostile.

Dutton (2007) draws on attachment theory to explain the batterers' typical overreaction to separation from loved ones. The strong attachment drives of the infant and small child are basic to survival into adulthood. Children deprived of love and security early in life do not know how to trust; they suffer from an attachment disorder that is destructive to their relationships. Men who have been so deprived in infancy have a striking inability to tolerate being alone. Because of their dependence on their wives, they resent them, even hate them. To diminish their anxiety about being abandoned, they establish an exaggerated control and isolation of their female partners. When the women balk or complain in any way, the men attack.

One especially striking finding of Adams's interviews concerns sexual practices. When asked about their sex life, the male inmates claimed they had sex daily with the women they killed; one-fourth of them claimed to have had sexual relations multiple times per day. The vast majority of the victim-survivors reported that they were pressured and coerced into sex on at least a weekly basis (90 percent) and that sex was demanded of them after they were beaten (70 percent). Adams speculates that this sexual abuse relates to the men's sense of ownership of these women and their possessive and obsessive behavior regarding them.

The dynamics of domestic homicide that ends in suicide is the subject of Chapter 3. Depression (which often has a biological basis) and anger are key components. Depression differentiates homicide-only perpetrators from these others (Aldridge Browne 2003). Alcohol abuse and a mental disorder are likely to be involved as well. The majority of all murder-suicides involve a situation that can be described as amorous jealousy. Men who commit such acts tend to be significantly older than their victims by six years or more and also when compared to murderers who do not commit suicide, they are more likely to be married to their partners. These are distinguishing features singled out by Adams (2007) from his review of the literature. Another curious factor mentioned by Adams is that often the men who committed murder-suicide had the wife's biological children residing in the home. Women very rarely commit murder-suicide; if they do, their children are the likely victims, and the motive springs out of some sort of deranged and suicidal impulse. Generally speaking, murders that involve multiple victims are male perpetrated crimes (Serran and Firestone 2004).

Women Who Kill

Up until now we have been focusing on male batterers, a subject on which social scientists have consensus. The literature on females who batter is sparse and also riddled with contradiction. All writers are agreed, however, that there are distinct male/female differences in interpersonal violence—differences stemming in part from physiology and in part from psychology.

Feminist criminologists, as most criminologists, stress that female perpetrated homicides most often are committed out of self-defense against a battering man. Indeed we know from research on the dynamics of female domestic homicide that most women arrested for murder have been battered by their victims; the victims were their victimizers (van Wormer and Bartollas 2007). Moreover, the overwhelming number of female arrests for domestic assault involve reciprocal violence with the victim fighting back. In contrast to men who kill, women, being the weaker sex, are not known to strangle or beat their victims to death; rather they will use a weapon such as a gun, or less frequently, a knife.

Aldridge and Browne (2003) in their review of research on female perpetrated homicide found that the large majority of women who killed used only as much force as was necessary. Almost half of the male homicides, in contrast, involved overkill. Evidently, such attackers were in a state of rage, because such killings involved multiple blows, cuttings, and shooting, far more than was required to kill the victim.

Consider also situations in which women beat on or beat up a passive male partner who refuses to fight back. We know little about such unilateral female-on-male attacks except anecdotally. Missing from the research data, as Dutton (2007) indicates, are reports of cases in which women batterers engage in unilateral, severe violence against a passive spouse or partner. The reason for this omission, as Dutton argues, is that researchers assume that female domestic violence is defensive and so they fail to ask women arrested for battering whether or not their male victims fought back. A small minority of women do attack nonviolent men, however. Such women tend to have an abusive personality and the same antisocial characteristics as some aggressive men. Poor self-control is a key characteristic. Research by Moffitt et al. (2001) further informs us about gender differences in antisocial or psychopathic behavior. Interestingly, these researchers found that male psychopaths in their study attacked strangers as well as intimates, but that female psychopaths attacked only persons close to them.

SOCIAL FACTORS IN INTIMATE HOMICIDE

We begin with a story of elephants. In a park in South Africa in the 1990s, a gang of delinquent young male elephants attacked and killed 39 white rhinoceroses (Barber 2006). The elephants causing the problems were orphans that had been moved from another park. The problem was solved when some bull elephants were brought in. This story can serve as a metaphor for the importance of healthy role modeling; it is being so used by organizers of a program called "Nurturing Fathers" to show the importance of adult male role models in the family. As we learned from Adams's interviews with men who had killed their wives and partners, these men consistently grew up in fear of their fathers or without fathers present in the home. Consider the case of Matthew, who, at age 23, killed his girlfriend after she broke off their relationship (Adams, 127):

> Matthew attributed his abuse and stalking of women to the absence of his father.... Asked how this specifically contributed to his violence, Matthew said, "I think just not having a father to teach me about life. Nobody ever taught me how to deal with rejection. It led to a dependency on women for love to fill that void."

The sociological analysis of partner homicide looks at the context of such violence and the demographics of the perpetrators. Although some theorists such as representatives of the Duluth Intervention Model would take a culturally deterministic view and attribute all domestic violence to patriarchal culture (see van Wormer 2007, and Chapter 11, this book), most theorists who write on domestic violence subscribe to a more holistic approach. All agree, however, that early childhood socialization and influences from the wider culture are key components in domestic partner violence. Early childhood socialization into cultural norms is paramount for healthy social development but it can also inculcate attitudes toward the treatment of women that are conducive to violence.

The fact that cultural norms are a key influence in family violence is seen in cross-cultural comparisons of domestic homicide rates. The lowest rates for this type of crime are found in Norway and Finland; the highest in India, Pakistan, and across the Middle East. (For a global view, see Chapter 7.)

In the most comprehensive study on femicide in the literature to date, Campbell, Koziol-McLain and their associates (2003) gathered information from persons closely connected to homicide victims. The following factors surfaced again and again in the interviews: access to a gun and previous threat with a weapon, stepchild in the home, estrangement and separation, and lack of police arrest for prior abuse. The strongest demographic risk factor for partner homicide was the abuser's lack of employment. In a study of gender-specific homicide in rural areas, Lee and Stevenson (2006) similarly found that unemployment and poverty were associated with male-on-female homicides but that they had no bearing in female homicide.

An additional demographic factor that has surfaced in the literature is age disparity, a factor in both homicide followed by suicide and homicide alone (Aldridge and Browne 2003). The highest risk for homicide victimization occurs in situations in which wives are 10 or more years younger than their husbands; sexual jealousy may be a possible cause (Dutton 2007).

CASE HISTORY RELATED TO MILITARY COMBAT

Investigative research by the *New York Times* uncovered 121 cases in which veterans of Iraq and Afghanistan committed a killing in this country after their return from war (Mitchell 2008). In many of those cases, combat trauma and the stress of military engagement along with alcohol abuse and family problems appear to have set the stage for tragedy. About a third of the victims were family members including children; others were fellow service members.

One article from the series entitled "When Strains on Military Families Turn Deadly" describes the tragic murder of Sergeant Erin Edwards who was killed by her husband, a fellow soldier (Alvarez and Sontag 2008). The murder followed a pattern of merciless violence. With a general's help the victim had secured a transfer to a different base and secured a protective restraining order. Her husband was ordered into treatment for substance abuse and anger management. Yet, as the article tells us,

> On the morning of July 22, 2004, William Edwards easily slipped off base, skipping his anger-management class, and drove to his wife's house in the Texas town of Killeen. He waited for her to step outside and then, after a struggle, shot her point-blank in the head before turning the gun on himself....After the murder-suicide, local police officers securing the scene noted that both bodies were dressed in military camouflage clothing with nameplates that said Edwards. Both were 24.

Clearly engagement in combat and the stress of multiple deployments are risk factors for family problems including substance abuse and domestic violence upon return. The best prevention would be the elimination of war. Under the present circumstances, close monitoring of high risk situations and assessments of the danger of homicide are tools that military social workers might rely upon in the development of a safety plan.

DANGER ASSESSMENT TOOLS

Jacquelyn Campbell and her associates developed a danger assessment tool based on their prior research findings on the characteristics of partner-wife killers. On the 15-point instrument that was constructed, the average score that would have been earned for the murder victims who were studied post-mortem was 8. These series of questions that comprise this instrument have been empirically validated by researchers to have predictive power to assess which battered women are most at risk of death (Campbell et al. 2003). The Danger Assessment study found that women who were threatened with a gun or other weapon were 20 times more likely than other women to be murdered. Just having a gun in the house increased the risk by six times. One major finding of the study was that almost half of the murdered women did not recognize the high level of their risk.

Stark (2002) finds Campbell's danger assessment tool useful in providing testimony as part of the defense strategy when a previously battered woman is on trial for the murder of her husband or partner. Risk assessment is designed to answer the following question: "Based on the prior history of battering in this relationship, what was the risk that the battered woman would be killed at the time she used violence against her partner?" More frequent use of this assessment instrument would be by practitioners to assist women clients in developing a safety plan. The instrument is simply scored by counting the "yes" responses, but question numbers 4 and 7 concerning gun availability and threats should be given special weight.

THE DANGER ASSESSMENT TOOL

Jacquelyn C. Campbell, Ph.D., R.N.

The Danger Assessment Tool was developed in 1985 and revised in 1988 after reliability and validity studies were done. Completing the Danger Assessment can help a woman evaluate the degree of danger she faces and consider what she should do next. Practitioners are reminded that the Danger Assessment is meant to be used with a calendar to enhance the accuracy of the battered woman's recall of events.

DANGER ASSESSMENT

Using the calendar, please mark the approximate dates during the past year when you were beaten by your husband or partner. Write on that date how bad the incident was according to the following scale:

1. Slapping, pushing; no injuries and/or lasting pain
2. Punching, kicking; bruises, cuts, and/or continuing pain
3. "Beating up"; severe contusions, burns, broken bones
4. Threat to use weapon; head injury, internal injury, permanent injury
5. Use of weapon; wounds from weapon

(If any of the descriptions for the higher number apply, use the higher number.)

Mark Yes or No for each of the following. ("He" refers to your husband, partner, ex-husband, ex-partner, or whoever is currently physically hurting you.)

_____ 1. Has the physical violence increased in frequency over the past year?
_____ 2. Has the physical violence increased in severity over the past year and/or has a weapon or threat from a weapon ever been used?
_____ 3. Does he ever try to choke you?
_____ 4. Is there a gun in the house?
_____ 5. Has he ever forced you to have sex when you did not wish to do so?
_____ 6. Does he use drugs? By drugs, I mean "uppers" or amphetamines, speed, angel dust, cocaine, "crack," street drugs, or mixtures.
_____ 7. Does he threaten to kill you and/or do you believe he is capable of killing you?
_____ 8. Is he drunk every day or almost every day? (In terms of quantity of alcohol.)
_____ 9. Does he control most or all of your daily activities? For instance: does he tell you who you can be friends with, how much money you can take with you shopping, or when you can take the car? (If he tries, but you do not let him, check here: ____)
_____ 10. Have you ever been beaten by him while you were pregnant? (If you have never been pregnant by him, check here: ____)
_____ 11. Is he violently and constantly jealous of you? (For instance, does he say "If I can't have you, no one can"?)
_____ 12. Have you ever threatened or tried to commit suicide?
_____ 13. Has he ever threatened or tried to commit suicide?
_____ 14. Is he violent toward your children?
_____ 15. Is he violent outside of the home?

_____ Total "Yes" Answers

> Thank you. Please talk to your nurse, advocate, or counselor about what the Danger Assessment means in terms of your situation.

Source: J.C. Campbell, D. Webster, J. Koziol-McLain, C.R. Block, D. Campbell, M.A. Curry, F. Gary, J. McFarlane, C. Sachs, P. Sharps, Y. Ulrich, and S.A. Wilt, "Assessing Risk Factors for Intimate Partner Homicide," *National Institute of Justice Journal* (NIJ), November 2003, no. 250: 15, http://www.ncjrs.gov/pdffiles1/jr000250e.pdf. Copyright 1985, 1988.

Jacquelyn Campbell and Anna D. Wolf generously extend permission for use of the above danger assessment instrument with proper citation.

DID O.J. SIMPSON FIT THE PROFILE?

Let us now review the items on the Danger Assessment Tool to determine if, using hindsight, O.J. Simpson would have met the profile. A search of the Internet and facts revealed in *The Batterer: A Psychological Profile* by Dutton (1997) fill us in on many details about Simpson's behavior that do show he was a person who would have been at high risk for homicide. Documentation from police calls reveal a pattern of accusations against Nicole that she was interested in other men, terrifying threats, and out-of-control temper outbursts. Simpson had been sentenced to a batterer's intervention program, but he had never attended. We know that Simpson had a gun because after Nicole's death, he threatened to kill himself with a gun. Later, he wrote in a suicide note, "If we had a problem, it was because I loved her so much." There is more than a hint of the kind of possessiveness and obsession that is consistent with cases of murder-suicide. We do not know about drugs or forced sex. Even when Nicole managed to end the relationship, as she thought, she was still being bothered by her ex-husband and had reason to be afraid of him.

Given the limited information that is available, it is clear that Lenore Walker was incorrect in her statement that O.J. Simpson did not meet the profile of the homicidal batterer.

CONCLUSION

Women in the United States are killed by their spouses and partners more often than by any other type of perpetrator, and the majority of these murders follow a pattern of physical abuse. The pattern of assault is clearly the first clue that a woman is at risk. In fact, to a lesser extent, the male batterer is also at some risk of being killed as a defensive reaction. For all parties concerned and for the sake of the children, determining the risk factors that can end in tragedy is vital.

This chapter has pursued this investigation of the risks of domestic homicide holistically, with a consideration of biological, psychological, and social components that together contribute to the abuse that can escalate into murder. Our review of the empirical literature revealed that in the male abuser a background of a personality disorder, heavy substance use, desperate fear of abandonment, access to a gun that he threatens to use, and unemployment are potential risk factors for violence escalating into murder. For females, the key risk factor for partner homicide is a history of having been victimized by a battering man and access to a gun.

Murder-suicide is almost exclusively a male perpetrated crime. Suicidal ideation, access to a gun, and a state of depression are risk factors for murder-suicide. The danger assessment devised by Jacquelyn Campbell can be used by mental health professionals and domestic services workers to gauge a battered woman's risk of being killed. It is especially important that men with a prior domestic violence conviction are prevented from gun ownership as mandated by federal law.

Immediate care for a woman in a potentially harmful or present abusive situation involves the development of a safety plan. A woman can be provided with temporary housing in a secret place, such as a shelter, and access to legal services so that she can get a restraining order. If a woman plans to stay with her spouse or parents, she can be helped in the development of plans that can be carried out if the abuse does not stop. Walker (2000) recommends helping battered women identify and verbalize the cues she perceives as signs of potential danger. Cues range from the woman's own feelings of anxiety to a change in the man's facial expressions. Practical plans are discussed. Examples are having access to available car keys, a telephone, cash, a personal bank account, and preparing children to leave on short notice. Finally, the escape plane is rehearsed.

In a British-based study on victim response to battering, Hoyle and Sanders (2000) raise an interesting point: that the perpetrators of violence move from the violent domination of one woman to the violent domination of the next. Future victims will only be protected if the batterer's violence is confronted and dealt with head-on.

To really deal with this form of violence, it is necessary, as Lenore Walker (2000) suggests, to establish a community-wide task force to assist the domestic violence divisions in the state attorney's offices and probation departments so that they can begin to identify which offenders should go directly to jail and which ones might benefit from post-adjudication diversion programs. Mandates that prosecutors, the police, and medical and mental health professionals be trained in implementation strategies and subsequent intervention protocol have been found to be effective in stopping the violence.

The next chapter explores the dynamics of the psychologically complex subset of domestic homicides—murder-suicide—in more depth.

REFERENCES

Adams, D. 2007. *Why do they kill? Men who murder their intimate partners.* Nashville, TN: Vanderbilt University Press.

Aldridge, M., and K. Browne. 2003. Perpetrators of spousal homicide: A review. *Trauma, Violence, & Abuse* 4:265–76.

Alvarez, L., and D. Sontag. 2008. When strains on military families turn deadly. *The New York Times,* February 15.

American Psychiatric Association (APA). 2000. *Diagnostic and statistical manual of mental disorders.* 4th ed. (DSM-IV-TR) (Text revision.) Arlington, VA: American Psychiatric Publishing.

Barber, M. 2006. Father figure. *The Honolulu Advertiser,* June 12. http://the .honoluluadvertiser.com/article/2006/Jun/12/il/FP606120311.html (accessed February 2008).

Campbell, J.C. 2006. Risk factors for femicide-suicide in abusive relationships: Results from a multisite case control study. *Violence and Victims* 21, no. 1: 3–21.

Campbell, J.C., D. Webster, J. Koziol-McLain, C. Block, D. Campbell, M.A. Curry, F. Gary, N. Glass, J. McFarlane, C. Sachs, P. Sharps, Y. Ulrich, S.A. Wilt, J. Manganello, X. Xu, J. Schollenberger, V. Frye, and K. Laughon. 2003. Risk factors for femicide in abusive relationships: Results from a multisite case control study. *American Journal of Public Health* 93, no. 7: 1089–97. http://www.ajph.org/cgi/content/abstract/93/7/1089.

Chang, J., C. Berg, L. Saltzman, and J. Herndon. 2005. Homicide: A leading cause of injury deaths among pregnant and postpartum women in the United States, 1991–1999. *American Journal of Public Health* 95, no. 3: 471–77.

Dabbs, J.M., and M.G. Dabbs. 2000. *Heroes, rogues and lovers: Testosterone and Dut behavior.* Hightstown, NJ: McGraw-Hill.

Dutton, D. 1997. *The batterer: A psychological profile.* New York: Basic Books.

Dutton, D. 2007. *Rethinking domestic violence.* Vancouver, Canada: University of British Columbia Press.

Gelles, R. 1991. Physical violence, child abuse, and child homicide: A continuum of violence, or distinct behaviours? *Human Nature* 2, no. 1: 59–72.

Gilligan, J. 1997. *Violence: Reflections on a national epidemic.* New York: Vintage Books.

Goetting, A. 1995. *Homicide in families and other populations.* New York: Springer.

Goetting, A. 1999. *Getting out: Life stories of women who left abusive men.* New York: Columbia University Press.

Hoyle, C., and A. Sanders. 2000. Police response to domestic violence: From victim choice to victim empowerment? *British Journal of Criminology* 40:14–36.

Jacobson, N.S., and J.M. Gottman. 1998. *When men batter women: New insights into ending abusive relationships.* New York: Simon & Schuster.

Koziol-McLain, J., D. Webster, J. McFarlane, C.R. Block, Y. Ulrich, N. Glass, and J.C. Campbell. 2006. Risk factors for femicide-suicide in abusive relationships: Results from a multisite case control study. *Violence and Victims* 21, no. 1: 3–21.

Kurst-Swanger, K., and J.L. Petcosky. 2003. *Violence in the home: Multidisciplinary perspectives.* New York: Oxford University Press.

Lee, M.R., and G.D. Stevenson. 2006. Gender-specific homicide offending in rural areas. *Homicide Studies* 10, no. 1: 55–73.

Leon-Carrion, J., and C. Ramos. 2003. Blows to the head during development can predispose to violent criminal behavior. *Brain Injury* 17, no. 3: 207–16.

Marano, H. 1993. Inside the heart of marital violence. *Psychology Today,* November/December: 50–53, 76–78, 91.

Mitchell, G. 2008. "War torn" series on G.I. murders debuts at "NYT." *New York Times,* January 12 http://www.editorandpublisher.com/eandp/article_brief/eandp/1/1003695837 (accessed July 2008).

Moeller, F.G., and D.M. Dougherty. 2001. Antisocial personality disorder, alcohol, and aggression. *Alcohol Research and Health* 25:5–11.

Moffitt, T.E., A. Caspi, M. Rutter, and P.A. Silva. 2001. *Sex differences in antisocial behavior.* Cambridge: Cambridge University Press.

Serran, G., and P. Firestone. 2004. Intimate partner homicide: A review of the male proprietariness and the self-defense theories. *Aggression and Violent Behavior* 9:1–15.

St. George, D. 2004. Many new or expectant mothers die violent deaths. *Washington Post,* December 19.

Stark, E. 2002. Preparing for expert testimony in domestic violence cases. In *Handbook of domestic violence intervention strategies,* ed. A. Roberts, 216–52. New York: Oxford University Press.

van Wormer, K. 2007. *Human behavior and the social environment, micro level: Individuals and families.* New York: Oxford University Press.

van Wormer, K., and C. Bartollas. 2007. *Women and the criminal justice system.* Boston: Allyn & Bacon.

van Wormer, K., and D.R. Davis. 2008. *Addiction treatment: A strengths perspective.* Belmont, CA: Thomson.

Walker, L. 1979. *The battered woman.* New York: Harper & Row.

Walker, L. 2000. *The battered woman syndrome.* 2nd ed. New York: Springer.

Websdale, N. 1999. *Understanding domestic homicide.* Boston: Northeastern University Press.

Wilcox, P. 2006. *Surviving domestic violence: Gender, poverty and agency.* Hampshire, UK: Palgrave.

Wrangham, R., and D. Peterson. 1996. *Demonic males: Apes and the origins of human violence.* Boston: Houghton Mifflin.

Zahn, M. 2003. Intimate partner homicide: An overview. *National Institute of Justice Journal* 250:2–3.

3

The Dynamics of Murder-Suicide in Domestic Situations[1]

In the United States and Britain, as elsewhere, a woman is more vulnerable to violence in her home than in public. In the United Kingdom, domestic violence costs the lives of more than two women every week (Home Office 2005b), and in the United States, with a much larger population, estimates are that more than three women a day are killed by their intimate partners (Rennison 2003).

Homicide is a leading cause of traumatic death for pregnant and postpartum women in the United States, accounting for 31 percent of maternal injury deaths (Family Violence Prevention Fund 2007). In the United Kingdom, pregnancy is a period of high risk as well.

Whereas in the United States women who are killed are most often killed by guns, in England and Wales three times as many women are killed by a sharp instrument or by strangulation as by shooting. Over the past decade, about four times as many females who were killed as males who were killed were partners or ex-partners of the murderer (Home Office 2005a). As in the United States, far more males than females are victimized by homicide of a general nature; they are killed often in fights with other men (Bureau of Justice Statistics 2005).

An extensive search by Aldridge and Browne (2003) revealed 22 empirical research studies on risk factors for spousal homicide. In the United Kingdom, 37 percent of all women who were murdered were killed by their current or former intimate partner compared to 6 percent of men. The most common cause of an intimate partner's death in England and Wales was being attacked with a sharp implement or being strangled. By contrast, the most common cause in the United States for spousal homicide was getting shot. Nine major risk factors are found that may help predict the probability of a partner homicide and prevent future victims (Aldridge and Browne 2003).

As anyone who reads or watches local or national news reports in the United States will be aware, a spate of murder-suicides is taking place. The dynamics are relatively similar; a battered woman had told her partner or he had inferred from her behavior that she was making a break in the relationship; the man loaded his gun and shot her and then himself, killing them both. Most of these domestic cases are not reported nationally; they are in headlines in the local paper.

Because government data in the United Kingdom and the United States providing national statistics on homicide that ends in suicide are hard to come by, other, less official and comprehensive sources must be consulted. A recent development in the United States is a promising development, however, for future research. The emerging state-based National Violent Death Reporting System recently has begun providing data on homicide-suicide for a sample of American states. Unfortunately for our purposes, the majority of the research that is available is not focused on domestic homicide situations.

HOMICIDE-SUICIDE IN THE UK

An analysis of the *London Times'* reports of murder (1887–1990) by Danson and Soothill (1996) revealed a total incidence of 6 percent of 2,274 cases of murder followed by suicide in the United Kingdom. Around the turn of the twentieth century, as the researchers suggest, this figure of murder suicides was much higher at approximately one in three. Murder-suicides, according to Danson and Soothill, are mostly family affairs, especially in cases of female perpetrators. There is a much higher proportion of British male murder-suicides, in general, however, and males are much more likely than females to commit their crimes with guns. Overwhelmingly the women committing murder-suicide in the study tended to kill their children and then themselves. Men, on the other hand, tended to kill their spouses or partners.

More recently, in the first epidemiological study of instances of homicide-suicide in England and Wales, Barraclough and Harris (2002) studied death certificates for all murder-suicides over a four-year time span. They found that 3 percent of male, 11 percent of female, and 19 percent of child homicides were of this type. Similarly, of all suicides, 0.8 percent male and 0.4 percent female deaths occurred in homicide-suicide incidents. The typical cases involved families of low socioeconomic status.

Data provided by the Home Office (2005b) for England and Wales, which are difficult to analyze because the circumstances and timing of suicides following homicide are not clearly spelled out, provide support for Barraclough and Harris's earlier findings of a low instance of murders ending in suicide. One can determine that of the 659 homicides that were committed in 2004, 19 individuals committed suicide before indictments could be issued. We do not know the nature of the homicides, however.

Personal correspondence with Kathryn Coleman on April 10, 2007 of the Direct Communications Unit of the Home Office provided data on suicide following homicide in which the victim was a partner or ex-partner. From the years 1997–2006, there were on average 12 cases each year of male-on-female homicides that ended in suicide. Official Home Office sources reveal there are around 100 male-on-female homicides for each year (for example, see Home Office 2004). So this means that only a small percentage—around 10 percent—of these intimate homicides ends in suicide in England and Wales. As further indicated in the government report, the methods of homicide were by means of a sharp instrument, poison or drugs, beating, or strangulation.

HOMICIDE-SUICIDE IN NORTH AMERICA

A rare find in the American literature is the research presented by Bossarte, Simon, and Barker (2006) who analyzed data from the National Violent Death Reporting System (NVDRS). This active state-based surveillance system includes data from 7 states for 2003 and 13 states for 2004. The incident-level structure facilitates identification of homicide/suicide incidents. Results revealed that within participating states, 65 homicide/suicide incidents (homicide rate is equal to 0.230/100,000) occurred in 2003 and 144 incidents (homicide rate is equal to 0.238/100,000) occurred in 2004. Most victims (58 percent) were current or former intimate partners of the perpetrator. Among all male perpetrators of intimate partner homicide, 30.6 percent were also suicides. A substantial proportion of the victims (13.7 percent) were the children of the perpetrator. Overall, most victims (74.6 percent) were female and most perpetrators were male (91.9 percent). A recent history of legal problems (25.3 percent) or financial problems (9.3 percent) was common among the perpetrators.

From Statistics Canada (2005) we learn that over the past 40 years, one in ten solved homicides were cases in which the suspect took his or her own life following the homicide. About three-quarters of these victims were killed by a family member. Virtually all of the incidents (97 percent) involved female victims killed by a male spouse. And, as Easteal (1994) demonstrated in an earlier study, one third of *spousal* homicides in the United States and Canada end in suicide. Few other varieties of homicide end in this way.

Probably related to the availability of guns, the homicide rate in the United States is much higher than the British rate, although the difference has diminished in recent years. According to an international comparative study, the homicide rate in the United States is 0.04 per 1,000 residents while in the United Kingdom the rate is 0.014 per 1,000 residents (NationMaster.com 2007). The difference in homicide rates between large American and British cities is even more pronounced.

Guns are by far the most common weapon used in these crimes (Violence Policy Center [VPC] 2008). One could speculate that if you shoot someone, it is relatively easy to then turn the gun on yourself. If you stab or strangle someone, however, suicide becomes much more difficult. In any case, the high rate of spousal murder-suicides is consistent with the murder-as-extended-suicide hypothesis of Palermo (1994).

Notably, in 1992, the *Journal of the American Medical Association* (JAMA) reviewed the epidemiology, patterns, and determinants of murder-suicide and made a strong case for the need for systematic data gathering so that prevention strategies can be developed (Marzuk, Tardiff, and Hirsch 1992). Although there is no standardized definition of murder-suicide, the *JAMA* report proposed that the term murder-suicide be restricted to a situation in which the suicide follows the homicide by one week at the most. Extrapolating from the test statistics available, it is probable that in the United States the murder-suicide represents 1.5 percent of all suicides and 5 percent of all homicides annually, according to this review. In Denmark, on the other hand, 42 percent of homicides are of this variety.

JAMA's summary of data on the mother/child murder-suicide indicated that only a tiny fraction of mothers who commit infanticide kill themselves although they often attempt or plan to do so. Mothers who kill their children typically suffocate, drown, or stab them; firearms are rarely used. The depressed, suicidal mother may psychotically perceive her child as an extension of herself. A form of "deluded altruism" may be the motive, according to this report.

According to the Violence Policy Center (2008), at least 662 people died in murder-suicides in the United States during the six-month period of the 2002 study. That averages out to about two such killings per day. Three-fourths of the murder-suicides involved "intimate partner" situations; of these, 94 percent involved male attacks on women.

The most recent study by VPC (2008) reported 554 murder-suicide deaths nationwide between January 1–June 30, 2007. This averages out to 9 murder suicide events each week. Of those, Texas had 24 cases and Florida had 24. Other statistics from the VPC include

- cases with male offenders: 95 percent;
- cases involving an intimate partner: 73 percent;
- cases that occurred in the home: 75 percent;
- case involving a firearm: 88.5 percent;
- average age difference between offender and primary victim: 6 years.

In Iowa, a midwestern state with a relatively low crime rate, between 1995 and 2005, 106 Iowans killed a partner or spouse in a domestic situation. The main factor appeared to be a pending breakup. Ninety-six of the killers were men; about half committed suicide shortly afterward. In Pennsylvania, of the 122 domestic homicide incidents in 2005, 100 of the perpetrators were male; 68 of the victims were shot; and 45 of the perpetrators committed suicide (Pennsylvania Coalition Against Domestic Violence 2006).

To determine the recent frequency of reports at the national level, I (van Wormer) went to www.google.com, typed in murder-suicide, pressed *search,* then went to news in the row above, which gives recent news stories for that item. Indeed, the frequency was high; there are at least two or more reports of these double or triple murders for each day, and we have to keep in mind that all newspaper headlines are not recorded on Google. Thus we can conclude that even two of these events per day is an underestimate. My search as of June 10, 2005 (reported in van Wormer and Bartollas 2007), yielded the following recent incidents for that week:

Ansonia, CT: A 27-year-old man strangled his wife and then jumped off the roof to his death. The two were Albanian; theirs was an arranged marriage, one reportedly fraught with difficulty.

Milwaukie, OR: A couple in their 80s who had often been seen strolling arm-in-arm was found dead of gunshot wounds, a case of suspected murder-suicide.

Union, SC: Problems with money and child custody seemed to be precipitating factors in this murder-suicide committed by a husband in his 20s.

New Providence, NJ: An elderly couple was found dead in what authorities called a murder-suicide. The husband's note seemed to confirm this.

Lakewood, WA: A couple in their 20s was found shot to death in an apparent homicide and suicide. Police said the man had broken into his ex-girlfriend's home with a hammer. There was a history of stalking.

Landenberg, PA: A man who shot and killed his wife and two sons before killing himself was said to be suffering from depression.

All of these cases took place in the space of several days. That the stories were typical was confirmed in later checks on www.google.com. As can be seen from these illustrations, this form of suicide, unlike other instances of suicide, is hardly a solitary act. During the six-month period of the VPC (2008) study, more people died from murder associated with the suicide—369—than from suicide itself—293. This means that a number of children in these families were orphaned, and that many others were left in a state of despair.

As reported by the Violence Policy Center (2008), the pattern of the murder-suicide is predictable: a male perpetrator, female victim, decision by the woman to leave the man, and a gun. The typical Florida pattern (Florida with Texas had the largest number at 24 of the 2007 total) involved an elderly male caregiver overwhelmed by his inability to care for an infirmed wife.

TYPES OF MURDER SUICIDE

From this Internet search, five basic patterns were delineated and the driving force for each is different. The basic types are as follows:

- suicide bombings;
- suicide by cop;
- murder-suicide in the family where murder is primary;
- suicide-murder—three types where suicide is primary;
- altruistic suicide-murder (of the elderly).

In some of the situations, such as that of mass terrorism performed by suicide bombers, homicide is the predominant motive; in other situations, the motives are a combination of murder and suicide; in still others the key element apparently is suicide.

Suicide by cop is the term used to describe a situation in which a person wants to commit suicide and die in a dramatic way, so he (almost always a man) threatens an armed police officer (sometimes with a toy gun) in order to have the officer pull the trigger on him first. There is no homicide here except for the police officer's killing of the suicide victim.

As an example of *murder-suicide in the family,* we can consider war veterans such as soldiers who have fought in Iraq. These returning troops have a high rate of both murder and suicide and sometimes both. A report from Washington state sees such events as a risk factor distinct to the military in which armed men are trained to kill, and many later carry the invisible scars of war. It is impossible to tell whether the externalized aggression (homicide) or internalized aggression (suicide) is primary. Consider these two cases from 2003:

- Army Specialist Thomas R. Stroh, 21, strangled his wife and son at their Fort Lewis home. He later committed suicide by driving head-on into a semitruck. The soldier had a record of abusing his wife and being drunk on duty.
- Young Marine Renee Di Li Lorenzo was shot and killed by her boyfriend who had been discharged earlier from the Marines. He then turned the shotgun on himself.

Some researchers argue that murder is the primary motive in such cases. Certainly, the urge to kill is the overwhelming factor; the urge can be described as self-destruction including the destruction of people who were once loved. Regarding murder and suicide in such cases, it may not be a case of either-or but of both-and.

Here we are introducing the term *suicide-murder* to refer to killings, in whichever age group, that is suicide driven. There are several basic types of suicide-murders. The first is the elderly couple situation in which an elderly man kills his frail, usually dying wife, and himself. The elderly man is old and feeble and does not want to go to a nursing home.

A second type of killing in which the suicide impulse is prominent is the *mass school or college shooting,* such as has occurred in the United States when boys (who had been bullied) brought guns to school and killed their fellow students and then themselves. Facts pertaining to the recent case of the largest such massacre on record—the killings of 32 students and faculty at Virginia Tech by Seung-Hui Cho, fit this category as well. Details from media accounts reveal a history of school victimization by taunting, a mental disorder, possibly autism from childhood, stalking women, referral by the campus police for suicidal ideation, and continual fantasies of extreme violence and revenge.

The third and most common variety of suicide-murder is the case of *intimate violence*. From the dozens of cases reviewed from news reports, a consistent pattern emerges. The intimate couple is usually in the 20- to 35-year-old range. The man is abusive, psychologically and/or physically. Obsessed with the woman to the extent that he feels he cannot live without her, he is fiercely jealous and determined to isolate her. Characteristically, suicidal murderers have little regard for the lives of other people; they would be considered, in mental health jargon, to be antisocial. So dependent are these men on their wives or girlfriends that they would sooner be dead than to live without them. But for them, suicide is hard —they cannot get the nerve—so they have to find a way to force themselves to do it. The speculating with this scenario is that for some they know if they kill another it will be easier then to turn the gun on themselves. After committing a homicide, the only way out is suicide.

An alternative scenario is that the urge to kill the source of their obsession is so strong in some men that if they cannot have these women, they want to end it all for them both. In the intimate-partner situation, the girlfriend/wife makes a move to leave. Her partner is absolutely distraught in the belief that he cannot live without her. This pattern of dangerously obsessive love often involves a history of stalking. The man decides at some point that if they cannot live together then they can die together; and if he cannot have her, no one will. He hates the woman he considers the source of his passion and pain and self-destruction. He kills her because he (obsessively) "loves" and wants to possess her. (O.J. Simpson once was quoted in the popular press as saying that if he did kill Nicole, his ex-wife, it would have been because he loved her.)

Milton Rosenbaum (1990) of the Department of Psychiatry at the University of New Mexico compared 12 cases of murder-suicide to 24 couple homicide cases, through interviews with family members and friends. The most striking finding was that the perpetrators of murder-suicide were depressed and almost all of these killers were men, while the perpetrators of homicide alone were not depressed and one-half were women.

Other studies by psychiatrists describe the young male perpetrators as intensely jealous with a history of suicide attempts. (See for example, Shaw and Flynn 2003.) Women who kill their children and then themselves are almost always depressed and highly suicidal.

Cases of *elderly murder-suicide,* as mentioned above, are more often defined by love and hate, but almost always there is depression based on serious health factors in old age. These cases can be considered altruistic because the belief is the world is better off without them. The typical scenario includes a wife with late stage Alzheimer's cared for by an increasingly frail husband who can no longer manage doing so. So instead of going to a nursing home, he takes both of their lives in his own hands. (See Malphurs, Eisendorfer, and Cohen 2001.)

REDUCING THE RISK

The prediction of the duration, intensity, and lethality of woman battering are among the most critical issues in forensic mental health and social work. Nevertheless, the courts, mental health centers, family counseling centers, intensive outpatient clinics, day treatment and residential programs, public mental hospitals, and private psychiatric facilities rely on clinicians to advise judges in civil commitment and criminal court cases. Based on interviews of family members and friends of 220 female victims of domestic homicide, compared to a control group of 343 victims of physical violence, Campbell et al. (2003) found that a combination of factors increased the likelihood of intimate partner homicide. The strongest risk factor that emerged in this study was an abuser's lack of employment compounded by a lack of education. Significant relationship variables are separating from an abusive partner and having a child in the home who is not the partner's biological child. Other factors that can help predict homicide are an abuser's use of illicit drugs and access to firearms. Threats of use of a weapon were common in cases where the partner actually did so.

The discussion in this chapter in terms of the lower rates of domestic homicide and murder suicide in the United Kingdom has implications related to the control of weapons. Tightening gun control laws and restricting the access to firearms by convicted batterers is a serious step in reducing rates of lethal violence. A striking fact, as reported by a former city attorney of San Diego and head of a domestic violence unit, and relevant to gun ownership, is the way in which domestic violence offenders use firearms to intimidate and threaten their partners, even when the gun is out of sight (Gwinn 2006, 239). "In fact," as Gwinn indicates, based on his personal experience, the "most common use of a firearm in the home of a batterer may well be to threaten the female victim." Firearm prohibitions involving domestic violence restraining orders, as he further asserts, do make a difference. States that carefully limit access to guns by individuals under a restraining order have significantly lower rates of intimate partner homicide than do states without these laws.

A further consideration more specifically relates to prevention of homicide in connection with suicide. Since the suicide rate is much higher among perpetrators of intimate homicide compared to homicide in general, suicidal ideation in battering men might be considered a possible risk factor for murder-suicide.

Because of imminent threats and danger, it is important to respond quickly to battered women and provide immediate crisis intervention in a systematic manner. To meet this need, Roberts (2000, 2005) developed and customized a seven-stage model for crisis intervention, a model which is a frequently used time-limited intervention model with battered women. Roberts's (2007) Seven-Stage Crisis Intervention Model crisis assessment and crisis intervention begins significantly with an assessment of risk to loss of life. Stage (1) provides for an assessment of lethality. Assessment in this model is ongoing and critical to effective intervention at all stages, beginning with an assessment of the lethality and safety issues for the battered women. With victims of family violence, it is important to assess if the caller is in any current danger and to consider future safety concerns in treatment planning and referral. In addition to determining lethality and the need for emergency intervention, it is crucial to maintain active communication with the client, either by phone or in person, while emergency procedures are being initiated.

Additional stages as delineated in the Crisis Intervention Model are (2) establishing rapport and communication; (3) identifying the major problems; (4) dealing with feelings and providing support; (5) exploring possible alternatives; (6) formulating an action plan; and (7) follow-up measures.

To plan and conduct a thorough risk assessment, the crisis worker needs to evaluate the following issues: (a) the severity of the crisis, (b) the client's current emotional state, (c) immediate psychosocial and safety needs, and (d) level of client's current coping skills and resources. In the initial contact, assessment of the client's past or pre-crisis level of functioning and coping skills is useful. However, past history should not be a focus of assessment unless related directly to the immediate victimization or trauma. The focus of crisis intervention is on assessing and identifying critical areas of intervention, while also recognizing the duration and severity of violence and acknowledging what has happened. Crisis intervention can be the starting point of a longer journey that will not end until the woman's health and life are no longer at risk.

A safety plan is crucial. The crisis worker must help the client look at both the short-term and long-range impacts in planning intervention. Such a plan is designed to ensure the woman's safety even if she chooses to remain in a threatening situation. The safety plan involves memorizing relevant phone numbers of domestic violence and legal services, a coded statement that can be conveyed to trusted relatives in telephone calls or email messages to signal that help is needed, the storing in another place duplicates of personal records and resources that the woman and her children might use later in the event of emergency relocation, and finally some thought given to a specific plan of a safe place to which one ultimately might escape.

CONCLUSION

Domestic violence is harmful, destructive of one's mental and physical health, and sometimes fatal. This chapter has focused on cases in which domestic violence ends in the death of one of the parties, most often the woman. In cases of domestic homicide, the gender differences are pronounced. The overwhelming majority of the women who had killed their partners and who were serving time in prison for this act received specific lethal threats in which the batterer gave every indication that he would kill her, maybe then, maybe later.

This chapter has revealed facts from government sources on the fatal victimization in domestic violence and cases of homicide followed by suicide. Domestic-type situations were contrasted with other forms of murder-suicide such as mass school shootings.

The Seven Stage Intervention Model by Roberts (2007) was discussed as an organizing framework for helping women choose a plan for their own and their family's safety.

It is important for all criminal justice practitioners to document the duration and intensity of battering histories among clients in order to provide the best possible safety planning, risk assessments, crisis intervention, and effective social services. Before court decisions are made, they should take into account whether or not battered women are at low, moderate, or high risk of continued battering, life-threatening injuries, and/or homicide. All assessments should start with an evaluation of the psychological harm and physical injury to the victim and the children in the family, the duration and chronicity of violent events, and the likelihood of the victim escaping and ending the battering cycle.

In knowing such facts about the dynamics of life-threatening situations that might end in the death of one or both of the partners, health care practitioners and social workers can be cognizant of the indicators that can serve as a basis for preventive intervention crisis and, in collaboration with the potential victim of domestic homicide, the development of a safety plan at the earliest possible moment.

NOTE

1. All of Chapter 3 is reprinted from K. van Wormer's article in *Brief Treatment and Crisis Intervention* 8, no. 3, 2008; doi: 10.1093/brief-treatment/mhn012.

REFERENCES

Aldridge, M., and K. Browne. 2003. Perpetrators of spousal homicide. *Trauma, Violence, and Abuse* 4, no. 3: 265–76.

Barraclough, B., and E. Harris. 2002. Suicide preceded by murder: The epidemiology of homicide-suicide in England and Wales 1988–92. *Psychological Medicine* 32, no. 2: 577–84.

Bossarte, R.M., T.R. Simon, and L. Barker. 2006. Characteristics of homicide followed by suicide incidents in multiple states, 2003–2004. *Injury Prevention* 12:33–38.

Bureau of Justice Statistics (BJS). 2005. *Homicide trends in the U.S.: Intimate homicide.* Washington, DC: U.S. Department of Justice, Bureau of Justice Statistics. http://www.ojp.usdoj.gov/bjs/homicide/intimates.htm (accessed February 2007).

Campbell, J.C., D. Webster, J. Koziol-McLain, C. Block, D. Campbell, M.A. Curry, F. Gary, N. Glass, J. McFarlane, C. Sachs, P. Sharps, Y. Ulrich, S.A. Wilt, J. Manganello, X. Xu, J. Schollenberger, V. Frye, and K. Laughon. 2003. Risk factors for femicide in abusive relationships: Results from a multisite case control study. *American Journal of Public Health* 93, no. 7: 1089–97. http://www.ajph.org/cgi/content/abstract/93/7/1089.

Danson, L., and K. Soothill. 1996. Murder followed by suicide: A study of the reporting of murder followed by suicide in *The Times* 1887–1990. *The Journal of Forensic Psychiatry* 7, no. 2: 310–22.

Easteal, P. 1994. Homicide-suicides between adult sexual intimates: An Australian study. *Suicide and Life-Threatening Behavior* 24, no. 2: 140–51.

Family Violence Prevention Fund. 2006. New system tracks homicides, suicides. December 22. http://www.endabuse.org/newsflash/index.php3?Search=Article &NewsFlashID=831 (accessed February 2007).

Gwinn, C. 2006. Domestic violence and firearms: Reflections of a prosecutor. *Evaluation Review* 30:237–44.

Home Office. 2004. *Crime in England and Wales 2002/2003: Supplementary volume / Homicide and gun crime.* London: Home Office. http:www.homeoffice.gov.uk/rds (accessed April 2007).

Home Office. 2005a. *Crime in England and Wales: Homicide and gun crime.* London: Home Office. www.homeoffice.gov.uk (accessed February 2007).

Home Office. 2005b. *Domestic violence: National plan for domestic violence.* London: Home Office. http://www.crimereduction.gov.uk/domesticviolence (accessed February 2007).

Malphurs J.E., C. Eisendorfer, and D. Cohen. 2001. A comparison of antecedents of homicide-suicide and suicide in older married men. *American Journal of Geriatric Psychiatry* 9:49–57.

Marzuk, P., K. Tardiff, and C. Hirsch. 1992. The epidemiology of murder-suicide. *Journal of the American Medical Association* 267, no. 23: 3179–83.

NationMaster.com. 2007. Crime statistics: Murder by country. http://www.nationmaster .com/graph/cri_mur_percap-crime-murders-per-capita (accessed February 2007).

Palermo, G.B. 1994. Murder-suicide—An extended suicide. *International Journal of Offender Therapy and Comparative Criminology* 8, no. 3, 205–16.

Pennsylvania Coalition Against Domestic Violence. 2006. *2005 Domestic violence report.* Harrisburg, PA: Pennsylvania Coalition Against Domestic Violence. http://www.pcadv .org/Resources/2005_fatality_report.pdf (accessed July 2008).

Rennison, C.M. 2003. *Intimate partner violence 1993–2001.* Washington, DC: U.S. Department of Justice, Bureau of Justice Statistics.

Roberts, A.R. 2000. An introduction and overview of crisis intervention. In *Crisis intervention handbook: Assessment, treatment and research,* 2nd ed., ed. A.R. Roberts, 3–30. New York: Oxford University Press.

Roberts, A.R. 2007. Overview and new directions. In *Battered women and their families: Intervention strategies and treatment programs,* 3rd ed., ed. A.R. Roberts, 3–31. New York: Springer.

Roberts, A.R., B.S. Roberts. 2005. *Ending intimate abuse: Practical guidance and survival strategies.* New York: Oxford University Press.

Rosenbaum, M. 1990. The role of depression in couples involved in murder-suicide and homicide. *American Journal of Psychiatry* 147, no. 8: 1036–39.

Shaw, J., and J. Flynn. 2003. Homicide followed by suicide. *Psychiatry* 2:32–35.

Statistics Canada. 2005. *Family violence in Canada: A statistical profile 2005.* Ottawa: Statistics Canada.

van Wormer, K., and C. Bartollas. 2007. *Women and the criminal justice system.* 2nd ed. Boston: Allyn & Bacon.

Violence Policy Center (VPC). 2008. *American roulette: Murder-suicide in the United States.* Washington, DC: VPC. http://www.vpc.org/studies/amroul2008.pdf (accessed July 2008).

4

The Role of Alcohol and Other Drugs in Domestic Homicide

Katherine van Wormer, Alissa Mallow, and Kelly Ward

The dead cannot cry out for justice; it is the duty of the living to do so for them.

—Lois McMaster Bujold
Diplomatic Immunity, 2002

The relationship between domestic homicide and substance abuse is complex. This relationship is best conceived as interactive rather than causative. Persons prone toward violence and especially lethal violence are likely to be risk takers, to go to extremes, and to be impulsive. Indulging in the use of a variety of addictive substances could be a part of their behavior pattern. We cannot, therefore, determine the degree to which the aggression is drug-induced or a product of the perpetrator's psychology. Furthermore, studies on the substance use-homicide nexus are clouded by the fact that perpetrators may exaggerate their drunkenness or drug use as an excuse for their wrongdoing. And then, sometimes the only witnesses to the crime—the victims—are dead.

Yet...researchers have found many ingenious ways to substantiate a case that alcohol and other drug abuse have played a role in domestic fatalities. Investigators, for example, have examined police and prosecution records for evidence that the offenders were using substances; they have interviewed family members and close friends of the victims; they have interviewed men and women incarcerated for murder; and they have consulted female survivors of attempted murder.

Drawing on the best, most empirically valid of these sources, this chapter explores the role that substance abuse plays in domestic homicide. Our concern is not only intimate partner violence by men and women but also the deaths of other family members as well, of the children in the family. The major risk factor for intimate partner homicide, no matter if a female or male partner is killed, is prior domestic violence (Campbell et al. 2007). Given that homicide within the family is generally preceded by such acts of nonlethal violence against the victim or victims (Adams 2007; Sharps et al. 2003; Walker 2008), our starting point is the role of alcohol and other drug use in domestic abuse. Concerning this substance abuse connection, we learn from the offices of the U.S. Department of Justice (Bureau of Justice Statistics 2007) the following:

ALCOHOL AND DRUGS
On average between 2001 and 2005—

- the presence of any alcohol or drugs was reported by victims in about 42 percent of all nonfatal intimate partner violence;
- victims reported that approximately 8 percent of all nonfatal intimate partner victimizations occurred when a perpetrator was under the influence of both alcohol and drugs;
- female and male victims of nonfatal intimate partner violence were equally likely to report the presence of alcohol during their victimization;

Average annual percent of nonfatal intimate partner victimizations, by offender alcohol and drug use and victim gender, 2001- 2005

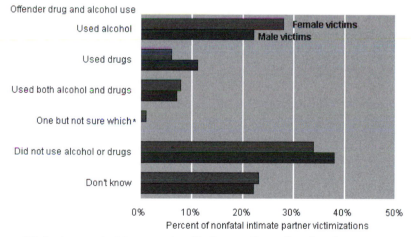

*Estimates on male victims are not provided because the small number of cases is insufficient for reliable estimates.

Note: Responses are based on perception of victim as to whether offender used alcohol or drugs

Source: Bureau of Justice Statistics, Intimate Partner Violence in the U.S., December 19, 2007.

- female and male victims of nonfatal intimate partner violence both reported their attacker was under the influence of drugs in about 6 percent of all victimizations.

For further information, concerning the battering-substance abuse link, we turn to clinical studies. For a start, here is a summary of findings gleaned from the domestic violence literature:

- Approximately one-half of batterers in batterer education programs have significant alcohol problems.
- Over one-half of married male alcoholics in treatment were physically aggressive toward their partners in the previous year.
- Cocaine, methamphetamine, and alcohol in high doses are all associated with a man's hyperactivity and violence; marijuana and heroin have not been proven to induce violence.
- Military studies on alcohol consumption in the army show that soldiers who drink heavily have a high rate of partner violence even when they are not drinking (Thompson and Kingree 252–53).

The reason for the correlation between alcohol and other drugs and any type of violence is generally attributed to the fact that intoxication lowers the person's inhibitions and the ability to think rationally; sometimes a state of paranoia results. The effect of alcohol, for example, contributes to a misreading of social cues through a cognitive impairment, and violent outbursts may result.

Researchers from the National Institute on Alcohol Abuse and Alcoholism today are testing people who are intoxicated at a blood alcohol level of .08 to determine their levels of sensitivity to stimuli related to danger (National Public Radio 2008). The tests are fairly simple, thanks to the new fMRI (functional magnetic resonance imaging) techniques for directly observing the brain at work. In an experiment devised by Jodi Gilman, intoxicated subjects view photographs of neutral and threatening faces. Under the influence of alcohol, the subjects fail to react. As the researchers conclude, intoxication decreases one's sensitivity to danger. This means that a person who is drunk might not know when to stop because he or she would not pick up on the warning signs.

A woman's substance use often parallels her partner's. Women arrested for battering—often fighting back—commonly are found to have been intoxicated at the time (Dutton 2007). Furthermore, research on women incarcerated for the murder of their partners shows they often had been drinking along with their partners just before they fired the fatal shots (Serran and Firestone 2004).

Women whose partners have been drinking are significantly more likely to be injured than are women whose partners have not been drinking (Thompson and Kingree 2006).

Cocaine is closely associated with violence as well, as we learn from a battered woman interviewed by Roberts and Roberts (2005, 91):

> He was especially jealous when he had been using cocaine. He threatened to kill me. He said I was a whore and deserved to die. This is when I really became scared. There were times I really thought I was going to die.

Sometimes the injuries are fatal. When men who are violence-prone by nature are under the influence of alcohol or other drugs, the risk of homicide is greatly increased (Goetting 1995). In one experiment described by Dutton (2007), for example, men were given either alcohol or a placebo (fake alcoholic) drink. The actual alcohol made the aggressive men more so but had no effect on the nonaggressive men.

Empirical data provided by David Adams (2007) who conducted in-depth interviews with 31 wife murderers who were serving time in prison revealed that 61 percent of the killers were heavy substance abusers. Critics would say this claim could just be an excuse for the behavior, and that there is no proof the offenders were intoxicated at the time of the crime. Yet even more of the female victims of attempted partner homicide (75 percent) stated that their partners fit this pattern. The pattern also included irrational bouts of jealousy, and sporadic employment.

Background factors pertaining to murder-suicide are difficult to determine as both victim and perpetrator are dead. Koziol-McLain et al. (2006) got around this problem by interviewing close friends and relatives of the murder victims. Their multisite study gathered data from over 300 individuals who knew the murder victims well and information from a comparison group of a similar number of domestic violence victims. They found from the reports that just over half of the murderers who killed themselves had had a substance abuse problem; this compared to just under one-third of nonlethal abusers.

RESEARCH ON MEN WHO KILLED THEIR WIVES—FEMICIDE

Partner homicides of females are approximately four to five times the male homicide rate, although the domestic homicide rates for both genders have steadily decreased during the past 25 years (Campbell et al. 2007). It should be noted that when talking to domestic violence abusers, researchers are told that their intention was rarely ever to injure, let alone kill. They claim that abuse just went too far or a fatal blow was struck inadvertently.

Research shows that severe problem drinking increases the risk for lethal and violent victimization of women in violent intimate partner relationships. There is strong evidence as well that the risk of homicide increases dramatically when the abusive man is abusing alcohol and other drugs on a daily basis (Adams 2007). Campbell et al. (2003) found that more than two-thirds of the homicide and attempted homicide offenders in their study used alcohol, drugs, or both during the incident while less than one-fourth of the victims did.

The connection between substance use and domestic homicide was also documented by David Adams (2007) in his extensive research on men in prison for
murder. Recall from Chapter 2 that Adams's interview subjects included 31
men who had murdered or attempted to murder their partners and 20 female
victims of attempted murder. Based on his interviews, Adams concluded that
the two most common types of male killers were jealous types and substance
abusers. Sixty-one percent of the men were substance abusers. One might think
the men were claiming to have been drunk as an excuse. Yet, these claims were
given some credibility by the fact that 75 percent of the women who were interviewed stated that their batterers were often drunk or on drugs. Adams further
found that the overlap between jealous types and substance abusers was considerable. This overlap is probably because of the interconnectedness between
intoxication and the arousal of jealous feelings in a man prone to violence. This
connection is deserving of further comment. If we have been exposed to people
high on drugs or drunk, we probably have seen how drug-induced states impair
thinking and reason. We now know, for example, from the new MRI technologies that the prefrontal cortex or judgment area of the brain is damaged by
chronic alcohol use (*News-Medical.Net* 2006). And as most of us are well aware,
if we have ever tried to reason with a drunk, a drug-affected brain is not a
clear-thinking brain. Irrational thoughts and baseless feelings of jealousy can rise
to the surface in an individual who is under the influence of drugs and alcohol. In
violence-prone people, such strong negative emotions can trigger violence.
Indeed there are many reasons for the close association of alcohol and other drug
use and violence. In addition to impaired thinking, intoxicated people may be
especially apt to commit violent as opposed to nonviolent crime because they
exhibit more risk-taking behavior in general than do nonsubstance abusers
(McClelland and Teplin 2001). Then, when intoxicated, their inhibitions are
lowered and they act on impulses that more sober people would control. Com-
pounding the problem, with batterers there is some speculation that if they are
feeling violent, they might get drunk on purpose in order to make it easier for
them to act on their impulses (Walker 2008).

Compared to the use of some other psycho-active substances, alcohol has
been shown to commonly increase aggression (Pernanen et al. 2002). But
research has also documented that chronic users of amphetamines, methamphetamine, and cocaine in particular tend to exhibit hostile and aggressive
behaviors (Inciardi and Saum 1996). In extreme cases, a cocaine-induced paranoia may result.

In a sample of men recruited from a domestic violence intervention program
and a sample of men entering an alcoholism treatment program, Fals-Stewart
(2003) found that male-to-female violence was 8 to 11 times more likely to occur
on a day that the male partner consumed alcohol compared to a day that the
male partner did not consume alcohol. On heavy drinking days, the likelihood
of violence was even greater. The significance of this research is in linking alcohol

problems in men to specific violent episodes. These findings are consistent with research that shows a decrease in partner violence among male alcoholics who received substance abuse treatment alone (Stuart 2005).

The correlation between drinking and femicide is especially pronounced in communities in which alcohol abuse is rampant. In some indigenous communities, for example, such as in Australia, alcohol abuse and lethal intimate partner violence are linked in a vicious cycle (Mouzos 1999). In 91.7 percent of indigenous femicide cases, the offender was under the influence of alcohol, compared to 54.2 percent in cases where the offender was nonindigenous. Overall, indigenous women accounted for approximately 15 percent of total femicide victims, even though they comprise approximately 2 percent of the total female Australian population.

RESEARCH ON WOMEN WHO KILLED THEIR BATTERERS

In his interviews with a sample of 105 incarcerated women who had killed their batterers and a control group sample of 105 battered women in the community, Roberts (2002) found that around 22–23 percent of the women in both groups had been abused by an intoxicated partner. The worst battering incidents, as reported by these women, were associated with the batterer's drunkenness and extreme jealousy. One interesting fact that emerged from this study was that most of the battered women who killed their spouses had first attempted suicide by taking an overdose of drugs.

This research is reminiscent of a previous study by Angela Browne (1987) of the Family Research Laboratory at the University of New Hampshire. Browne compared 42 women charged with murdering or seriously injuring their spouses with 205 abused women who had not killed their husbands. She found that almost a third of the women in the homicide group had been married to men who had used drugs daily or almost daily. This compared to only 7.5 percent of the battered women in the other group. There were even sharper differences in reported alcohol use. Twice as many (80 percent) of the men who were killed by their wives reportedly were drunk every day, compared with 40 percent of the abusive men not killed by their spouses.

Concerning the women's use of substances, Spunt et al. (1996) in their interviews with 215 female homicide offenders in New York found widespread substance use. About 7 out of 10 respondents had been regular users of some drug including alcohol prior to their incarceration, while over half had been addicted to a substance. Over one-third of the respondents were "high" on a drug at the time, while about half of the victims of these homicides had used drugs. Alcohol, crack, and powdered cocaine were the drugs most commonly used. We do not know if these were domestic homicides but can assume that the majority were based on our knowledge that women's victims overwhelmingly are their partners and family members (van Wormer and Bartollas 2007).

Sometimes a woman takes advantage of a battering man's inebriated state to kill him while he's incapacitated. Lenore Walker (2008) discusses this phenomenon in her book, *The Battered Woman Syndrome.* Walker, who often serves as an expert witness in domestic homicide cases, has researched and testified in numerous cases in which women are on trial for murdering their husbands. The defense of such women is especially problematic when the woman has killed her husband when he is asleep or passed out from drinking. Walker's basic argument is that such women who are often afraid for their lives seize the opportunity to get the man when he is down, incapacitated in some way. (See Chapter 8 to learn more of legal advocacy work when battered women are charged with murder.) Common features of such cases are autopsies that show that the homicide victims had blood alcohol levels of up to three times greater than the measure normally defined as intoxicated; a history of arrests for drinking and driving; and the wife's ignorance of her husband's prior arrests.

PARENTAL MURDER OF A CHILD—FILICIDE

If women who murder their spouses are considered an anomaly, women who kill their children are regarded as downright monsters. The typical scenarios are chilling. McKee (2006), a forensic psychologist who evaluated over 30 girls and women who have killed their infants and children, and the author of *Why Mothers Kill,* presents two case histories of women whose homicides were connected in some way to substance abuse. The story of "Samantha," for example, tells of a mother who killed her nine-year-old daughter while she was impaired by heavy cocaine use. Her daughter had just been raped by Samantha's boyfriend and was threatening to tell her teacher. McKee also recalls from his case book the case of Harriet, a chronically alcoholic woman whose repeated abuse of her four-year-old son while she was intoxicated resulted in his death.

Studies of women in psychiatric populations who killed their children document high incidences of psychosis, social isolation, depression, lower socioeconomic status, suicidality, substance use, and difficulties in their own childhood (Friedman, Horwitz, and Resnick 2005). Mothers and stepmothers kill about half of all children murdered; whereas mothers tend to kill infants, fathers more often kill children aged eight or older. Mothers, of course, in general spend a great deal more time with children, especially small children, than fathers do.

Because the innocence and vulnerability of children typically arouse feelings of nurturance and protectiveness, how do we understand the mother killings? To discover the answer, Crimmins et al. (1997) conducted life history interviews with 42 women convicted of killing children. They found that repeated experiences of damage to the self, including physical and sexual victimization, suicide attempts, and substance abuse, were evident throughout the lives of these women. Pregnant mothers who endanger their unborn children by using drugs also fall into this pejorative category of mother child killers. The shocking image of monstrously deformed "crack babies" proliferated in the mass media in the early 1990s led to numerous prosecutions of women for "fetal abuse." This criminalization of pregnant drug users has resulted in prosecution of mothers in accordance with mandatory reporting laws of those who fail drug tests (Drug Policy Alliance 2007; van Wormer and Bartollas 2007). Alcohol and drug use in pregnant women have been found to be closely associated with battering, and both substance abuse and being beaten are closely associated with miscarriage (Jasinski 2004). Recall from Chapter 2 that a man who beats a pregnant woman is at high risk of eventually killing her.

Studies of maternal filicide are abundant in the literature, whereas there is little attention to father-child murder. Fathers and stepfathers who kill their children tend to be of low socioeconomic status, lack parenting skills, and misinterpret the child's behavior. Based on their review of the literature on paternal child murder, Bourget, Grace, and Whitehurst (2007) report a high incidence of substance abuse in these situations. A British study of fatal child abuse cases showed that 60 percent of cases recorded a history of parental substance abuse and heavy drinking by parents as a contributory factor (Robinson and Hassle 2001).

The two case histories that follow are those of two women whose lives were shortened because of intimate partner homicide. While their names and characteristics have been altered to protect their anonymity, their stories are based on actual cases known to one of the authors.

CASE OF LISA AND JEFF

Lisa and Jeff had been together for six years; both actively involved in heroin addiction, Lisa often would engage in prostitution to support the couple's habit. Jeff was aware of Lisa's behavior, but would often turn a "blind eye." When financial problems occurred, the couple would enter a methadone program or inpatient detoxification in an attempt to obtain sobriety. Important to note is that they never went into programs separately, always together. If one was discharged early, the other left as well even if it was against medical advice.

The relationship between the two was stormy at best with bouts of physical violence. Lisa often reported that even in sobriety they were violent toward each other, stating that it must "have been because of the passion." Jeff, at times, was extremely violent when high. Lisa said that during these times she thought he was "speedballing" (that is, using a combination of cocaine and heroin). Sometimes, he would go into a rage after a night where Lisa did not make "a lot of money" or when he believed that she was "keeping it for herself."

Lisa stated she was not particularly concerned about his rages as she could "handle herself." Nonetheless, she had suffered blackened eyes and bruises on her torso, which she said made it difficult to work. Prior to her demise, Lisa stated that Jeff had relapsed and was becoming increasingly more agitated and she thought that his cocaine use was increasing. Attempts to contract for safety were often met with resistance from Lisa and she stated that she "had a plan" and to "get away."

The program Lisa and Jeff had attended was informed that Lisa had been hospitalized following a fall from a six story window. Lisa had sustained multiple injuries and surgery was unsuccessful. Lisa died after being on life support for approximately one week and never having regained consciousness. It was reported to the program that neighbors heard the couple fighting and then the sound of broken glass. It was hypothesized that Jeff may have pushed Lisa so violently that she broke through the glass and fell from the window.

ANGELA

In therapy sessions, Angela reported that she was a "good and dutiful" wife. She felt that keeping her family together had been important to her and since Bill was able to sustain periods of abstinence from alcohol, that things would be okay. Occasionally, Angela would miss scheduled sessions. Answers regarding her missed appointments were often vague with Angela stating, "Sometimes I just got so busy I forgot."

Once when the worker explored the origins of a bruise, Angela began crying and revealed that Bill had relapsed and was violent towards her. She stated that this type of violence had been going on throughout their marriage but only when he was intoxicated. Angela was desperate to help Bill regain sobriety. During that time, Bill entered inpatient rehabilitation and began attending a 12-step program. Angela was "delighted" feeling that "everything would be fine again." Nonetheless, the worker often spoke with Angela about plans for safety should Bill relapse.

Angela missed two consecutive appointments after attending consistently for six months. Attempts to reach her were unsuccessful and the worker made the decision to contact Angela's emergency contact number—her sister. The sister informed the worker that Angela had been run over by a motor vehicle in front of her home while running across the street. She further stated that Angela had "other types" of injuries as well. When the worker inquired how Bill was, her sister stated, "He's in jail" and then requested that the telephone call end. It was surmised that Bill had relapsed, begun beating Angela, and to escape him, she ran from the house and in running across the street was struck by the car.

In both of these cases, a history of intimate partner violence preceded the homicide. There are several commonalities in these cases. First, the women were both hopeful that their relationships would improve if their partners entered into recovery. Second, both women felt relatively assured that they could "handle" their partner's violence, stating that the violence stemmed from substance intoxication. Third, the suggestion that when substance abuse is involved, the propensity for violence can be exacerbated is evident in each case. However, although there was a history of violence in both cases, we cannot conclusively state that the deaths were caused by such as we have no conclusive information about the actual cause of death for both these women. Suffice it to say, in couples where there is a history of violence and addiction, workers need to maintain caution and contract for safety whenever possible.

CONCLUSION

Despite some differences in the estimated rates of alcohol and drug involvement in these various studies, together they can make us pause to look at the connection between substance abuse and domestic violence. Although as we have seen in this chapter, alcohol and other drugs may not directly cause violence, they may be present when violence occurs. While many men and women can drink without becoming violent, others are only violent when they are under the influence. And some are violent whether they are drunk or sober. Substance abuse impairs rational thinking, heightens aggression, and promotes recklessness in human relations just as it does when one is behind the wheel of a car.

If the treatment choice is whether to treat an alcohol- or substance-abusing batterer for the battering or the substance abuse, research seems to indicate treatment for the substance abuse should be the greater priority. However, it is likely that batterers would have the most favorable outcomes through integrated programming or the incorporation of substance abuse treatment as a standard component of batterer intervention. The challenge for the future is to devise programs that will address substance abuse problems and partner violence concurrently. Providing effective interventions to reduce hazardous alcohol use among partner-violent men could significantly improve both substance use and batterer intervention outcomes, lowering the risk of subsequent violence, which in turn would reduce the risk of homicide (see Chapter 11).

REFERENCES

Adams, D. 2007. *Why do they kill? Men who murder their intimate partners.* Nashville, TN: Vanderbilt University Press.

Bourget, D., J. Grace, and L. Whitehurst. 2007. A review of maternal and paternal filicide. *Journal of the American Academy of Psychiatry and Law* 35, no. 1: 74–82.

Browne, A. 1987 *When battered women kill.* New York: The Free Press.

Bujold, M.L. 2002. *Diplomatic immunity.* Newport, TN: Baen Books. http://www .quotationspage.com/ (accessed April 16, 2008).

Bureau of Justice Statistics (BJS). 2007. *Intimate partner violence in the U.S.* Washington, DC: U.S. Department of Justice, December 19. http://www.ojp.usdoj.gov/bjs/intimate/ circumstances.htm (accessed May 1, 2008).

Campbell, J.C., N. Glass, P.W. Sharps, K. Laughon, and T. Bloom. 2007. Intimate partner homicide: Review and implications of research and policy. *Trauma, Violence, & Abuse* 8, no. 3, 246–69.

Crimmins, S., S. Langlety, H. Brownstein, and B. Spunt. 1997. Convicted women who have killed children. *Journal of Interpersonal Violence* 12, no. 1:49–69.

Drug Policy Alliance. 2007. Drugs, police, and the law. http://www.drugpolicy.org/law/publicbenefi/index.cfm (accessed December 2007).

Dutton, D. 2007. *Rethinking domestic violence.* Vancouver, Canada: University of British Columbia Press.

Fals-Stewart, W. 2003. The occurrence of partner physical aggression on days of alcohol consumption: A longitudinal diary study. *Journal of Consulting and Clinical Psychology* 71:41–52.

Friedman S. H., S. M. Horwitz, and P. J. Resnick. 2005. Child murder by mothers: a critical analysis of the current state of knowledge and a research agenda. *American Journal of Psychiatry* 162: 1578–87.

Goetting, A. 1995. *Homicide in families and other populations.* New York: Springer.

Inciardi, J. A., and C. A. Saum. 1996. Legalization madness—legalizing drugs. Public Interest, No. 123, Spring: 72–82.

Jasinski, J. 2004. Pregnancy and domestic violence: A review of the literature. *Trauma, Violence, and Abuse* 5, no. 1: 47–64.

Koziol-McLain, J., D. Webster, J. McFarlane, C. R. Block, Y. Ulrich, N. Glass, J. C. Campbell. 2006. Risk factors for femicide-suicide in abusive relationships: Results from a multisite case control study. *Violence and Victims* 21, no. 1: 3–21.

McClelland, G., and A. Teplin. 2001. Alcohol intoxication and violent crime: Implications for public policy. *The American Journal of Addictions.* National Institute of Alcoholism and Alcohol Abuse (NIAAA), Special Supplement, Winter.

McKee, G. 2006. *Why mothers kill: A forensic psychologist's casebook.* New York: Oxford University Press.

Mouzos, J. 1999. *Femicide: The killing of women in Australia 1989–1998.* Australian Institute of Criminology Research & Public Policy Series, No. 18.

National Public Radio. 2008. Peering into the human brain with fMRI techniques. *Talk of the nation,* May 2.

News-Medical.Net. 2006. Prefrontal cortex in the brain damaged by both alcoholism and chronic smoking. April 26. http://www.news-medical.net/?id=17584 (accessed April 2008).

Pernanen, K., M.-M. Cousineau, S. Brochu, and F. Sun. 2002. *Proportions of crimes associated with alcohol and other drugs in Canada.* Canadian Centre on Substance Abuse. http://www.ccsa.ca/NR/rdonlyres/2322ADF8-AF1E-4298-B05D-E5247D465F11/0/ccsa0091052002.pdf.

Roberts, A. R. 2002. Comparative analysis of battered women in the community with battered women in prison for killing their intimate partners. In *Handbook of domestic violence intervention strategies,* ed. A. Roberts, 49–63. New York: Oxford University Press.

Roberts, A. R., and B. S. Roberts. 2005. *Ending intimate abuse: Practical guidance and survival strategies.* New York: Oxford University Press.

Robinson, W., and J. Hassle. 2001. *Alcohol problems and the family—from stigma to solution.* London: ARP (Alcohol Recovery Project)/NSPCC.

Serran, G., and P. Firestone. 2004. Intimate partner homicide: A review of the male proprietariness and the self-defense theories. *Aggression and Violent Behavior* 9:1–15.

Sharps, P., J. C. Campbell, D. Campbell, F. Gary, and D. Webster. 2003. Risky mix: Drinking, drug use, and homicide. In Intimate Partner Homicide, *NIJ Journal* 250:8–13. Washington, DC: National Institute of Justice, U.S. Department of Justice.

Spunt, B., H. H. Brownstein, S. M. Cummins, and S. Langley. 1996. Drugs and homicide by women. *Substance Use and Misuse* 31, no. 7: 825–45.

Stuart, G.L. 2005. Improving violence intervention outcomes by integrating alcohol treatment. *Journal of Interpersonal Violence* 20: 388–93.

Thompson, M.P., and J.B. Kingree. 2006. The roles of victim and perpetrator alcohol use in intimate partner violence outcomes. *Journal of Interpersonal Violence* 21, no. 2: 163–78.

van Wormer, K., and C. Bartollas. 2007. *Women and the criminal justice system.* Boston: Allyn & Bacon.

Walker, L. 2008. *The battered woman syndrome.* 3rd ed. New York: Springer.

5

Issues of Power and Control in the Death of a Loved One

Kelly Ward and Carolyn A. Bradley

In the media, on the Internet, and even in most academic journals, domestic violence is most often examined through the lens of the victim. Moreover, some attention might be devoted to the perpetrator of the violence. This focus continues into the area of services and resources that are more readily available for the victim, and to a lesser extent for the perpetrator. Missing in the equation is attention to the needs of family members and compassion for what they must be going through when a loved one is injured or even killed.

Loss of a loved one through murder is a traumatic experience that inevitably leaves a great deal of pain and anguish in its wake. When the murderer is another family member, the pain and anguish are compounded exponentially. The suddenness, preventability, and violent nature of a death of this sort places family members at risk for post-traumatic stress disorder and mourning that may continue indefinitely (Asaro 2001). This chapter begins with a discussion of the dynamics of domestic violence, facts of which family members should be aware. By way of illustration of the principles of the early stages of escalating violence, a case history is presented. As we lay out the details of this case, we identify some of the strategies of power and control that are commonly used by batterers. In recognizing such strategies, family members can sometimes provide the help their loved ones need to prevent the violence from escalating. But sometimes homicide is so sudden, there is nothing that outsiders can do. The final section of the chapter deals with the worst case scenario—murder of a loved one. Our focus then turns to the therapeutic challenges in helping family survivors cope with their loss. Finally, we list some recommended resources for family members.

Before we present the case history, consider the following facts on domestic homicide. These statistics are provided by the Federal Bureau of Investigation for the year 2005:

- In 2005, 1,858 women were murdered in "a single episode" between a man and a woman; 129 were killed by strangers and 92 percent (1,574) were killed by intimate partners (spouse, ex-spouse, common law spouse, or boyfriend), 150 were unidentified as to relationship with the victim.
- 62 percent of women were killed by an intimate partner.
- 317 were killed by their partners during an argument (notice most killings are not during an argument).
- 52 percent of the homicides in 2005 against women were with firearms, 21 percent knives, 14 percent bodily force, and 7 percent by a blunt object.
- The report indicates that 9 percent of victims were under 18, 10 percent over 65 years old, and the average age of victims is 38 years old (Violence Policy Center 2007).

While most people would realize that domestic violence can end in the death of the victim, the portrayal of such situations in media such as made-for-TV movies tends to blunt that reality with portrayals of strong, resourceful survivors who triumph in the end. The reality, however, is that in the United States more than three women a day are murdered in domestic violence incidents (Family Violence Prevention Fund 2008). All cases of domestic violence can scar the individual who survives these incidents; and for those that do not survive, the family and friends carry the emotional scars.

THE POWER AND CONTROL WHEEL

Experts in the field of domestic violence have long recognized that the violence is interlocked with issues of power and control. The Domestic Abuse Intervention Project of Duluth, Minnesota, has developed a Power and Control Wheel that outlines a variety of signs that people can observe when looking at relationships for domestic violence. These signs include (1) coercion and threats, (2) minimizing denying and blaming, (3) using male privilege, (4) using intimidation, (5) using emotional abuse, (6) using isolation, (7) using children, and (8) using economic abuse. Signs may intersect with each other and more than one type of abuse could be occurring simultaneously (Domestic Abuse Intervention Project, n.d.). We will use the Power and Control Wheel to demonstrate the signs of abuse that were present in the case of Alice in the section below.

THE STORY OF ALICE

Alice was the only daughter in a family of four children, having an older brother and two younger brothers. She grew up in an upper middle class family

Figure 5.1 The Power and Control Wheel. Courtesy of Domestic Abuse Intervention Project, 202 E. Superior Street, Duluth, Minnesota, 55802, 218-722-2781, www.duluth-model.org.

in Monmouth County, New Jersey, with a stay-at-home mother and a father who was a mathematician. Both of Alice's parents had grown up in homes with alcoholic fathers. Alice's mother was extremely anxious and took various medications to "make her less nervous." Alice's father did not drink but was very rigid and controlling. Alice was a compulsive overeater. Her oldest brother was a workaholic. Her two younger brothers were marijuana users.

Alice attended public schools and was an excellent student, consistently making honor roll throughout her high school years. While academically advanced, Alice encountered social problems with peers due to her weight problem. She did not date in high school and was somewhat socially isolated. Alice interacted better with adults than with people her own age. She was also teased by her brothers who were athletes and had numerous friends.

Upon graduation from high school, Alice went to college in the Midwest with the intention of becoming a child psychologist. Again in the college setting, she excelled academically but was socially isolated. She was very lonely in the first semester and thought about dropping out of school or transferring to a New Jersey college.

At the end of the first semester, Alice met Jim while networking to secure a ride back to New Jersey for semester break. Jim was a junior from Pennsylvania. They carpooled back and forth to school.

Jim was a business major, slightly overweight but very self-assured. He was kind to Alice and seemed interested in her studies and her career goals. They saw each other as friends during the second semester of Alice's freshman year.

During Jim's senior year, he began to pursue Alice. They became a couple during the first semester of her sophomore year, when she was just 19. At Christmas, Jim presented Alice with an engagement ring. Despite her parents' objections, Alice accepted the ring. Her parents felt that Alice was too inexperienced in dating in general and really did not know Jim that well.

Jim graduated and returned to Pennsylvania to seek employment. Alice returned to her Midwest college as a junior. During the fall semester, Jim and Alice stayed in contact and visited each other as often as their schedules permitted.

Jim got a job as a sales manager for a local beer distributorship in the Poconos. He seemed to do well. He felt that he could do better if Alice was closer and he did not have to juggle his schedule to visit. He suggested that Alice transfer to a college closer to his work or just quit school and live with him. *This is coercion on the Power and Control Wheel.*

Alice felt very pressured by Jim's request. While she loved him, she also felt very committed to completing her degree. She thought that Jim understood and respected her career goals. She was doing very well in school and was concerned about loss of credits should she transfer. Her parents were adamant that she remain in school. They felt that they were not in a position financially to have Alice complete college on a "five-year plan."

Alice felt caught between Jim and her parents. Jim insisted that Alice's parents did not like him and were trying to sabotage the relationship. Alice capitulated to Jim's unrelenting badgering and dropped out of college at the end of the first semester of her junior year. Her parents refused to allow her to return home. She moved in with Jim. *This dominance and pressure is disrespectful and could fall under coercion or perhaps subtle intimidation on the Power and Control Wheel.*

Jim had purchased a small house in a vacation community in the Poconos. It was isolated in a wooded area several miles off a main road. Alice got a job for minimum wage as a receptionist at a construction company. Her parents refused to visit; Jim discouraged Alice from taking the three hour trip home, thus essentially cutting off family contact. Her older brother stayed in touch while communicating to Alice his concerns about the relationship and disappointment about not completing her degree. *This move and lack of contact is clearly isolation, but starts the cycle of economic abuse with Alice making only minimum wage.*

Jim worked irregular hours depending upon the season. Alice's job had fairly regular hours with weekends off. The relationship began to encounter problems due to Jim's expectations that Alice be available for him all the time. Although Jim's work schedule was unpredictable, Jim felt that Alice should be home after work every day and not schedule activities with anyone on the weekends. He was very jealous and possessive which Alice interpreted as showing that he cared about her. Because of the need to be available to Jim, Alice did not develop new friendships in the area. *More isolation is seen here.*

Despite problems in the relationship, Alice and Jim moved forward with their wedding plans. Alice's family mellowed toward the idea of the wedding. Alice's mother, although anxious about all the planning required, seemed to enjoy the idea of being "mother of the bride." Alice's father was more apprehensive about the wedding but accepted that it was "Alice's life." Neither parent spoke of their concerns to their daughter again since it seemed her mind was set.

Following the wedding, Alice and Jim's relationship experienced a "honeymoon" period. They focused on planning a life together, talking about having children, moving to a less isolated location, and so on. In the interim, they decided to start their family with a cat, a dog, and a bird.

About a year after the wedding, Jim lost his job as a sales manager with the beer distributorship. Accounts were complaining that Jim was not making regular sales calls and when he did show up the orders were not being properly processed. After the loss of his job, Jim went from being "a beer with dinner" drinker to a six pack a night. As time passed and Jim was unemployed for a more extended period of time, his drinking progressed to a case a day and starting the day with a beer. His moods fluctuated frequently and his behavior became unpredictable. Often withdrawn and sullen, he became increasingly controlling and verbally abusive. *This area shows emotional abuse but also intimidating behavior.*

Alice did not know much about Jim's family. His father was deceased and his mother lived in central Pennsylvania. Jim was an only child and surprisingly did not seek much connection with his mother; she never met her mother-in-law or any other family member from Jim's side of the family. *Again more isolation from the Power and Control Wheel.*

Alice tried expressing her concern to Jim regarding his lack of employment after he was without a job for about six months. She also expressed concern about his increased drinking. Jim's response was to assure her that they were financially fine and that he was looking for employment. He needed to find "the right position" and couldn't take just any job as she had done. He did not address her concerns about his drinking. *This conversation shows so many areas of power and control: minimizing/denying, emotional abuse, and male privilege.*

Alice continued her employment at the local construction company. As she was a bright, conscientious worker, her employer approached her about her intentions regarding the company. He was aware that she had some college. He was interested in having her pursue computer classes to learn how to create computer generated blueprints. Alice was very motivated to return for any type of education, especially as her company was willing to pay for the classes at a local community college.

When Alice shared the idea with Jim, he exploded verbally. He felt that such a plan would entail more time away from home and would have a negative impact on the marriage. Additionally, he told Alice she was not bright enough to pursue design work as it required excellent math skills and she was "just a receptionist." He told Alice she was not to pursue the idea. After the discussion, Jim retreated to the living room and proceeded to get drunk. *Evident in this exchange is emotional abuse and again the isolation factor.*

Alice was becoming more concerned about Jim's drinking and his mood swings. He was gaining weight and showing less and less interest in pursuing employment. Additionally, although he was home all day, he felt that Alice should continue to do the food shopping, the cooking, the cleaning, and the laundry. *Male privilege.*

As Alice really wanted to pursue the community college classes, she decided to approach Jim again regarding the matter. She framed the discussion around the idea that the increased education would lead to more responsibilities at the office, which would mean a salary increase. She pointed out that Jim had not been able to find a new position after almost a year of searching.

Jim exploded physically. He threw the can of beer he was drinking at Alice and then charged at her. Grabbing her by the throat, he threw her against a wall. Jim then grabbed her by an arm and ejected her from "his house," locking the door behind her. Bruised, scared, and crying, Alice tried unsuccessfully to gain entry to their home through the two other entrances. She spent the night in the shed in the yard. *Obvious here are threats, male privilege, intimidation, physical and emotional abuse.*

The next morning, when Jim let the dog and cat out in the yard, Alice came back to the house. Jim was very contrite and showed concern about the bruise on Alice's neck and arm. He was, however, adamant that Alice had provoked him by bringing up a subject that he said was closed. He felt that Alice's "constant nagging" about employment and money questioned his abilities as a husband. He stated that they would never talk about this subject again. *Here are minimizing, denying, blaming, economic abuse, male privilege, and intimidation.*

By Monday, when Alice returned to work, the bruises were faded but still evident. Alice was very self-conscious and embarrassed. She wore long sleeves and a blouse that buttoned at the neck.

Alice's boss requested her decision about the college courses. Alice suddenly felt sick to her stomach and excused herself from the meeting. After exiting the bathroom, she asked her boss for the afternoon off, feigning food poisoning from a bad lunch.

Alice drove around for the afternoon. She didn't feel safe at home and now work, where she felt valued, was no longer stress free. She felt angry and scared. Alice felt like she needed someone to talk all of this out with. She called her older brother.

After listening to all that was going on, her brother wanted to come and bring Alice home. He insisted that the situation she was living in was unsafe and hopeless. Alice insisted she didn't need to be rescued but just needed some emotional support. Her brother recommended she move out temporarily if she wouldn't come home. He felt that she should pursue the offer for more schooling, especially as he was certain this marriage wasn't going to last. *This is minimizing on Alice's part.*

After talking to her brother, Alice felt better. He had confirmed that she was thinking rationally and that Jim was the problem. She called her boss, said she was feeling better and would be in tomorrow. She scheduled a meeting with him to work out the details for her to take the college courses to be able to do design and blueprint drafting.

Feeling more confident, Alice headed home. She got to the house about an hour later than she would usually get home from work. As she walked through the door, Jim, extremely drunk, grabbed her and threw her to the floor. He then jumped on top of her, pinning her down. Screaming in her face, he demanded to know where she had been. She was late and he called work to find out where she was. Her boss told him that she had gone home sick. So who had she been with? *From the Power and Control Wheel here are intimidation, jealousy coercion and threats, and physical abuse.*

Alice struggled to get from beneath Jim. She began to scream and sob that they could talk this out. Jim began to slap her and called her many accusatory names and attacked her personally. Alice screamed louder. Their dog, a 70-pound hound, charged Jim, unbalancing him and knocking him off Alice. Alice scrambled to her feet and ran for the phone. Jim came after her again. This time the dog came between them, snarling at Jim. Jim retreated from the room. Alice fell to the floor, holding the phone, trying to think who to call. Where they lived, there was only state police coverage. The dog stayed by Alice on the floor. *Here again is physical and emotional abuse.*

Jim reentered the room with his hands behind his back. Alice stumbled to her feet and started toward the door with the phone in her hand. The dog squared off toward Jim. Jim, bringing his hands from behind his back, revealed a handgun with which he shot and killed the dog. Alice ran screaming into the woods outside the house. *Intimidation, coercion, and threats are shown here.*

Jim followed her into the woods but lost her in the increasing darkness. Alice spent another night in their shed. But she did place a call to her brother, told him what had happened, and asked him to come to get her in the morning.

Alice's three brothers arrived early the next morning. Alice had remained in the shed, trying to inconspicuously watch for their arrival. Upon their arrival, she ran out to them, sobbing. Her brothers consoled her and told her she was leaving Jim today and they were there to get her and whatever she wanted to take from the house. Her older brother wanted to know if Jim was still in the house, what other weapons Jim had, and suggested calling the police. Alice felt that things would be okay as it was early morning and Jim probably would either be asleep or not drunk yet.

So, Alice and her brothers entered the house. The house had been ransacked. Things were strewn about and smashed. A small fire had been started in the fireplace, destroying pictures of Alice and Jim. Alice's clothes had been torn and thrown in a pile by the dead dog. Jim was passed out on the floor of the kitchen, which was littered with empty beer cans. The handgun was visible, stuffed in the waistband of his jeans. *This shows more intimidation, threats, emotional, and economic abuse.*

Alice's older brother told Alice and the two younger brothers to go gather quickly whatever Alice felt was essential. He would watch Jim. He also told Alice to call the state police. He felt that Jim could be violent if he woke up while they were still there. Alice called the police and was told that the nearest patrol was about 20–30 minutes away but would be dispatched to the scene. She was advised to leave the house and wait for a trooper. Alice felt she could be gone before the police arrived.

Alice and her brothers gathered up her things and began packing her car. She was distraught over the death of her dog and felt that there was very little that she wanted from the house except the cat and the bird. The packing took next to no time.

Jim had stirred a few times but never got up. Both cars were packed and Alice was doing a quick walk through of the house to see if there were any other items to be taken, when the trooper arrived with lights and siren. Her brothers hurried out of the house to speak with the trooper.

Alice was in the living room, looking sadly at her dead dog, when Jim entered from the kitchen. Alice heard a sound, and turned thinking it would be her brothers and the trooper. Jim and Alice stared at each other. Alice screamed and ran for the door leading to the deck. Her scream was heard by her brothers and the trooper.

Jim followed Alice onto the deck. There he was confronted by the trooper and Alice's brothers but not before he could grab Alice and draw his handgun. Without a word, he shot Alice in the head and turned the gun toward the trooper and the brothers. Jim was shot and killed by the trooper before Jim could get off a round.

INSIGHTS FROM THE POWER AND CONTROL WHEEL

In Alice's story, we see warning signs throughout the relationship which may not have been recognized because of Alice's belief that she loved Jim as well as her lack of a social support system and experience. Using the Wheel of Power and Control categories we can see that Jim used coercion and threats. The coercion included the pressure to give up her career plans and her goal to graduate from college. Although there were no verbal threats, Alice may have felt she would lose him if she did not do as he pressured. This request gave Alice fewer job opportunities, forced her to give up her professional career plans, and in the process she may have not felt equal to her husband who had a college degree. Giving up a goal can also decrease self-esteem and leave a person more dependent on the other for finances, and for self-worth.

The second area of the Power and Control Wheel is minimizing, denying, and blaming. The first time that Jim struck Alice, he took no responsibility for his behavior and blamed the outburst on her actions. He firmly states that the topic which Alice wished to discuss was off limits forever and that she was not smart enough to benefit from the educational opportunity her job was offering.

Jim used male privilege when he stated that he bought the house, when he did not share with Alice their financial status when he was laid off, and when saying that he was not able to just settle for any job, like she had. Jim also used intimidation, both physical and emotional. Throwing things at her, coming into her face and grabbing her throat, and saying "We will never discuss this topic again" would have been intimidating to Alice since she was in a very vulnerable position.

Jim resorted to emotional abuse when commenting that she was not smart enough to take the class, or when he verbally abused her as he hit her. His jealousy and insecurity were the basis of his accusation of her being unfaithful. His perception of her as his property to do things for him and with him held her hostage to a position which was increasingly becoming intolerable for her and destroying her sense of self.

Next from the Wheel is isolation. The choice to live in the Pocono Mountains was very isolating. This location was three hours from her family and even further from his family whom she had never met. There also was no contact with either side of the family except Alice's older brother by phone. That isolation fostered dependence on Jim for all activities and maximized her social isolation. The next area of the Wheel is the use of children, which they did not have. But the final area of the Wheel is finances. When Jim was fired Alice was the sole financial resource for the family, yet he still did not share with her what their financial situation was while he was unemployed.

Each of these areas of the Power and Control Wheel that Jim used violated Alice more and more. As he gained more power and control she lost not only power and control but also her happiness, her voice in her own life, the freedom to choose, and her self-respect. Although she finally made a phone call it was too late, as it is for so many. Likely you recall that alcohol was involved in this domestic violence relationship. Keep in mind that much physical abuse takes place in the absence of substance use. In this situation the fatal shot occurred the following morning, but we do not know how long it had been since Jim's last drink.

FAMILY ROLES AND ISSUES

Most family members are genuinely interested in meeting each others' significant others—their dates, boyfriends, and girlfriends. Desiring the best for their loved ones, they are often disappointed with the choices that are made. Yet they are inclined to keep their thoughts to themselves, whether to avoid an argument or in the belief that the relationship will not last.

Oftentimes the family sees no signs of abuse, does not know the signs of abuse, or has their own history of abuse and does not see the behavior as unusual. When family members do recognize the signs of abuse they still may keep quiet but become more wary. When they do verbalize concerns, they run the risk of antagonizing the victimizer and isolating their loved one even more. Alternatively, the expression of concern and perhaps offer of a way out may be appreciated. Sometimes it takes an outsider to point out the obvious before it hits home.

When the family suspects abuse they should try to somehow get the victim to recognize the reality of a dysfunctional and dangerous relationship and leave before it is too late. But, how does a family go about doing that without alienating the batterer or the victim? Trying to spend as much time with the victim as possible as well as asking thought provoking questions may be useful.

Following is a list of questions one can ask to reveal possible signs of abuse that a close friend or family member might be in danger from her significant other. (Assume the potential victim is a female.)

- Does the object of your concern show signs of fear of her partner? If so, how much of the time?
- Does she seem to be avoiding certain topics with her partner and hushing others up who broach these topics?
- Are there changes in her personality (for example, passivity) since she moved in with her partner?
- Have you seen her partner humiliate, criticize, or yell at her?
- Does he treat her so badly that she is embarrassed for you to visit?
- If there is a separation, is stalking involved?
- Does he have a bad and unpredictable temper?
- Is there indication that a pet has been injured by the partner?
- Do the children seem afraid of their father? Does he threaten to take them away or harm them?
- Does he threaten to commit suicide if the other family members leave?
- Do you suspect forced sex is taking place?
- Is there substance abuse by either party?
- Does he allow her any privacy?
- Does he act excessively jealous and possessive?
- Does he control where they go or what they do?
- Does he keep her from seeing friends or family?

- Does he limit her access to money, the phone, or the car?
- Does he constantly check up on her?

One of the areas of domestic violence that is frustrating to family members, friends, and even professionals is that many women do not always leave the batterer. Although most people who are watching want to stop the relationship and open the eyes of the victim, those looking into the relationship from the outside are frequently powerless to make any changes. All they can really do is offer information and support. Beyond asking questions that help them gain insight into the relationship, family members and friends can educate them on having a safety plan to get out of the relationship. Safety plans include making sure there are no weapons in the house (including putting kitchen knives in less accessible places), notifying neighbors and police that there is trouble, saving up money on the side, keeping a phone in a room with the ability to lock it once inside (or keeping a cell phone on one's person), keeping a bag packed with clothes and important papers and identification, and finally sharing a secret code word with children and family that means to contact the police.

WHEN MURDER HAPPENS

Unfortunately, as the statistics indicate, even with all the planning, education, and support families members can offer to the victim, batterers still kill their victims at a rate of three per day. So what do the families do then? Families can gain help and guidance through victim advocacy programs. Many states cover therapy for homicide survivors under crime victim compensation funds; information about this resource is available through the local district or state attorney's Victim/Witness Assistance Office. If family members feel threatened by the person whom they suspect of murder or of the family of the person suspected of the crime, they may obtain a restraining or protective order. For psychological support, they may be referred to a self-help or bereavement group in the area or to the national self-help clearing house that can be accessed at http://www.selfhelpgroups.org.

It is also important that family members realize they will all go through the grief process. The grief process, as explained by Elisabeth Kübler-Ross (1997), has five stages: denial and isolation, anger, bargaining, depression, and acceptance. Every person goes through these stages at his or her own pace and sometimes repeats stages or stays in a stage longer than others. With such a violent death, and given that the domestic violence homicide victim is often in the prime of life, the reactions of denial and anger can be expected to last longer than the other stages for the family. In such situations, joining a support group, obtaining professional counseling and engaging in open dialogue about the murder, sharing family memories, and honoring the victim can enhance the healing process.

Guilt in family members, as the next chapter will reveal, is a common emotion following the murder of one's loved one. "If only I had asked more questions... if only I had rescued her while there was still time"—these are common responses. When children are killed too, or even if they survive the horrible violence, an outpouring of regret and remorse over their suffering is inevitable. Friends and outsiders, trying to help, often say the wrong thing at this terrible time. Even worse, they may stay away or just send flowers. This is why a professional counselor can be immensely helpful. Family members have to remember that open, honest communication will be critical for them to heal the wounds created by this violent murder. Some family members might heal by becoming an advocate against domestic violence, while some will find comfort in making sure the batterer is punished, and others may take comfort in religion or in other ways. Unfortunately, many experience a crisis in their religious faith at this time, so pastoral counseling may or may not be a major benefit to some (Asaro 2001). The ramifications of not dealing with the feelings of pain and guilt related to the murder in the long term can result in depression, self-medication through substance abuse, negative impact on future relationships, and/or the breakup of the family. Often one survivor's method of coping or speed of recovery is different with another's and serious misunderstandings ensue. If the death penalty is an issue, these differences may come to the head in a courtroom with some testifying for the death penalty and others in the same family arguing the other way. In the role of mediators, therapists perhaps can help family survivors maintain their close ties despite such different responses to the tragedy. Hopefully, however, if the death penalty is an issue, the family members will be on the same side. Consider this response by a pair of sisters in the loss of their father and stepmother. This example is provided on the Web site of Murder Victims' Families for Reconciliation (2008, 1):

> Terry and Lucy Smith, Linell and Megan Smith's father and stepmother, lost their lives on Sept. 6, 2001 when they were awakened in their home, tortured, and murdered by Lucy's adopted teenage son Michael, as well as some of his friends. One of these friends is currently on death row. In their own words this is why Megan and Linell oppose the death penalty:
>
> "Our definitions of justice and healing did not match those of the newspapers or the court system. To think that yet another person would die and another family would suffer is haunting, and is something we want no part in. Death does not equal justice and does not promote healing, nor will it honor the ones we lost."

Therapy is essential if small children lose a parent or their parents, and especially if they witness the homicide. This is the case even if on the surface they do not appear outwardly distressed. Often adults make the mistake of not discussing what happened in the hopes that the children will somehow forget. Children are too young, however, to process what they have seen and heard on their own. Beyond the help they need in talking about the trauma, they also need to learn how to express their own anger without resorting to violence. Research suggests that children who witness relationship violence, not to mention homicide, have many issues to work through. With small children, play therapy can be immensely helpful. Mental health professionals, by working with child witnesses to family violence, can play a key role in teaching children nonviolent methods of resolving conflict and thereby can help break the generational cycle of violence (Barnett, Miller-Perrin, and Perrin 2005). We have focused on the family survivors of homicide from the perspective of the victim's family. The sympathies of the literature and media do tend to be with the victim's family, not the family of the perpetrators. Consider the O.J. Simpson case, for example. Media coverage of relatives of Simpson was practically nil in comparison to the coverage of the Brown and Goldman families. It is rare, besides, for the families of the accused murderer to risk speaking to the press as a court case may be pending. Then in cases of murder-suicide the guilt feelings of these parents and relatives of the perpetrator can be tremendous. The typical pattern is this: through feelings of shame and guilt, the family members of the murderer grieve for their son or other relative, grieve for the daughter-in-law or partner who was killed, and for grandchildren who might have gotten caught up in the bloodshed as well, and they are consumed with anger as well as grief. Typically, cut off from their support systems, and having to deal with law enforcement and other authorities, these people need professional help so that they can get through this trying time. Major tasks for the grief counselor or pastor are to help normalize the family members' strong and seemingly irrational emotional responses and to help them refrain from blaming themselves or each other. In a murder-suicide, only rarely does the community come together and mourn the loss of human life of all parties. Even rarer still do the families on both sides of the murder-suicide have a common funeral. But, recently, this was exactly what happened in Iowa City, Iowa. Following the conclusion of this chapter, we present one of the many articles that appeared on this nationally publicized case. We have chosen to include coverage of this case, not because it is typical but because it captures in graphic detail the family tragedy that is murder-suicide, the tragedy both of the persons killed and of the family members left behind.

CONCLUSION

Domestic violence is a difficult social issue, compounded when the victim is killed by the batterer. Prevention efforts can offer a life line to those who are willing to take it. This chapter presented the Duluth model's Power and Control Wheel for its didactic value. All family members including the youths in the family would do well to be familiar with strategies that are used in domestic abuse situations, strategies that ultimately may place the victim in danger. When victims and family members do not recognize the danger signs, in some rare cases, the abuse may be fatal. When prevention fails, the society through victim assistance programming needs to reach out to those left behind. The survivors themselves are at high risk of suicide and/or self-destructive behaviors that arise from unresolved grief and loss, but most especially feelings of guilt. The challenge in working with the surviving families in the aftermath of murder is enormous, yet the difficulty of assisting survivors to cope with such tragedy should not deter clinicians from taking on this challenge. The use of a variety of strategies—including crisis intervention; individual, family and group therapy; peer support; and pharmacological and other approaches—may promote the client's ability to cope with the trauma and loss and facilitate personal growth in the aftermath (Asaro 2001). This chapter has described the situation facing family survivors of murder generally; the following chapter reviews case studies of such survivors and further describes the clinical challenge in doing such work.

FORGIVENESS FRAMES FUNERAL FOR FAMILY OF SIX

Anelia K. Dimitrova

Two Iowa City families mourned their loved ones Saturday at a 90-minute ceremony at St. Mary's Catholic Church in Iowa City. Six white hearses took the Sueppel family to their final resting place in a single grave at St. Joseph's Cemetery.

Ethan and Seth to the left, Mira and Eleanor to the right. Dad Steve and mom Sheryl in the middle.

They could have been posing for a portrait before leaving on a family vacation.

But on this bright Saturday afternoon, March 29, the Sueppels arrived at their final resting place at St. Joseph's Cemetery.

When the mourners left, a truck pulled in to hoist the caskets one after another and place them in the embrace of a single grave.

A last loving gesture fulfilling the family's wish of unity.

Mom and Dad in the middle in their silver-gray caskets, the kids in their baptismal-white coffins, flanking their parents in order of seniority.

Placing the mother and her children in the same eternal home with the husband and father who killed them was the ultimate act of true forgiveness, family members say.

"The thought of having them laid to rest separately was unthinkable," says David Kesterson, Sheryl's older brother, in a telephone interview with *Waverly Newspapers* after the funeral. "They were a family in life, they are a family in death. Their legacy is love. That's what they will be remembered for."

Such togetherness in another life seemed the only possibility for Steve Sueppel, the 42-year-old former banker who killed his family on Easter Sunday and the early morning hours on Monday. He then took his own life.

In October, the Iowa City native was charged with embezzlement and money laundering. His trial was scheduled for April 21.

The Sueppels attended the 9:30 a.m. Easter Sunday service at St. Mary's Catholic Church, the same church in which Steve grew up, in which he and Sheryl said their vows and in which the couple's children were baptized.

But no one saw it coming, says the Rev. Ken Kuntz, St. Mary's pastor.

On Saturday, relatives and community members turned to their faith to understand why a peaceful Easter celebration had turned into one of the most heinous mass murders in Iowa's history.

FORGIVENESS

The family's forgiveness framed the final ritual at the church and humbled the pastor.

"I will never be able to pray the Lord's prayer the same way again," Kuntz said after the burial, adding that he had never seen forgiveness in such a powerful and immediate way. "It's embedded in my mind how the families have witnessed that in the face of that tragedy."

In a genuine display of shared grief, Bill and Patricia Sueppel, Steve's parents, and Jack and Gisela Kesterson, Sheryl's parents, leaned on each other and comforted one another during the emotional 90-minute funeral service.

Kuntz commended the parents' decision to hold the Mass for the entire family.

"Gisela, Jack, Pat and Bill, what a witness you are for the meaning of forgiveness," Kuntz said. "We all need healing.... We all need God."

Choking back tears at times as he described his own ordeal, David Kesterson, Sheryl's brother, said that forgiving Steve was the "easiest thing" he had to do last week.

"There is nothing that we have done that God can't rectify," he said later, echoing thoughts he had expressed at the funeral. "Unfortunately, down the line, Steve missed that lesson because if he hadn't, we wouldn't have this tragedy."

"Forgiveness was not a conscious decision," he said Sunday. "It was a non-issue. When we couldn't find Steve and were unsure of his whereabouts, we hoped to find him alive not so that justice could be served, but because we loved him. Not only did I lose my sister and those four beautiful kids, but also my brother-in-law that was more like a brother."

Contemplating the loss, Kesterson added: "Nobody won. The unfortunate thing is that the enemy won the battle, but if you read the rest of the Book, you know who won the war."

THE VICTIMS

The scion of a prominent Iowa City family, Steve climbed to the vice presidency of Hills Bank & Trust on his own merit.

Born on Aug. 13, 1965, in Iowa City, the son of William and Patricia Tierney Sueppel, Steve graduated from Regina High School and the University of Northern Iowa.

His wife Sheryl Kesterson was born Feb. 21, 1966, in Sioux City, the daughter of Jack and Gisela Frey Kesterson. She graduated from Iowa City High School and the University of Iowa with a master's degree in education.

When Steve and Sheryl married on June 13, 1990, they hoped to raise a big family in accordance with their faith.

They adopted four children from South Korea.

When Ethan, the couple's first son, showed up at the Omaha airport, held by a nanny, there was not a dry eye in the arrivals area, Kesterson told about 1,000 mourners who had gathered at the church Saturday morning.

Ethan was born Nov. 2, 1997. The Longfellow Elementary School fourth-grader played the cello, golfed and loved soccer.

Seth was born on July 1, 1999. A second-grader at Longfellow, he played the violin, raised rabbits and gardened.

Mira, a kindergartner at Longfellow, would have celebrated her sixth birthday one day after she was killed. Kuntz remembered her at the funeral for her exuberant personality.

The family's baby, Eleanor, 3, was born on Oct. 31, 2004. The little princess loved to dress up. She showed great courage in the face of adversity, dealing with kidney problems.

WHY

Why Steve Stueppel, a man who family and friends describe as non-confrontational and an involved father and husband, ended six lives so violently will always remain a mystery.

During the funeral service, Kuntz attributed the tragedy to the "scourge of mental illness," and said that "only a merciful God is able to untangle the mess."

"I don't know why or how Steve could do what he did," he said, "but I do know that he loved his wife and his children."

Kuntz later added that anyone who commits such violent acts "must have experienced a break from reality.... It was so out of character for the Steve we knew and loved."

QUESTIONS

Steve left behind a detailed suicide note, telling survivors he could not live with the disgrace he had brought on his family in this life.

In his savior's promise for resurrection, a message still fresh in his mind from the Easter service, he must have gleaned an exit, a way to regain some of the honor he had lived by, but squandered somewhere along the way.

Who knows how long Steve must have tormented himself as he saw everything he had built slip away?

Was this final act of destruction a cry of desperation, his twisted way of regaining his honor, eroded by his own actions?

Death may have been the only path to salvation Steve saw. Taking his family along was just an extension of his duty to take care of his wife and children, just like he always had.

Who knows why he turned a baseball bat, a father's proverbial bonding badge to his children, into a murder weapon?

Who knows why the family Toyota Sienna, the van in which Sheryl took the kids to school events, became, in his final script, a suicidal pyre?

In five deaths and a suicide, he must have seen relief.

Who knows why?

But he did.

HOW

As Easter Sunday drew to an end, he first claimed wife Sheryl, 42, as if he wanted to spare her the devastation of knowing what he had planned next. She died of trauma to the head in the master bedroom.

Police say Sueppel left a message at his father's law office saying that his family is in heaven.

Early morning Monday, police say, he loaded Ethan, 10, Seth, 8, Mira, 5, and Eleanor, 3, in the family van and turned the ignition key on.

When carbon monoxide failed to bring about a peaceful ending for all, he took charge again, bringing the children back into the house.

Were they whimpering? Dazed? Scared? Was he blind? Dazed? Scared?

Eager to take away their suffering just like a dutiful dad would?

Eleanor, the youngest, was found in the toy room in the basement. Mira was found in the guest bedroom downstairs. Their brothers were found in their bedrooms.

At 6:31 a.m., Steve made a 911 call.

"What's the address?"

"629 Barrington Road," Steve says, speaking calmly over road noises in the background. "Please go there immediately."

A click answers the dispatcher's last question, "What's going on there?"

Steve's sober voice, articulating every word with dispassion, curdles the blood now that investigators know that the killing was over by then.

Police say Steve tried to document his every move, leaving a timeline he knew investigators would follow to reconstruct the crime scenes.

Like a man putting his final affairs in order, Steve even had the presence of mind to write a lengthy note describing his actions.

Life was not worth living, he said in the note, mentioning his despair over the indictment and the shame he had brought on his family.

He asked forgiveness for what he had caused and what he was about to cause his relatives, but explained he was sparing his wife and children the pain.

The dad took care of them all to the end, even putting Post-It notes on library books with instructions on where to return them.

In a second unsuccessful attempt to end his own suffering, Steve drove the van to the Iowa River at Lower City Park where he tried to drown himself, but failed to sink. He left a message to this effect on his home answering machine.

Less than half an hour after the 911 call, Steve took the final step ... he steered the family van east on Interstate 80 and slammed it into the base of a sign, where it burst into flames and charred his body beyond recognition.

The magnitude of the tragedy shook Mike Bartlett, the soft-spoken caretaker of St. Joseph's Cemetery, who watched Saturday from afar as family members hugged and held one another.

The stark reality of the separation had started to sink in as extended family listened to the brief prayers and began to realize that they were going to have to let go of the caskets, the last physical reminder of their loved ones.

"Oh, God," a woman sobbed disconsolately. "Oh, God."

Leaning on his wife, with a trembling hand Bill Sueppel plucked a white rose from his daughter-in-law's coffin. Other family and friends stepped in to take flowers from the decorations atop the caskets as mementos of better times.

Parents in the crowd clutched their children and a father kissed his son on the top of the head as if to protect him from the intensity of the grief.

When the mourners left, it was Bartlett's time to attend to his duties of placing the coffins in the single hole.

It awaited, covered, about 25 feet from the blue tent where the cemetery ritual took place.

"They will always be together," he said. "They will always be touching each other, side by side."

Source: "Forgiveness Frames Funeral for Family of Six," *The Cedar Falls Times,* April 5, 2008. Reprinted with permission by Anelia Dimitrova, author and publisher.

REFERENCES

Asaro, M. R. 2001. Working with adult homicide survivors: Helping family members cope with murder. *Perspectives in Psychiatric Care* 37, no. 4: 115–24, 136.

Barnett, O. W., C. Miller-Perrin, and R. Perrin. 2005. Family violence across the lifespan: An introduction. Thousand Oaks, CA: SAGE.

Domestic Abuse Intervention Project. n.d. Duluth, MN. http://www.duluth-model.org/ (accessed February 2, 2008).

Family Violence Prevention Fund. 2008. Domestic Violence is a Serious, Widespread Social Problem in America: The Facts http://www.endabuse.org/resources/facts (accessed April 2008).

Kübler-Ross, E. 1997. *On death and dying.* New York: Scribner.

Murder Victims Families for Reconciliation (MVFR). 2008. www.mvfr.org (accessed April 2008).

Violence Policy Center. 2007. When men murder women: An analysis of 2005 homicide data. Females murdered by males in single victim/single offender incidents. Washington, DC: VPC. http://www.vpc.org/studies/wmmw2007.pdf (accessed February 2008).

RESOURCES

Individual State Coalitions. http://www.ncadv.org/resources/StateCoalitionList_73.html.
National Coalition Against Domestic Violence. http://www.ncadv.org/.
National Domestic Violence Hotline. http://www.ndvh.org/. 1-800-799-SAFE (7233);
   1-800-787-3224 (TTY).
U.S. Department of Agriculture Safety, Health and Employee Welfare Division. http://
   www.usda.gov/da/shmd/aware.htm.

6

Portraits of Life in the Aftermath of Domestic Homicide

Marilyn Peterson Armour

There are approximately 20,000 homicides in the United States annually. In 2002, 8.6 percent of victims were killed by their spouse, 5.5 percent were children killed by a parent, 7.4 percent were killed by a family member, other than their spouse or parent, and 7.3 percent were killed by their boyfriend or girlfriend (Durose et al. 2005). The vast majority of these deaths are related to domestic violence. When children murder parents, for example, most of them have witnessed partner violence or were victims themselves of child abuse (Marleau, Auclair, and Millaud 2006). Fathers who kill children and then themselves often meet the criteria for domestic abuse of their partners, including contact with the police (Johnson 2006). Even many suicides by women are thought to be associated with battering (Fox and Zawitz 1999).

Although the problem of domestic violence has received considerable attention, the study of domestic homicide is relatively recent and limited to precipitating conditions or the act itself. Most of the literature on familicide focuses on the personality characteristics of the victim and perpetrator or tries to answer the question, How did the death happen? Indeed, 35 states have now developed domestic violence fatality review teams (DVFRT) to uncover possible causes and institute mechanisms to prevent future intimate partner fatalities (Wilson and Websdale 2006). Little notice, however, has been given to the members of the victim's family who, in the midst of their loss and extreme suffering, inherit the fallout from their loved one's death including massive upheaval, psychiatric disturbance, ill health, financial difficulties and the propensity for future intrafamilial violence. Even determining the numbers of potential survivors is difficult because records on domestic homicide, for example, do not specify if children were involved (Steeves and Parker 2007), agencies such as the child welfare system do not gather information on what happens to these children after their parent dies (Steeves et al. 2007), and studies of survivors do not differentiate between familicide and stranger homicide (Armour 2002). This chapter describes what is known about the children and the adults who survive in the wake of a domestic fatality. Although many of their experiences are similar to the experiences of homicide survivors generally, this chapter will highlight some of their unique circumstances and the paucity of services particular to their needs. Names and circumstances of people in case examples have been changed to protect their confidentiality.

THE CHILDREN WHO REMAIN

Based on the number of women of childbearing age killed by their partners (Fox and Zawitz 2004), U.S. Census population data from 2000 (Lewandowski et al. 2004), and a conservative estimate of the number of children such women are raising, it is calculated that between 3,000 and 4,400 children are affected by a domestic homicide annually (Steeves and Parker 2007).

Many of these children may already have the scars from witnessing the domestic violence that likely precedes the murder. They may observe the actual event, or their exposure may be more indirect, such as hearing violent encounters or later witnessing the results from a violent exchange. Both direct and indirect exposure to domestic violence is negatively associated with children's emotional, behavioral, and developmental well-being (Ybarra et al. 2007; English, Marshall, and Stewart 2003).

In recent years an increasing body of evidence describes the deleterious effects exposure to domestic violence can have on the health, cognitive functioning, and emotional health of children (Fantuzzo and Mohr 1999; Groves 1999; Spilsbury et al. 2007; Ybarra et al. 2007). Indeed, a child's age and stage of development can be an important determinant for what those consequences may be. For instance, children who are preschool age and younger should ideally be learning to think in egocentric ways, begin the process of gender identification, develop language skills, and explore a moral schema (Newman and Newman 2006; Baker et al. 2002). For children this age, exposure to violence has been established as a positive correlate of disrupted developmental milestones such as language development, toilet training, and motor skills acquisition (Ybarra et al. 2007; Fantuzzo and Mohr 1999; Mbilinyi et al. 2007). In addition to disrupted development, exposure to domestic violence is positively associated with reduced empathy and prosocial behaviors, poorer communication skills, and increased behaviors that undermine the development of a social network (Ybarra et al. 2007).

Older children who are exposed to domestic violence face complex emotional and identity problems. Because they take social, gender, and behavioral cues from their adult role models, they are at risk, for example, for developing stereotyped notions of gender, such as women are victims and men are perpetrators

(Baker et al. 2002). Although peer identification is considered a key developmental task of adolescence (Newman and Newman 2006), exposure to domestic violence may promote behaviors, which inhibit membership in a peer group. For example, several reports link exposure to domestic violence to aggressive behavior, conduct problems, depression, anxiety, low self-esteem, and impaired social competencies (see for example Baker et al. 2002; Ybarra et al. 2007).

In contrast to the amount of research on children up to the time they experience domestic violence, little is known about what happens to these children in the aftermath of the murder. Besides being neglected in the literature, they are often overlooked in the chaos that follows the parent's death and feel alone, lost, and invisible (Clements and Burgess 2002). Far from being distant spectators, many of these children were actually in the home when the homicide occurred and may have witnessed it or found their parent's body. Consequently, they not only have to deal with the trauma of death by homicide but may be haunted by the sights and sounds that occurred during the incident (Lewandowski et al. 2004) including the mutilation of their mother's body or the "blank, evil, and frightening look in their father's eye immediately after he committed the homicide" (Steeves and Parker 2007, 1279). As bystanders, they may also witness the reactions of family members to the death notification. In one case, a girl worried that the grandma had been shot because of the way she fell down on the floor and started screaming when she learned of the murder (Clements and Burgess 2002). Ironically, these children are often the primary source of information about the homicide because of their proximity to the event.

Immediate Effects

The impact of the homicide varies, in part, based on the child's proximity to the event. Although post-traumatic stress disorder (PTSD) symptoms, physical health problems including psychosomatic concerns, and sleep disturbances are common, they are more often reported in children who witnessed the murder (Burman and Allen-Meares 1994; Eth and Pynoos 1994). In particular, PTSD is a frequent response to trauma that includes the persistent reexperiencing of the trauma, avoidance of stimuli associated with the trauma, and symptoms of increased arousal such as frequent anger outbursts or difficulty with sleep. Reactions to trauma vary based on the child's age (National Coalition for Child Protection 2007). Younger children, for example, may start wetting the bed whereas older children may show an obsessive fascination with guns and violence. Many have distressing nightmares and flashbulb memories of their parent's mutilated body including images and sounds of the incident. The Hennepin County fatality review team (2002, 24). describes the level of terror that some children have endured.

> Visions of children attempting to intervene to protect their mother from a perpetrator's assault and in doing so being struck themselves, crawling along the floor

with the lights out for fear of being seen through a window by a mother's ex-boyfriend, leaving bicycles "just so" in front of an entry door in order to detect whether the perpetrator had entered the home while they were gone, all painted an extraordinarily troubling picture of the terror that permeates every aspect of these young lives.

Other short-term effects include fears of being separated from the current caregiver and a tendency to be either overly emotional in response to everyday situations or overly in control of emotions (Black and Kaplan 1988). Indeed, because some children may be in a state of shock or numbness, adults may erroneously assume that their quietness indicates little or no reaction. Uniformly children feel sad, depressed, lonely, preoccupied, guilty, and angry (Clements and Burgess 2002).

Some of their difficulties are related not just to the murder but to the level of disruption that hits their young lives. If their home is sealed off as a crime scene, they cannot get clothes or familiar toys (Hendricks, Black, and Kaplan 1993). Even if they remain in the original home, it is now "like an empty shell, filled with haunting reminders and echoes of the person who is now dead" (Clements and Burgess 2002, 36). Moreover, their losses are multiple and sudden. Besides losing both parents simultaneously, they frequently lose their home, neighborhood, school, and friends. Concomitantly, they have to adjust quickly to unfamiliar environments. Studies indicate they usually live with a member of the victim's family after the murder (Steeves and Parker 2007). Although, some live with a member of the perpetrator's family, in institutional settings, with distant relatives, or with families who adopt them. Rather than remaining in their new home location, however, many of these children move as many as 4 to 5 times (Hendricks, Black, and Kaplan 1993). They may even move back with the perpetrator when that person is released from prison. In addition to being relocated to a new home, they also find themselves in different schools with teachers who cannot tend to their needs because the caregivers want to give the children a new start and, therefore, withhold information from the school about the murder. In contrast, children may be teased about being the child of a murderer and not be able to escape comments from peers, at school or in the neighborhood, who make them feel different (Clements and Burgess 2002). Without their usual support network and familiar surroundings, they feel rootless, disoriented, and dislocated.

Loyalty Conflicts and Long-Range Effects

In domestic fatalities, children lose either parents or their equivalent at once. They become both a victim-survivor and offspring of a murderer. The conflict inherent in this dual and seemingly irresolvable identity struggle plays out legally and in the family. If children's testimony, for example, results in an acquittal, they may feel traitorous to their mother. If their testimony results in a conviction, they may feel responsible and guilty for making their father spend years, or even the rest of his life, in prison (Zeanah and Burk 1984). This split and the confusion it creates may continue for children as they deal with their relatives who also have strong emotions about what happened. The conflict between the victim and perpetrator may be replicated in ongoing conflict between their extended families (Black and Kaplan 1988). Each side may blame the other, vie over who will raise the children, or differ about the children's contact with the perpetrator in or out of prison. These wars place children in difficult and untenable positions. If they are placed with the mother's family, for example, their antagonism with the perpetrator may prevent access to him. If the children are placed with the perpetrator's family, family members may disparage the mother, even accusing her of provoking her own murder, in an effort to protect the perpetrator and family's reputation.

Children need a rounded picture of their parents in order to resolve their own inner identity struggles. When a father, for example, has no redeeming qualities, the child's self-image can be damaged because of the conflict inherent in trying to identify with the father. "If daddy is bad, then half of me must be bad because half of me comes from daddy." These kinds of fears are common. Children worry that they may inherit the badness or sickness of the perpetrator (Hendricks, Black, and Kaplan 1993). They may fear that they will end up like the parent who was killed or even that the perpetrator will come back to kill them too. Children's apprehensions are not without merit. A small study of adult survivors found that the women participants were abused in their later personal lives as adults and the male participants indicated that they had been abusive (Parker et al. 2004).

Children also have difficulties with attachment. Such difficulties are expected given the nature of the crime itself, the unresolved loss, and the aftermath of disruption. The dimensions of the attachment are also influenced by self-image and the ambivalence over children's post-homicide identification with either the victim or perpetrator. Indeed, existing studies show that although many children have no discernible attachment problems, the majority have difficulty attaching at all or may be underattached to their caregivers (Hendricks, Black, and Kaplan 1993) and, as adults, have trouble establishing and/or maintaining love relationships (Steeves and Parker 2007).

Not talking about the homicide is a significant characteristic that contributes to loyalty conflicts, fears, and attachment issues (Steeves et al. 2007). Some children manage the loyalty conflicts by not conversing with others. "You don't want to hear how terrible your parents are, you don't really want to hear it when you're little" (Steeves et al. 906). Others are explicitly told not to talk about it because of the worry that saying something might hurt others. They may also protect themselves from the insensitivity of others by not speaking. In response to this taboo, family members state that no one talked to them about the homicide or their family after the murder or that their adoptive or guardian family did not talk about the murder believing that it was best to just move on. Although this silence seemingly keeps the trauma at bay, it also freezes it in time and may distort children's development and functioning as adults. Indeed, talking is particularly important for children because it is the mechanism that allows them to readapt to the violent death of their caregiver at each new stage of their development.

Instead of stability, many children confront additional fears and trauma after the death of their loved one. New caregivers who feel overwhelmed by their own grief and the sudden task of caring for young charges may be emotionally unavailable (Hardesty et al. 2008). In one study, 24 percent of children were sexually attacked or abused by a member of their new household (Steeves and Parker 2007). Post event illnesses and deaths of caregivers also occur (Hardesty et al. 2008). There may be permanent alienation between the maternal and paternal families which costs the children still more (Johnson 2005). If adopted or institutionalized at a young age, children may know little about their families of origin. As adolescents, they may end up abusing alcohol or drugs and engage in suicidal behavior (Steeves and Parker 2007), perhaps as a way of reuniting with a lost loved one. They also live haunted by fears. Because they lost one parent, they may fear losing the other one too or losing their new caregiver. They may closely monitor that person or hide their feelings to ensure that the person does not get angry or upset or disappear too. They are scared to be alone yet frightened that getting close to someone new could result in still more loss. They may also worry that they will become violent or psychiatrically ill (Hendricks, Black, and Kaplan 1993). This stacking up of never-ending crises or living in the shadow of survival-level fears further complicates recovery.

THE ADULTS WHO REMAIN

Intrafamilial homicide can include partner homicide, child murder, homicide-suicide, and nonpartner intrafamilial homicide. Consequently, the experiences of adult survivors vary, in part, based on their familial role to the victim and perpetrator. Similar to the children who remain, little is known, however, about adult survivors' unique needs. Indeed, this subgroup of homicide survivors appears to have been sidestepped in the literature with the explanation that their issues are extremely complex due to previous family history, family dynamics, and the fact that the relationships to the victim and perpetrator, whether by blood or through marriage, endure into the future.

For many adult survivors, threats to kill the victim were communicated to family, friends, relatives, and neighbors prior to the homicide. They subsequently struggle with having had some sense of the risk and question whether they could have prevented the murder. Other adult survivors are stunned to learn that the murderer is a family member. They wrestle with their ignorance while trying to absorb the fact that they were duped by the perpetrator into believing that he was someone other than who he was. They may also recognize that the victim was not fully disclosing about the direness of her circumstances. A mother who lost her only daughter to a former boyfriend did not know that telephone contact had been reestablished between them and the perpetrator was again pursuing her daughter. Although the mother did not realize it at the time, her daughter likely stayed late at her mother's home on the night she was killed in order to evade him. In these cases, parents are left with guilt and a sense of responsibility about what they might have done to stop the murder. One family reflected on how they had misjudged the perpetrator's potential for violence because they erroneously believed that they could control his moodiness.

> He'd never done anything physical to anyone but he still acted like he was about to explode. I felt like I was walking on eggshells with him the last five to ten years. The slightest criticism would just send him off the roof. Everything was personal to him.

Because family members know the perpetrator, are aware of the domestic violence that often precedes the lethality of the act, or assume that the victim is not withholding information, they frequently expect themselves to have known better. They wrestle, therefore, with guilt either over the murder, given what they knew, or guilt for what they should have known, which might have allowed them to rescue the victim. This guilt along with other feelings can hold adult survivors hostage. They can also feel bound by their responsibility for the children who are left, loyalty binds to both victim and perpetrator, and chronic conditions that emerge as a result of the homicide.

Parenting Stress

Although there are no definitive statistics, many adult survivors become instant parents because the actual caregivers are now imprisoned or dead because of murder or murder-suicide. In a study of 146 children, 59 percent moved into the homes of their maternal or paternal kin (Lewandowski et al. 2004). Another study found that 37 out of 47 children lived with either the victim's or perpetrator's family after their parent was killed (Steeves and Parker 2007). These relatives not only manage their own grief reactions but also deal with their reluctance to become parents and the stress of not knowing how to parent severely traumatized children.

Taking on the responsibility of parenting by default creates additional problems. Adult survivors commonly report health problems as they put their own needs secondary to caring for the children. In interviews with 10 participants selected from a 10-city study, two caregivers had suffered heart attacks, two underwent major surgeries, and one was hospitalized with a heart condition (Hardesty et al. 2008). These health and adjustment challenges are compounded by other harsh realities including the fact that caregivers may already have limited financial resources, have to quit jobs to care for children, and lack ongoing external support.

Adult survivors feel particularly challenged by the fact that children in the same household respond differently to the homicide, in part, because they have diverse needs and are at different ages and stages of development. In one family, the caregiver describes how four grandchildren have varied needs and responses four years after the intimate partner familicide (IPF) (Hardesty et al. 2008, 114).

> [The] five-year-old grandson (who was 11 months old at the time of the IPF) does not remember his mother and father from before the murder. He has developed a relationship with his father through phone calls and visits to the prison. [The] seven-year-old granddaughter (three years old at the time) believes that another man killed her mother, not her father. [The] nine-year-old grandson (five years old at the time), unlike his siblings, refuses to visit his mother's grave or visit his father in prison. In contrast, [the] 10-year-old grandson (6 years old at the time) is angry that his father is in prison and believes that he should not have been sentenced to prison.

Indeed, it may be common for parenting stress to reflect the reality of having to confront unusual and complicated situations. A mother described some of the challenges she faced raising her son and two-month-old granddaughter after her daughter's boyfriend killed her daughter and tried to kill her son when he attempted to protect his sister.

> My son had about a 10% chance of living but he made it through. He thought I was angry at him because he didn't protect his sister....One day he blew up and said, "I did the best I could. I promise you I did." I said, "Well Donald, it's not your fault. It's Jaime's fault. You did better than what most men would have done. Cause you were only 17 at the time. Most men when they see a domestic abuse, they turn their head. To me you're a hero even though she didn't live. To me you're her hero. You're a treasured hero." He could have killed my granddaughter too.

In an unsolved murder, a woman described her response to her grandson when his mother who allegedly killed the woman's son sent the grandson to spend time with his grandmother.

> The little boy came to visit us for about a month when he was about six and [his mother] would say, "If you don't act right, I'm going to send you to stay with relatives." He said that his mother told him that his dad died in a car accident. That was number one. She wouldn't even tell him the truth. We didn't talk about [his father's death] while he was here. I figured he'll find out if he wants to. He'll find out when he gets older. I haven't seen or heard from her in over five years. You wonder about the little boy but not much you can do.

Parenting stress is also extreme for the remaining parent when a family member kills one or more children as part of a murder-suicide. These domestic homicides are often associated with a perpetrator's separation from a partner and/or mental illness (Finkelhor 2001). Besides physical problems such as insomnia, hair falling out, high blood pressure, and losing considerable weight, caregivers have long-term mental illness and substance abuse problems, which frequently develop in response to the homicide. Mothers find that involvement in later relationships, if possible, and the birth of additional children do not lessen their suffering. In some instances, their extended families fight to keep them from killing themselves. One mother reported that she "had no interest in surviving" without her children. Another mother reported, "I never went outside to shop for three years. I was on tranquillizers" (Johnson 2005, 79).

Loyalty Binds and Chronic Conditions

Recovery for adult survivors is complicated by estranged family relationships, emotional impasses, and conflict between victim's and perpetrator's extended families (Armour 2002). Irresolvable binds contribute to chronic conditions including loneliness, anger, and feelings of betrayal. Indeed, intrafamilial homicide divides the loyalties within a person, as well as between family members. For example, children may both grieve the loss of their father and feel angry at him which can complicate feelings of love and loyalty to both parents. Parents of the perpetrator may feel both protective of their child but also shame for what he did and guilt for trying to protect someone who has also killed their grandchildren.

The Lonaper family had lived with a mentally ill son/brother for years; his frequent hospitalizations were triggered by a refusal to take his medications. Victor killed his sister Brenda after convincing her to let him into the home she shared with her mother Pat. The family lives in fear of another murder because Victor took an insanity plea and will be released at some point from the hospital for the criminally insane. The remaining siblings, Darlene and Tony, are upset with their mother, Pat. She continues to maintain contact with Victor even though she is convinced that Victor really meant to kill her instead of Brenda and will likely do so when he gets out of the hospital. Darlene and Pat describe how their concerns about the future have driven a wedge between them.

> Darlene: "My mother told me that she intends to keep some contact with Victor after he gets out and trying to monitor him, make sure that he's taking his medication. And this just threw me for a loop because I have been intensely planning my future of how I am going to get away from here and cut contact and hide from Victor basically, completely hide. And the fact that my mother intends to keep some contact, that makes it very difficult. How am I going to keep the contact with my mother when I am trying to hide? I am looking at total exclusion from my family. It's my only choice because I feel I need to be safe."
>
> Pat: "My first reaction when I heard he murdered Brenda was, 'Oh, poor Victor. He must feel so terrible.' And the farther I get from that and the more I see him I just realize that he really doesn't have a clue as to the impact of her death on so many people. I always had hope that he would get better but now I don't care. If Victor gets out. I want to be the magnet that he's drawn to, the one that he comes to first so that the rest of them don't get it."

In addition to splitting the family, adult survivors struggle with reactions that are likely more intense because the survivors are related to the perpetrator by blood or marriage. Darlene Lonaper continues to feel terror about the murder because the nightmare continues since she is related to Victor and, therefore, may have possible contact in the future. "If he ever gets out, I'll be changing my name, moving, cutting virtually all my contacts with my past life in an effort to protect me and my family," she said.

It is also common for family members to feel betrayed because the person they knew and trusted turned out to be someone else. A couple whose son-in-law, Jeff, murdered their daughter still cannot comprehend the level of his deception. "He's a person who came inside this house. He slept overnight. He sent me flowers. He was the father's golfing buddy. How could we be so taken in? How could we be so stupid?" The perpetrators' legal defense often feeds the betrayal because it now appears duplicitous. "Jeff went into the house and staged a break-in and decided he would plead not guilty. He didn't say he didn't kill her or he did kill her. He just said 'I didn't do anything wrong.'"

Although homicide survivors generally feel unremitting rage, the anger felt by survivors of domestic fatalities can be differentiated because it is often tied not only to their helplessness but also to their profound sense of betrayal, which is made even stronger because people have a history together and are still related to each other even if they have no contact. A father whose daughter was killed by her husband described the size and unrelenting quality of his fury and his efforts to distance himself from the murderer.

> For a long time I thought about him a lot and more than I thought about my daughter. That bothered me. And every time I would try to move my daughter forward, I couldn't seem to get her by him. I can tell you right now how much I hate him. He is like a bad seed. He is like sin and I hate all those things. It borders on rage at times so you see spots in front of your eyes. We go down to the prison and just look at that damn prison. Can you believe that? The betrayal. We even buried our daughter with her maiden instead of her married name. I just can't even call her...so she's buried under....

The trauma from domestic homicide is enduring and causes long-range changes in the way people function. Moreover, recovery has a chronic quality because of the ongoing stressors and conflicting responses following the murder. Some adult survivors increase their alcohol consumption to deal with the aftermath (Johnson 2005). Others keep themselves exceptionally busy. Others succumb to a life-long depression. A man who lost his sister said, "I think the day my Mom heals is probably going to be the day she dies. I don't think she'll ever get over it."

SEEKING HELP AND AVAILABLE SERVICES

For the children who remain, many of them are left to manage on their own (Burman and Allen-Meares 1994; Lewandowski et al. 2004). In the short run, they need help navigating the various agencies they have to deal with. Children interviewed by police may worry that they will be accused of being responsible for the death. Autopsies may be confusing because the child perceives additional violence is being done to the victim. In the long run, they will need help throughout their development because as they grow older and their vocabulary increases, they may have new memories and begin to understand things differently which can add to their stress. The majority of children affected by domestic homicide are under 10 years of age (Lewandowski et al. 2004). Studies indicate that many of them never receive therapy (Robertson and Donaldson 1997), delay getting help (Black and Kaplan 1998), or see a professional only once (Lewandowski et al. 2004). Indeed, children may even resist counseling because it feels to them like forced self-revelation (Steeves and Parker 2007). Goals of treatment for these children include relief of suffering and resolution of trauma symptoms, clarification of cognitive or emotional distortions about the homicide, provision of a supportive environment in which the child may continue to work through the experience in the future, and minimization of future problems as a result of the trauma (Zeanah and Burk 1984). The behavior of adult survivors who were children when the murder happened also gives some indication of what they needed as children. Specifically adult survivors try to make meaning of their lives by discovering as much as possible about the homicide, assigning a reason for what the perpetrator did, relying on religious prescription for understanding, or finding some way to make peace with the perpetrator (Steeves and Parker 2007).

Studies indicate that the presence of a strong figure in the lives of these children helps bolster them through the turmoil (Steeves and Parker 2007). Other protective factors include effective coping skills, bonding with trusted adults, and a safe place to go outside the home. Education regarding interpersonal relationships including healthy and unhealthy behaviors and their consequences (Lewandowski et al. 2004), achievements including success at school, and good relationships between siblings (Hendricks, Black, and Kaplan 1993) are other important elements for these children.

Adult survivors follow an unusual pattern in obtaining services. A study of help-seeking behavior found that they used services in the initial eight weeks following the homicide more than adult survivors of nonfamilial homicides (Horne 2003). However, their outreach decreased in the subsequent eight weeks. It is possible that their conflicted feelings toward the relationships with the perpetrators and their guilt and shame may have resulted in self-isolation, keeping issues in the family, or the avoidance of experiences that can trigger painful and ambivalent emotions (Hardesty et al. 2008).

Services for families of the perpetrators may also be limited. Although they too grieve the loss of children in a murder-suicide as well as the loss of their son, victim service agencies may not contact them because the agencies are already providing services to members of the mother's family (Johnson 2006). It is likely, therefore, that both children and adults need special services because of their unique survivor issues. For example, families may need help determining whether children should have or not have contact with the perpetrator. Few services exist, however, and survivors often report that the therapist has little understanding of their problems. An observer made the following remarks about survivors (Johnson 2005):

> [They] were obliged to find their own ways to heal, because their suffering was so deep and intense that existing services lacked the experience or capacity to deliver what was needed. The survivors' families came and went in a haze, and were in no doubt affected by their own grief and the lack of services. Overall, I was left with the feeling that the survivors' families were all, in some ways, isolated by their own trauma, and the inability of others to meet their needs.

The vast majority of states have DVFRT that review the facts and circumstances of all fatal family violence incidents that occur within a designated geographic area. The purpose of these agencies is to utilize a multi-agency and confidential process to identify gaps in the system that can lead to more effective prevention policy and coordinated strategies. Although these teams have been in existence since the mid 1990s, almost no information has been gathered on either the children or adult survivors. Past and current studies continue to show that family members are in need of considerable help in the aftermath of the homicide (Hennepin County 2002). DVFRTs provide avenues for both the gathering of information about survivor's needs and the recommendation of services. If DVFRTs could expand their focus of inquiry, survivors of intrafamilial homicide might be given advocates who could speak on their behalf and support them through the tragedy.

REFERENCES

Armour, M.P. 2002. Experiences of covictims of homicide: Implications for research and practice. *Trauma, Abuse, and Violence: A Review Journal* 3, no. 2: 109–24.

Baker, L.L., P.G. Jaffe, L. Ashbourne, and J. Carter. 2002. *Children exposed to domestic violence: A teachers handbook to increase understanding and improve community responses* London, ON: Center for Children and Families in the Justice System.

Black, D., and T. Kaplan. 1988. Father kills mother: Issues and problems encountered by a child psychiatric team. *British Journal of Psychiatry* 153:624–30.

Burman, S., and P. Allen-Meares. 1994. Neglected victims of murder: Children's witness to parental homicide. *Social Work* 39, no. 1: 28–34.

Clements, P.T., and A.W. Burgess. 2002. Children's responses to family member homicide. *Family & Community Health* 25, no. 1: 32–42.

Durose, M.R., C.W. Harlow, P.A. Langan, M. Motivans, R.R. Rantala, and E.L. Smith. 2005. Family violence statistics: Including statistics on strangers and acquaintances. Washington, DC: Department of Justice, NCJ 207846, Bureau of Justice Statistics. http://www.ojp.usdoj.gov/bjs/abstract/fvs.htm (accessed December 22, 2007).

English, D.J., D.B. Marshall, and A.J. Stewart. 2003. Effects of family violence on child behavior and health during early childhood. *Journal of Family Violence* 18, no. 1: 43–57.

Eth, S., and R.S. Pynoos. 1994. Children who witness the homicide of a parent. *Psychiatry* 55: 287–306.

Fantuzzo, J.W., and W.K. Mohr. 1999. Prevalence and effects of child exposure to domestic violence. *The Future of Children* 9, no. 3: 21–32

Finkelhor, E., and R. Omrad. 2001. Homicides of children and youth. *Juvenile Justice Bulletin.* Washington, DC: U.S. Department of Justice, Office of Justice Programs, Office of Juvenile Justice and Delinquency.

Fox, J.A., and M.W. Zawitz. 1999. Homicide trends in the United States. Washington, DC: U.S. Department of Justice, Bureau of Justice Statistics.

Fox, J.A., and M.W. Zawitz. 2004. Homicide trends in the United States. Washington, DC: U.S. Department of Justice, Bureau of Justice Statistics.

Groves, B.M. 1999. Mental health services for children who witness domestic violence. *The Future of Children* 9, no. 3: 122–32.

Hardesty, J.L., J.C. Campbell, JM. McFarlane, and L.A. Lewandowski. 2008. How children and their caregivers adjust after intimate partner femicide. *Journal of Family Issues* 29, no. 1: 100–24.

Hendricks, J.H., D. Black, and T. Kaplan. 1993. *When father kills mother: Guiding children through trauma and grief.* New York: Routledge.

Hennepin County. 2002. *Domestic fatality review pilot project report.* http://wwwa.co .hennepin.mn.us/images/HCInternet/Static%20Files/112799246Domestic_Fatality _Review_Pilot_Project_Report.pdf (accessed January 12, 2008).

Horne, C. 2003. Families of homicide victims: Service utilization patterns of extra- and intrafamilial homicide survivors. *Journal of Family Violence* 18, no. 2: 75–82.

Johnson, C.H. 2005. *Come with daddy: Child murder suicide after family breakdown.* Crawley, Western Australia: University of Western Australia Press.

Johnson, C.H. 2006. Familicide and family law: A study of filicide-suicide following separation. *Family Court Review* 44, no. 3: 448–63.

Lewandowski, L.A., J. McFarlane, J.C. Campbell, F. Gary, and C. Barenski. 2004. "He killed my mommy!" Murder or attempted murder of a child's mother. *Journal of Family Violence* 19, no. 4: 211–20.

Marleau, J.D., N. Auclair, and F. Millaud. 2006. Comparison of factors associated with parricide in adults and adolescents. *Journal of Family Violence* 21, no. 5: 321–25.

Mbilinyi, L.F., J.L. Edleson, A.K. Hagemeister, and S.K. Beeman. 2007. What happens to children when their mothers are battered? Results from a four-city anonymous telephone survey. *Journal of Family Violence* 22, no. 5: 309–17.

National Coalition for Child Protection. 2007. *When children witness domestic violence: Expert opinion. Summary of expert testimony on the impact on children of witnessing domestic violence.* New York. http://www.nccpr.org/index_files/page0007.html (accessed January 12, 2008).

Newman, B.M., and P.R. Newman. 2006. *Development through life: A psychosocial approach.* 9th ed. Belmont, CA: Wadsworth.

Parker, B., R. Steeves, S. Anderson, and B. Moran. 2004. Uxoricide: A Phenomenological study of adult survivors. *Issues in Mental Health Nursing* 25, no. 2: 133–45.

Robertson, M., and M. Donaldson. 1997. No place like home: Family murder, the child victims. Center for the Study of Violence and Reconciliation. http://www.csvr.org.za/wits/articles/artfamur.htm (accessed January 12, 2008).

Spilsbury, J.C., L. Belliston, D. Drotar, A. Drinkard, J. Kretschmar, R. Creeden, D.J. Flannery, and S. Friedman. 2007. Clinically significant trauma symptoms and behavioral problems in a community-based sample of children exposed to domestic violence. *Journal of Family Violence* 22, no. 6: 478–99.

Steeves, R., K. Laughon, B. Parker, and F. Weierbach. 2007. Talking about talk: The experiences of boys who survived intraparental homicide. *Issues in Mental Health Nursing* 28, no. 8: 899–912.

Steeves, R, and B. Parker. 2007. Adult perspectives on growing up following uxoricide. *Journal of Interpersonal Violence* 22, no. 10: 1270–84.

Wilson, J.S., and N. Websdale. 2006. Domestic violence fatality review teams: An interprofessional model to reduce deaths. *Journal of Interprofessional Care* 20, no. 5: 535–44.

Ybarra, G., S. Wilkens, and A. Lieberman. 2007. The influence of domestic violence on preschooler behavior and functioning. *Journal of Family Violence* 22, no. 1: 33–42.

Zeanah, C.H., and G.S. Burk. 1984. A young child who witnessed her mother's murder: Therapeutic and legal considerations. *American Journal of Psychotherapy* 38, no. 1: 132–45.

Part II

The Sociology of Domestic Homicide

7

Domestic Homicide Worldwide

Katherine van Wormer and
Woochan S. Shim

The study of domestic homicide is incomplete without consideration of the treatment of women worldwide and the impact of global market economics on that treatment, whether directly or indirectly. The revolution in communication technologies, this phenomenon that is drawing the world in closer and closer, is one significant factor affecting the lives of women. Globalization can be looked at in a number of contexts, both positive and negative, that are relevant to women in the world today. From a positive standpoint, women of the world are uniting individually through the Internet and collectively through international organizations and conventions. At the same time, the exchange of information about lifestyles and women's roles has raised the consciousness of educated women across the globe. Internationally, women have organized to advocate for human rights at conventions, the most famous of which was that held in China in 1995 at the United Nations Fourth World Conference on Women. It was only after the Beijing conference, in fact, that Amnesty International, the well-known non-governmental organization (NGO) that has done so much to publicize human rights abuses worldwide, took up the call to investigate crimes specifically against women (van Wormer and Bartollas 2007). "Women's rights are human rights" has become the mantra of this organization. Attention to such issues and to human rights violations today has been catapulted to the forefront of international media concerns.

And yet...this positive form of globalization—the communications revolution—has generated fears in certain quarters across the globe of cultural change that could be threatening to age-old traditions. The basic fear is that if women's consciousness is raised, women will demand their rights. A counterreaction, in short, has taken place—a backlash by entrenched forces with a vested interest in the status quo. This backlash is especially pronounced in regions of the world where religious fundamentalism has been used to threaten women and suppress them.

Economic competition undoubtedly plays a role in what has been termed the "world's war against women" as well. Worldwide, as competition for well-paying and secure jobs in a global economy heats up, dangerous right-wing extremist movements are seizing political power. The mistreatment of women globally tends to be expressed in the guise of an attack on modernization, including the threatened liberation of women (van Wormer 2004).

This commercial "flattening" of the world (see Friedman 2005) has an effect to bear not only on the lowering of trade and political barriers, but on the nature of crime, the passage and enforcement of transnational laws, and, on the victimization of women. Poverty and pressures from the global market that are associated with family breakdown interact with traditional ideologies and can exacerbate women's victimization. Every social movement breeds a counter reaction, and as some individuals are losing their place in the world, even from forces that have nothing to do with women's increasing equality, some men are lashing out at the most vulnerable people in their lives—women. Psychologists call this *displaced aggression.* In some non-Western nations, the form that the displaced aggression takes is a virtual war on women's self-expression and their rights. Today, in many places, as the stress on families and communities is severe, men whose "sense of their own manhood flowed out of their utility in a society" as Faludi (1999, 607) terms it, are often seen to be "fighting a world transformed by the women's movement" (413).

The macroeconomic policies associated with the global economy have important human rights implications in that they increase inequalities among nations and people. Macroeconomic policies require that the nonindustrialized nations reduce their indebtedness to the world banks by reducing social welfare spending; this in turn increases the gap between the rich and the poor within as well as between nations.

Relevant to economic inequities, women perform two-thirds of the world's work but earn only one-tenth of all income; women own less than one-tenth of the world's property (Human Rights Watch 2002). People in a position of economic servitude to others who have control over the resources are generally vulnerable to mistreatment, and they have little recourse for justice.

Indeed, the low social and economic status of women combined with a value on materialism can be both a cause and a consequence of violence against women. Take the dowry bride burnings in India, for example. Dowry bride burning is an illegal custom in which a bride is set on fire by her in-laws if the demands for dowry payment from the bride's family are unmet. Indian feminists use the term *femicide* to fit the reality of such systematic female killing in their country. As India has shifted to a market cash economy, the new consumerism has put more value on the size of the dowry itself than on the woman.

Low economic status of men and the inherent stress of trying to eke out a living also can be a factor associated with violence, most likely in the form of displaced aggression by the husband onto the wife. In their investigation of correlates of domestic violence, Campbell et al. (2003) found that the strongest contextual risk factor for intimate partner homicide is an abuser's lack of employment. In fact, unemployment increased the risk of intimate partner homicide fourfold. Abusers who were more highly educated were less apt to murder their partners than those abusers who were uneducated. Although this study was conducted in cities across the United States, one can assume that the basic psychology would apply elsewhere inasmuch as earning a living and supporting a family are basic human needs.

It stands to reason that as the economy improves in a country, more girls are educated, birth control is practiced more widely, women move into the work force, and the lives of women improve, or so the proponents of "free trade" and global economics argue. The United Nations (UN 2005) in a news report has reversed the proposition—instead of saying education stops the violence, the report states that stopping the violence is the key to promoting education for girls and eliminating poverty. This claim is premised on the argument that women who are not terrorized by violence and who enjoy some degree of gender equality are free to make decisions concerning family size. Liberated women also are apt to have access to health care for themselves and for their children and to be able to successfully oppose harmful traditional practices. Moreover, as studies show, when women control the family spending, they are more likely than men to invest a higher percentage of their earnings in family needs (UN 2005).

From our perspective, both education for women (including career access) and government action to provide protection (including economic support) for women who wish to leave a battering situation are essential to a woman's well-being. Human rights standards affirm that everyone has a fundamental right to be free from violence, and economic security is essential for the achievement of this goal. But across the globe, women are rarely in control of the economy or of the family spending.

That women's rights are human rights is an underlying assumption of this chapter. The focus here is femicide worldwide. After looking at the basic statistics on the extent of this problem, we focus on ritualistic murder through honor killings and dowry deaths. Economic globalization, poverty, and violence against women are seen as intertwined.

STATISTICS ON FEMICIDE

Domestic homicides, especially of women killed by male members of the family, often are misclassified as suicides or accidents. This lack of accurate reporting is a hindrance to global human rights organizations in their effort to prevent domestic homicide. In Palestine, for example, even when women are burned, strangled, beaten, stabbed, and shot to death, the death is frequently declared a suicide (Emery 2003). Despite such active concealment and misclassification of domestic homicide, however, such available worldwide statistics on domestic homicide as do exist reveal that the overwhelming majority of victims are women and that the majority of perpetrators are their intimate partners.

Studies in Australia, Canada, Israel, South Africa, and the United States have shown that 40 to 70 percent of women who have been murdered were killed by their intimate partners, usually in the context of an abusive relationship (World Health Organization [WHO] 2002). A study of 249 court records in Zimbabwe revealed that 59 percent of female homicides were committed by the intimate partner of the victim (Watts, Osam, and Win 1995). National figures for intimate femicide suggest that this most lethal form of domestic violence is prevalent in South Africa. In 1999, 8.8 per 100,000 of the female population aged 14 years and older died at the hands of their partner in South Africa, which is the highest rate ever reported in research anywhere in the world (Mathews et al. 2004). In the United States, domestic homicides have decreased 71 percent for men and 25 percent for women since the mid 1970s (U.S. Department of Justice 2007). However, homicide victim rates for women are still much higher than male rates, with a four to one ratio. In the United Kingdom, 37 percent of female homicide victims are killed by their husbands or boyfriends whereas 6 percent of male victims were murdered by their wives or girlfriends (Simmons 2002, cited by Aldridge and Browne 2003). Canadian homicide data reveal a history of domestic violence in the majority of partner killings, that separation can trigger killings of women, and that young separating women are at the highest risk (United Nations Economic and Social Council 2006).

An estimated 14,000 Russian women are killed every year, on average, by partners or other family members, according to a Russian Government report to the Committee on the Elimination of all Forms of Discrimination against Women (United Nations Population Fund [UNFPA] 2007). Nearly 20 percent received regular and/or severe beatings, almost half of them while pregnant, ill, or unemployed, according to the study. Many are victims of systematic abuse. The death toll by domestic homicide is higher than the number of Russian soldiers who were killed during the 10-year war they fought in Afghanistan.

Honor killing is the ancient practice in which men, often brothers, kill female relatives who have disgraced the family through sexual activity, including rape victimization. In Jordan, according to the UNICEF (2003) report, there are around 23 such murders per year; another 300 took place in 1997 in Pakistan and Yemen, and 52 in Egypt. The United Nations estimates that as many as 5,000 young women are killed every year in the name of "honor killings" primarily in Western Asia, North Africa, parts of South Asia, and in Pakistan, where at least 1,000 women were murdered in 1999 (UN 2000b). Relocating or immigrating into a Western country does not seem to decrease the problem. In London, a Muslim father was found guilty of "honor killing" when he ordered his own daughter's murder. Britain is home to some 1.8 million Muslims and more than 100 homicides are under investigation for being potential "honor killings" (Associated Press 2007).

According to the United Nations Children's Fund (UNICEF), in India alone, more than 5,000 brides die annually because their dowries are considered insufficient (United Nations Children's Fund 2000, 14), while hundreds of women in Bangladesh are subjected to acid attacks.

Domestic homicide, honor killings, dowry deaths, and crimes of passion all have similar dynamics in that the women are killed by male family members and the crimes are perceived as excusable or understandable (Mayell 2002). In the following section, we elaborate further on these family homicides inflicted by male family members on female family members along with the "not-so-domestic" aspects of domestic homicide. The cases illustrated in each section have been developed after reviewing specific types of domestic homicide cases that were published in various news media in order to demonstrate the common aspects of each type of domestic homicide.

ISLAMISM AND HONOR KILLING

Honor killings are known to be more prevalent in countries where the majority of the population identifies as Muslim. Honor killings have been especially prominent in Bangladesh, Egypt, India, Israel, Italy, Jordan, Morocco, Pakistan, Turkey, and Uganda (UN 2000a). The view of women as property with no rights of their own seems to be deeply rooted in Islamic culture and reinforced in some teachings in the Qur'an (Koran), the book of basic Islamic teachings:

> Men are in charge of women, because Allah hath made the one of them to excel the other, and because they spend of their property [for the support of women]. So good women are obedient, guarding in secret that which Allah hath guarded. As for those from whom ye fear rebellion, admonish them and banish them to beds apart, and scourge them. Then if they obey you, seek not a way against them (sura 4:34 cited in Shehadeh 2003, 19).

Islamic fundamentalists believe that women are to be treated equally with men as long as men are heading the household, leading prayers, and holding the office of a caliph or supreme imam (Hiro 1989 cited in Shehadeh 2003).

Others argue that the Muslim religion granted to women rights they have never had before: the right to choose their marriage partner, the right to divorce, and the right to inheritance (Mernissi 1987). It is argued that through distorted use of religion, such as "selective preference of one verse from the Qur'an over many other verses that talk about kindness and justice towards women has created an atmosphere that tolerates and allows violence toward women" (Ayyub 2000, 242). Recently, Islamic feminists are pushing for reinterpretations of the Qur'an to use it as the ideological basis for fighting for human rights and democratic societies (Khan and Langman 2005). Some Islamic leaders have condemned the practice of honor killing and say it has no religious foundation by saying that there is nothing in the Qur'an that permits or sanctions honor killings. In addition, some of their religious practices that have been interpreted as oppressive toward and discriminatory against women have an alternative interpretation. The religious practice of men praying in front of women or women not allowed to pray in front of men depicts the men's awareness of their own powerlessness toward sexual drive and their desire to avoid distractions when worshiping God.

In her memoir, *Iran Awakening,* Shirin Ebadi (2007), a Muslim feminist attorney who won the Nobel Prize for Peace in 2003, advocates for the universality of human rights and debunks cultural relativism and the U.S.-led "war on terrorism." She singles out the patriarchal religious authorities and theocracy rather than religion as the basis for the repressive state laws and customs in Iran. Similarly, we can see that the cause of honor killing is not so much due to the Muslim religion as due to the historical interpretation or misinterpretation of certain religious beliefs. As explained by Emery (2003, 6):

> The murder of females in the Middle East is an ancient tradition. Prior to the arrival of Islam in AD 622, Arabs occasionally buried infant daughters to avoid the possibility that they would later bring shame to the family. This practice continued through the centuries. It may still occur today among Bedouins, who consider girls most likely to sully the family honor. Honor killings occur for a variety of offenses, including allegations of premarital or extramarital sex, refusing an arranged marriage, attempting to obtain a divorce, or simply talking with a man. Among Arabs, marriage is traditionally a family affair, not a personal choice. Girls are often pressured into arranged marriages, while boys are not. If a woman brings shame to the family, her male relatives are bound by duty and culture to kill her.

Since honor killings have been a part of Turkish culture for a long time and are often tolerated if not condoned by public officials, women's advocates face major challenges in protecting women from these crimes (Kardam 2005). Perpetrators often receive light sentences or are excused by the court entirely because the defense of the family's honor is treated as a mitigating circumstance (UN 2000a). Joining the global effort in decreasing violence against women, Turkey has tightened their punishment for honor killing. However, instead of saving women's lives, changes in their penal code in turn have led young women to be pressured to take their own lives. Honor killing has now become honor suicide as illustrated in the following case reported by Bilefsky (2006, 1):

> Derya lives in Batman, Turkey. She is [a] 17 year old and recently received a text message from her uncle that read, "You have blackened our name; kill yourself and clean our shame or we will kill you first." Her crime was that she liked a boy in her school, and showed her desire to wear a short skirt and to go to the movies with him. She was not raped by a stranger or relative nor had consensual sex, which is often considered as ruining the family honor. She received a similar type of death threat from her uncles and brothers, as many as 15 messages a day. Not being able to tolerate constant harassment, she decided to follow wishes of her uncles and

brother. In order to die with dignity, she jumped into the Tigris River but only to be rescued. She then hanged herself but one of her uncles cut the rope just in time to save her life. She slashed her wrists with a kitchen knife but only ended up being hospitalized. From the hospital, she was referred to a women's shelter.

This can be interpreted as a cultural clash between rigid moral structures of Islamic families and the secular values of young women who are influenced by exposure to the Internet and the popular channel MTV. People from rural areas and those who are uneducated are more likely to be less tolerant toward women's liberation and are more likely to subscribe to traditional notions of family honor (Kardam 2005). Young women like the one in Batman, Turkey, who are from areas that are poor, rural, and deeply influenced by conservative Islam, are at risk of victimization by traditional sanctions if they stray from traditional norms and mores of the society (Bilefsky 2006). The cultural clash between old and new ways related to globalization is often associated with cruel repression of women in a vain attempt to "keep them in line."

DOWRY BRIDE BURNINGS

Giving or receiving any dowry of more than 7,000 rupees (£90/US$150) is a crime in India. Yet within the country's booming economy, the middle class is spending a fortune on dowries. Dowries may include items such as bikes, refrigerators, microwaves, cars, and large amounts of cash. These gifts are made in an attempt to find a suitable husband. Families that are unable or unwilling to provide such items risk the loss of their daughter through dowry related femicide (Mynott 2003). India's illegal dowry system is still thriving, leaving women vulnerable to abuse, degradation, and murder by "accidental" kitchen fires. Because impoverished families cannot afford the expense of a daughter, many resort to abortion of the fetus if the ultrasound shows it is female or infanticide after the birth of a girl. Accordingly, over the past two decades, millions of girls have been found to be "missing" from the population of India (Mapp 2008).

As dowry related crimes have spiraled out of control, the government has taken drastic measures. A law has been passed that if a bride dies in the first seven years of marriage, her family can file a charge alleging dowry crime, and anyone remotely connected to the death of a wife faces jail time. Adam Mynott, a BBC reporter, came across mothers, sisters, sons, daughters, aunts, nieces, and nephews who were all behind bars in Tihar Jail (Mynott 2003). He found that most of the time the husbands of the victims do not get charged because they are not the ones setting a woman on fire or even present when execution is in place. The Tihar Jail has a "mother-in-law" cell block which is exclusively for women who have killed or harassed their daughters-in-law. The cell is full of elderly women, some of whom are serving 20-year sentences for murder (Mynott 2003).

Dowry disputes are not the only reason for these horrors inflicted upon women, according to Mapp (2008), but rather, the low status of women in general in Indian culture. In Pakistan, women are also victims of deliberate burnings blamed on stoves, deaths that are not related to disputes over dowries.

Universally, suicide rates for women are typically lower than the rate of male suicide rates by a ratio of 2.8 to 1. This excludes China and India where suicide rates in young married women are higher than male rates (Brockington 2001). These findings may be explained by the way domestic homicides get recorded in those countries. In India, the familiar pattern in dowry killings is the following: A woman is burned to death in her kitchen but when the police arrive, the family of the husband claim that it is a "cooking stove" accident. The police are then assisted toward this conclusion with a wad of rupees.

As the world grows ever smaller and as developing countries become more Westernized, inhumane practices that hark back to an ancient culture get exposed to outside criticism. Those traditional practices, if evaluated to be inhumane by the world community, should be expected to clash with external political influences and eventually to be relinquished. However, in many lands, the opposite seems to be the case. The more that people in India become Westernized, for example, the more a materialistic way of life is desired. People want expensive clothes and other consumer objects that are constantly advertised through media, such as motor scooters which are quite popular in Bangalore. And the more expensive and materialistic things that are requested for a dowry payment, the more danger the women of lower middle class families will face if their family is unable to afford the requests.

CRIMES OF PASSION

The term *crime of passion* "refers to homicides resulting from conflicts related to love and/or sexual relations...involving the killing of women and/or their suitors by husbands, fiancés, lovers, or fathers and brothers" (Besse 1998, 653). This form of homicide became a social concern in Brazil in the 1910s through the 1930s, mainly with a campaign against the tolerance of crimes of passion by a group of male professionals, the Conselho Brasileiro de Hygiene Social (CBSH: Brazilian Council on Social Hygiene). In 1940, the penal code was revised to criminalize wife killers; this act caused the social concern over crimes of passion to diminish. Yet, the change in the penal code did not necessarily result in changes in practice, and offenders were only lightly punished under this law based on the argument that they did not pose as much danger to the society as other criminals.

France, similarly, has been known to have an ambivalent attitude toward crimes of passion. Under the Napoleonic Code, "excusable murder" was used to describe the killing of a woman caught in an extramarital affair by her husband, while it did not excuse a woman who discovers her husband in such act. In 1975, this term was removed from the judicial lexicon. However, a crime of passion is often viewed in a much more sympathetic light than other murders in France as in many other countries (Hunt 2007, 1):

> Marie, a well-known actress in France, fell into a coma and died at the hospital in the summer of 2003. Her injuries were from being beaten severely by her boyfriend, Cantat. Cantat was passionately jealous of her relationship with all and any men who were around her. He also wanted Marie to end her relationship with the three fathers of her four children. He was jealous of her acting co-stars at work and pressured her to try to get the love scenes cut from her films. When she did not comply with his demands, she had to face his punishment, a violent beating. Cantat was originally sentenced to eight years in prison. However, since French law grants parole once half the sentence has been served, there is a possibility for Cantat to be released from jail after he serves his half sentence.

This example and that of the ineffectual campaign of CBSH in Brazil illustrate that changes in the penal code alone are not sufficient in themselves to protect women in a patriarchal society—social belief systems must change as well.

DOMESTIC HOMICIDE IN SOUTH KOREA

Just like any other culture, domestic homicides in South Korea, especially women being killed by their intimate partners, have a long history. During the Joseon Dynasty (1392–1910 AC) under Jeongjo's ruling (1724–1776 AC), there were 70 (7.3 percent) domestic homicide cases among the 1,112 felony cases. Of those, 964 were homicide cases, according to the Record of Investigation called *Simrirok* (Shim 2007). The majority of cases were among low to middle class citizens, and all of the victims from 70 cases were either wives or mistresses killed by their husbands/lovers. Victims' "crimes" for which they were murdered included being disrespectful toward parents-in-law, being neglectful in farming, showing jealousy toward the mistress or the wife, having an affair, or being intoxicated with alcohol.

In South Korea in the past, homicides of women based on adultery and power struggles were common. In more recent times, when South Korea suffered a severe recession that struck in 1997 and was related to a "fast track capitalism" encouraged by the International Monetary Fund, the pattern of family homicides changed. From 1997 to 2001, wife murders were increasingly related to financial difficulties. In a social structure based on patriarchal and Confucian cultural norms in which the head of the household is expected to be the provider for the family, many fathers in the family experienced failure to fulfill their role expectations as head of the household. As the financial stress became intolerable, some decided to kill those whom they were supposed to care for and some ended up killing themselves as well. As we learn from a South Korean news report (Yonhap News 2001),

> Kang was running a fancy American franchised family restaurant. It was a thriving business until 1997. As a growing number of people would travel abroad or live a

few months to a few years abroad, there was a growing need for Westernized tastes and looks. However, as the whole country started to experience financial difficulties, people were less likely to eat out. He started to notice that franchised restaurants were turning to smaller scale Korean style restaurants; a few were starting smaller scaled food-cart business on the street, and a few were going bankrupt. He started to experience hardships as well. However, downsizing or changing his business meant losing his dignity. The more stressed he was and the more his wife suggested making changes to their business, the more he fought. He fought with everybody around him but his wife was getting the most of it. He started beating her more often and more severely. One day, he decided to kill his wife who was 47 years old, and then killed himself by jumping off of his apartment complex. He was 56 years old.

In the first national survey of domestic violence rates in Korea, involving over 6,000 males and females who are or have been married, Byun (2007) found that 15.7 percent of the households experienced physical violence in the previous year. Only around 3 percent of this was female-on-male violence. Little difference in social class was found.

The Korean-American community in Los Angeles has seen a spate of murder-suicides, most related to financial issues (Pelisek 2006). We need to take into account as indicated by the Family Violence Prevention Fund (2005) the fact that immigrant women are at higher risk for domestic violence than are U.S.-born women, and that the rate of domestic violence among Korean Americans is exceptionally high. Studies of Asian immigrant groups in general reveal that during immigration resettlement, men's economic status can worsen; there may be a gender role reversal, and men can try to reassert their male power through aggression (Bui 2008). Like immigration, involvement in military combat creates a situation conducive to later violence in the home.

LEGACY OF THE IRAQ WAR

Unique to the military is the training of men (and women) to kill. Combat in warfare conditions the soldier to kill almost as a reflex in a situation of danger. Military socialization "to make a man out of the boy" not only attempts to obliterate all that is feminine but also breeds misogynous heterosexuality in the soldier as well (Farr 2005). The degradation of traits such as weakness in battle, squeamishness, and compassion of traits associated with femininity, helps create or preserve masculine detachment and aggression desirable for battle. Such conditioning can be devastating for later family functioning.

On the home front, a condition such as post-traumatic stress disorder (PTSD) or a state of intoxication, and even being suddenly aroused from sleep, can trigger violence. Depression related to PTSD can lead to suicide. In a recent *New York Times* article, Alvarez and Sontag (2008) discuss the spate of murders and murder-suicides that have been committed by soldiers returning from combat.

They describe, for example, the murder of Erin Edwards, herself a soldier, who like her husband had served in Iraq. After being severely beaten by her husband, she left town and obtained a restraining order:

> Yet on the morning of July 22, 2004, William Edwards easily slipped off base, skipping his anger-management class, and drove to his wife's house in the Texas town of Killeen. He waited for her to step outside and then, after a struggle, shot her point-blank in the head before turning the gun on himself.

This case was reminiscent of several murder suicides that took place within a six-week period in 2002 when three Special Forces sergeants returned from Afghanistan and murdered their wives at Fort Bragg in North Carolina. Two immediately turned their guns on themselves; the third hanged himself in a jail cell. A fourth soldier at the same Army base also killed his wife during those six weeks (Alvarez and Sontag 2008). There was a barrage of media attention to these homicides and much speculation about the link between combat duty and domestic violence when the men came home. But as Alverez and Sontag suggest,

> National attention to the subject was short-lived. But an examination by *The Times* found more than 150 cases of fatal domestic violence or child abuse in the United States involving service members and new veterans during the wartime period that began in October 2001 with the invasion of Afghanistan. In more than a third of the cases, *The Times* determined that the offenders had deployed to Afghanistan or Iraq or to the regions in support of those missions.

Similarly, Anderson (2005) investigated seven homicides and three suicides that have taken place in western Washington State by returning soldiers from the war on Iraq. Five wives, one girlfriend, and a child have all been killed. Two of the suicides were committed after the murders. These cases and others like them reported across the United State seem to suggest that as an antiwar slogan popular in the sixties said, "War is not good for people or other living things."

CONCLUSION

There are two kinds of backlash—institutionalized and personal. *Institutionalized backlash* operates at the societal level, typically as laws that are written or enacted as a reaction against progress by a minority group. *Personal backlash* may have its origins in extreme stress such as that pertaining to war-related combat or to stress related to work in a highly competitive global economy or to the lack of work stemming from the same source. This form of backlash is manifest as displaced aggression onto another person such as a family member. Both forms of backlash, whether at the macro- or micro-level, are cultural in origin and derived from basic prejudice against girls and women combined with a sense of fear of loss of male power and control in the home and in society.

In parts of the Middle East, as we have seen, knowledge of the progress of affirmative action for women's rights in Western societies and attempts to import Westernized "reform" are met by the male authority structure with resistance and a reinforced suppression of women. In effect, women from another part of the world seemingly are being punished for the advances made by women far away. Such a cultural clash of ideologies can lead to violence out of a desperate attempt to keep girls and women down. Backlash at this most basic level is a response to anger and resentment by individual males whose place in society is undergoing rapid change, often faster than they can psychologically handle.

Institutional backlash is played out in the Middle East in the enforcement of traditional laws that keep women in the home and in a subordinate position in relation to men. In the Western part of the world, there is evidence of institutional backlash as well; this is played out not in terms of inequality but in the treatment of women as equals even in situations in which it works against women, for example, in the United States' prison system which are now modeled on prisons for men (refer to Chapters 1 and 8). Much of the backlash that we have considered in this chapter has taken the form of attempts to reverse feminist-inspired policies and activities. Attacks on women's reproductive freedoms have effectively established family planning roadblocks with a drastic impact on services in the United States and abroad. So in both the West and the East, women are increasingly being punished whether through the introduction of new laws or the removal of traditional protections based on gender.

The study of domestic homicide from a global perspective focuses not only on gendered inequities and situations of interpersonal conflict, but it also takes note of the impact of forces from the global market on the family. We have strived to show how one form of violence is connected to other systems of disadvantage and marginalization. Women's experiences, especially of exploitation and violence, effectively bring into sharp relief the underlying elements of globalization as a complex system of oppression.

The adoption of a human rights framework is increasingly relevant today, given the realities of the global market. A human rights discourse can provide a basis for awareness of, and alternatives to, the global regime that reinforces structures of disadvantage "through blatantly undemocratic processes which result in benefits for the few rather than the many" (Ife 2001, 202).

A high priority is providing women and girls safe communities in which they can realize their potential and exercise their social, legal, and human rights (Erez 2007). To address this priority, it is important to understand the interconnections between the global and the particular, and between paternalistic attitudes in the culture and the tolerance of violence against girls and women. Failure to address these issues in the development of policy and responses will result in missed opportunities to create change at optimal levels. The victimization of women is one of the most difficult issues to redress because it is related to deep-seated gender ideologies (such as prevalent notions that women are inferior to or dependent on men) which often tolerate, and in some instances even encourage, victimization (Erez 2007). The struggle to eradicate gender violence such as that discussed in this chapter—for example, rape, honor killings, bride burnings, and wife beatings—must be a global struggle. Such an effort will benefit from the adoption of a human rights approach and the effective utilization of the strategies of human rights advocacy.

REFERENCES

Aldridge, M.L., and K.D. Browne. 2003. Perpetrators of spousal homicide: A review. *Trauma, Violence, & Abuse* 4:265–76.

Alvarez, L., and D. Sontag. 2008. When strains on military families turn deadly. *The New York Times,* February 15.

Anderson, R. 2005. Home front casualties. *Seattle Weekly,* September 6. www.seattleweekly.com (accessed November 2007).

Associated Press. 2007. Father found guilty of ordering daughter's murder in "honor killing." http://www.iht.com/articles/ap/2007/06/11/europe/EU-GEN-Britain-Honor -Killing.php (accessed September 24, 2007).

Ayyub, R. 2000. Domestic violence in the South Asian Muslim immigrant population in the United States. *Journal of Social Distress and the Homeless* 9, no. 3: 237–48.

Besse, S.K. 1998. Crimes of passion: The campaign against wife killings in Brazil, 1910–1940. *Journal of Social History* 22, no. 4: 653–66.

Bilefsky, D. 2006. How to avoid honor killing in Turkey? Honor suicide. http://www .nytimes.com/2006/07/16/world/europe/16turkey.html?_r=2&pagewanted=1&oref =slogin (accessed September 24, 2007).

Brockington, I. 2001. Suicide in women. *International clinical psychopharmacology* 16, no. S2: S7–S19.

Bui, H. 2008. Immigration, masculinity, and intimate partner violence from the standpoint of domestic violence service providers and Vietnamese-origin women. *Feminist Criminology* 3, no. 3: 191–215.

Byun, W. 2007. Violence against women in Korea and its indicators. Invited paper. United Nations Division for the Advancement of Women, October 5. http://www.un.org/ womenwatch/daw/egm/vaw_indicators_2007/papers/Invited%20Paper%20Korea% 20Whasoon%20Byun,.pdf (accessed August 2008).

Campbell, J.C., D. Webster, J. Koziol-McLain, C. Block, D. Campbell, and M.A. Curry. 2003. Risk factors for femicide in abusive relationships: Results from a multisite case control study. *American Journal of Public Health* 93, no. 7: 1089–97.

Ebadi, S. 2007. *Iran awakening: One woman's journey to reclaim her life and country.* New York: Random House.

Emery, J. 2003. Reputation is everything: Honor killing among the Palestinians. *Worldandi.com.* http://www.worldandi.com/newhome/public/2003/may/clpub.asp (accessed September 24, 2007).

Erez, E. 2007. Women as victims and survivors in the context of transnational crime. Sidebar in *Women and the criminal justice system,* 2nd ed., K. van Wormer and C. Bartollas, 282–84. Boston: Allyn & Bacon.

Faludi, S. 1999. *Stiffed: The betrayal against the American man.* New York: William Morrow & Co.

Family Violence Prevention Fund (FVPF). 2005. The facts on immigrant women and domestic violence. FVPF. http://endabuse.org/resources/facts/Immigrant.pdf (accessed August 2008).

Farr, K. 2005. *Sex trafficking: The global market in women and children.* New York: Worth.

Friedman, T. 2005. *The world is flat: A brief history of the 21st century.* New York: Farrar, Straus and Giroux.

Hiro, D. 1989. *Islamic fundamentalism.* 2nd ed. London: Paladin Grafton Books.

Human Rights Watch. 2002. *Human Rights Watch world report: United States.* www.hrw.org (accessed February 2008).

Hunt, C. 2007. Why passion is no excuse for murder. *Independent* (Ireland), September 30. http://www.independent.ie/opinion/analysis/why–passion-is-no-excuse-for-murder-1092421.html (accessed October 22, 2007).

Ife, J. 2001. *Human rights and social work: Towards rights-based practice.* Cambridge: Cambridge University Press.

Kardam, F. 2005. The dynamics of honor killings in Turkey: Prospects for action. United Nations Population Fund. http://www.unfpa.org/upload/lib_pub_file/676_filename_honourkillings.pdf (accessed September 24, 2007).

Khan, M.F., and L. Langman. 2005. Islamic fundamentalism, modernity, and the role of women. In *Religious Innovation in a Global Age: Essays on the Construction of Spirituality,* ed. George N. Lundskow, 138–59. Jefferson, NC: McFarland.

Mapp, S.C. 2008. *Human rights and social justice in a global perspective: An introduction to international social work.* New York: Oxford University Press.

Mathews, S., N. Abrahams, L.J. Martin, L. Vetten, L. Van Der Merwe, R. Jewkes. 2004. Every six hours a woman is killed by her intimate partner: A national study of female homicide in South Africa. MRC Policy Brief no. 5. http://www.mrc.ac.za/policybriefs/woman.pdf (accessed September 24, 2007).

Mayell, H. 2002. Thousands of women killed for family "honor." http://news.nationalgeographic.com/news/2002/02/0212_020212_honorkilling.html (accessed September 24, 2007).

Mernissi, F. 1987. Beyond the veil: Male-female dynamism in modern Muslim societies. Bloomington: Indiana University Press.

Mynott, A. 2003. Fighting India's dowry crime. http://news.bbc.co.uk/2/hi/programmes/correspondent/3259965.stm (accessed September 24, 2007).

Pelisek, C. 2006. Community in pain: Korean Americans deal with five murder-suicides. *LA Weekly,* April 13. http://www.laweekly.com/2006-04-13/news/community-in-pain/ (accessed August 2008).

Shehadeh, L.R. 2003. *The idea of women in fundamentalist Islam.* Gainesville, FL: University Press of Florida.

Shim, W.J. 2007. The Organization of Korean Historians. Social history of sins and punishments: Is intervening in a couple conflict similar to cutting water with a knife? (Translation from Korean). July 16. http://www.koreanhistory.org/ (accessed February 2008).

Simmons, J. 2002. Crime in England and Wales 2001/2002. Great Britain, Home Office Research, Development and Statistics Directorate.

United Nations. 2000a. *Civil and political rights, including questions of: Disappearances and summary executions: Report of the special rapporteur, Ms. Asma Jahangir: Submitted Pursuant to Commission on Human Rights Resolution.* http://www.unhchr.ch/Huridocda/Huridoca.nsf/TestFrame/8b28981c68a13fd7c12569f2005b1513?Opendocument (accessed September 24, 2007).

United Nations. 2000b. *The state of world population.* http://www.unfpa.org/swp/2000/english/index.html (accessed September 24, 2007).

United Nations. 2005. *The promise of equality: Gender equity, reproductive health and the millennium development goals.* The State of World Population 2005. New York: United Nations Population Fund, October 12.

United Nations Children's Fund (UNICEF). 2000. *UNICEF executive director targets violence against women.* http://www.unicef.org/newsline/00pr17.htm (accessed September 24, 2007).

United Nations Children's Fund (UNICEF). 2003. *The state of the world's children 2003.* New York, United Nations.

United Nations Economic and Social Council. 2006. *Violence against women: Assessing the prevalence of violence against women in Canada.* http://www.unece.org/stats/documents/ece/ces/ge.30/2006/8.e.pdf (accessed September 24, 2007).

United Nations Population Fund (UNFPA). 2007. Domestic violence in Russia: Ending the silence. UNFPA, December 10. http://www.unfpa.org/gender/docs/fact_sheets/domestic_violence_russia.doc (accessed February 2008).

U.S. Department of Justice. 2007. FBI supplemental homicide reports. www.ojp.usdoj.gov /bjs/ (accessed September 24, 2007).

van Wormer, K. 2004. *Confronting oppression, restoring justice: From policy analysis to social action.* Alexandria, VA: CSWE.

van Wormer, K., and C. Bartollas. 2007. *Women and the criminal justice system.* 2nd ed. Boston: Allyn & Bacon.

Watts, C., S. Osam, and E. Win. 1995. *The private is public: A study of violence against women in Southern Africa.* Harare, Zimbabwe: WiLDAF (Women in Law and Development in Africa).

World Health Organization (WHO). 2002. World report on violence and health. Geneva: WHO.

Yonhap News (YTN). 2001. A death leap after a homicide. December 11. (Translated from Korean.) http://search.ytn.co.kr/ytn/view.php?s_mcd=0103&key=200112110114384090 (accessed February 2008).

8

Response of the U.S. Criminal Justice System

Laws both reflect and shape the cultural norms in society. In a law abiding society, what is legally wrong is often thought to be morally wrong. Consider what happened in the Deep South, USA, when segregation first was the law, then was against the law. Public opinion shifted accordingly, and a new generation sprang up who took the new ways for granted.

Going back even further into history, we can see this phenomenon with wife beating. As the law changed, attitudes changed and vice versa. Sometimes, though, the old attitudes hung on, and resistance showed itself in unanticipated yet predictable ways. This is called backlash, as we saw in the last chapter.

As we review the history of laws protecting women from abuse in this chapter, we must recognize the inexorable force of backlash in how the laws are played out. We are talking here not only of the legal statutes themselves but of the judicial interpretation of these statutes and of police practices in their enforcement.

The law, the courts, and law enforcement—these are the concerns of this chapter. Transcending all three is the theme that, following Chesney-Lind (2002), we term "equality with a vengeance." This term refers to a strategy that is hostile to women's rights, a strategy that says, "so you want to be the equals of men; we will treat you like men—no more privileges, no more double standards." The equality-with-a-vengeance motif is seen in the police arrests of the battered women who fought back and in the trend toward awarding custody of children to the father (including known batterers). It is seen in the substantial increase in the prosecution of women (many of whom were forced into crime) for drug conspiracy, and in the continuing struggle to prove self-defense when battered women have killed their abuser.

Admittedly, women have won great victories through activism and legislation, and many have thrived professionally, but poor and minority women all too often have had to pay the price for the professional advancement of their more privileged sisters (van Wormer and Bartollas 2007). So while some at the upper echelons of society have achieved equality, others at the lower echelons have had equality thrust upon them. To see how this uneven state of affairs came about, a historical overview is in order.

HISTORICAL OVERVIEW

In the early days the man was "lord and master" of his household and he could physically chastise his wife and children for disobedience. There was no formal concept of wife abuse (or child abuse), not until well into the nineteenth century (Kurst-Swanger 2003). A man's right to punish his wife was affirmed in church doctrine as well as in Roman law and English common law. Historically, the family was viewed as a private entity within the context of the privileges of the patriarchal society. All through the years, even after physical punishment of one's wife was outlawed (in the late 1800s), domestic violence was considered a private matter, not one for intervention by the state (Presser and Gaarder 2004). One may recall testimony in the O.J. Simpson trial that when Nicole Simpson called the police for help, her husband persuaded the authorities that the problem was "a family matter" (see Ingrassia and Beck 1994). So the legacy of the past has continued into modern times.

In the 1970s, when the women's liberation movement took hold, attention was drawn to rape as a crime of power, and to domestic violence in the home. The tendency to blame women for their own victimization was exposed for what it was. Exposing this victim-blaming not only produced new theoretical understandings but also laid the groundwork as well for collective political action and social support. The efforts of this movement for justice culminated in the landmark Violence Against Women Act (VAWA) of 1994. This federal legislation, which was reauthorized in 2000 and again in 2006, provided for improved prevention and prosecution of violent crimes against women and children and for the care of victims (Kurz 1998). The law also provided funding for violence prevention, shelter services, and legal advocacy. In its recent enactments, the VAWA includes protections for immigrant, rural, disabled, and older women (Family Violence Prevention Fund 2008).

Unfortunately, however, as Kurz was quick to point out, other legislation such as the welfare "reform" legislation has put poor women who are trying to escape from family violence at grave risk, because they have no means of support or shelter. Restrictions on welfare recipients crossing state lines to receive benefits has shut off this avenue of escape, while the lack of affordable housing has left large numbers of runaway families homeless.

Although the response of the criminal justice system to battered women has generally improved since the 1970s, compelling criticisms have been leveled against law enforcement policies and the way police officers carried them out.

Officers were faulted for their failure to arrest perpetrators and for routinely supporting offenders' positions while trivializing victims' fears (Miller 2005). Some of the fault for the low arrest rate was not theirs, because even when they wanted to make an arrest, the police, in most states, could not do so unless they had personally witnessed the assault. In any case, as a result of the problems with law enforcement, a deluge of class action lawsuits were filed on behalf of battered women against police departments. Among the cases were some involving women who were murdered despite the fact that they had obtained valid court orders of protection, restraining orders that were ignored by law enforcement officers (Kurst-Swanger 2003). These class action lawsuits, in conjunction with political activism by feminists and victims' advocacy groups, helped set the stage for change.

Another influential factor in promoting change came in the form of enhanced data collection thanks to the Department of Justice's recognition of the need to gather solid and detailed documentation of the extent of intimate partner violence and intimate homicide (Kurst-Swanger 2003). For the first time, national victimization surveys now made it possible to monitor domestic violence trends. Published as press releases, the survey findings were distributed across the wire news services and the Internet.

Meanwhile, parallel developments have taken place all across society in increased funding for victim assistance programming; the construction of women's shelters and the providing of domestic violence services such as courtroom advocacy; legislation requiring batterer educational programs in lieu of serving jail time; and restrictions of gun ownership rights of known batterers. Efforts to increase the numbers of women in policing and to include women in responding to domestic violence calls were initiated to give assaulted women a better chance of being heard. Special training programs on family violence were provided for police personnel in many states. All such efforts were instituted to ensure greater protection for vulnerable women.

By 1993, marital rape was criminalized in all 50 states; then in 1994 new legislation required that the police make arrests where there is probable cause to believe that a felony or misdemeanor was committed or that an order of protection was violated. A major impetus for this latter policy change from the police perspective was to prevent homicides, not necessarily to prevent domestic violence. Miller (2005) discovered this rationale in her extensive interviews with state troopers and city police. So it was a fear of lawsuits if the police did nothing and the victim was injured or killed that helped shape the mandatory arrest practice.

Legally, there were setbacks. One such setback for victim protection came with the Supreme Court decision in the *Castle Rock v. Gonzales* case. In this tragic case, a battered woman, Jessica Gonzales of Colorado, had a protective restraining order against her husband. Her estranged husband drove off with their daughters, and Gonzales pleaded with the police for help but the police ignored her pleas (Richey 2005). Gonzales's husband then killed the children and had himself killed in a suicide-by-cop shoot-out. Gonzales sued the police, and her case landed at the Supreme Court. Then surprisingly, the Court ruled in favor of the police department. This ruling leaves victims at the mercy of their police departments.

THE IMPACT OF MANDATORY ARREST POLICIES

The perfect solution to the reluctance and inability of the police to make arrests seemed to have been found in the introduction of the new law enforcement policies. Following the Duluth, Minnesota, model, this criminalization of domestic violence represented the most progressive thinking of the 1980s through the 1990s. No longer would the police have to witness the abuse; now they would in fact be required to make an arrest based on probable cause that an assault had occurred. In response to media campaigns related to the women's movement, such mandatory arrest policies became standard practice. Not only was the arrest of batterers mandatory but also jail terms often were mandatory too, and victims who filed charges were not allowed to later drop them. Sometimes prosecutors forced reluctant victims to testify against partners. All this was done for the victim's protection, and it seemed to make a lot of sense at the time.

This paradigm shift in law enforcement strategy was catapulted in part by research results that seemed to show a significant decrease in homicides and domestic violence incidents. The most influential of the research findings supportive of mandatory arrest policies came from the Minneapolis Domestic Violence Experiment that was undertaken in 1981 (Miller and Peterson 2007), methodological problems notwithstanding. Research limitations pertained to the small sample size and the possibility of an alternative explanation of the reduced number of incident reports that emerged with mandated arrests. The fact that many battered women only wanted to stop the violence, not to have her partner arrested, was not considered. Before the research findings could be verified through more rigorous testing, word was out of the seemingly effective policies in Minnesota in reducing violence, and the policies of police departments nationwide followed suit (Hirschel and Buzawa 2002; Miller 2005; Sherman and Cohn 1989). That early research and premature release of the findings, as Chesney-Lind (2002) indicates, seemed to silence many of those who doubted the wisdom of a law enforcement-centered approach to the problem of domestic violence. When later more empirical-based research revealed little or no deterrent effect resulting from the mandatory arrest of a battering male, it was too late to change the policies back.

One evidence-based study in Milwaukee did indicate a small deterrent effect on persons who were employed and had a lot to lose through an arrest (Sherman 1992). Nevertheless, as we saw in Chapter 1, the nationwide homicide rates of women killed in domestic situations are not substantially down since the new

arrest policies have been introduced. Furthermore, women remain disproportionately the victims of intimate personal violence, representing more than 70
percent of the victims of intimate lethal violence and 85 percent of victims of
nonlethal violence (Rennison 2003).

A major development that came out of Duluth, Minnesota, ("the Duluth
model") is the "no-drop" policy of prosecutors. This policy is now in place in
many jurisdictions in the United States and Canada. Instead of dropping charges
of assault and battery, which the victim often requests under duress or a change
of heart, prosecutors continue the case based on evidence produced by the police.
Batterers are viewed as a menace to other potential victims, including their own
children, and as potential homicide/suicide risks. Victim-support units attached
to the prosecutor's office assist with these cases. Requirements for the perpetrators to enter specialized treatment programs are generally a part of any probation
plan. Noncompliance, ideally, results in a lengthy prison term. The use of
restraining orders to keep offenders away from the survivors offers protection
to women in cases of low-level abuse but offers no security in life-threatening
situations. A man who is suicidal as well as violent has a high potential to kill
his wife or partner (van Wormer and Bartollas 2007).

UNINTENDED CONSEQUENCES OF THE NEW LAWS

"The best laid schemes o' mice an' men Gang aft a-gley" (translation—"The
best laid plans of mice and men gone awry"). This line from Robert Burns's
(1979/original 1785) poem comes to mind as we contemplate the benefits and
drawbacks of policies that were designed for the protection of battered women.

One factor that we have to take into account in our analysis is the impact of
attitudes on how the laws are carried out, the impact of backlash, when laws seem
too extreme, or sexism still prevails in certain circles. Women's advocates could
not have anticipated how the mandatory arrest laws have been played out. In a
strange twist of fate, the more stringent arrest policies have resulted in arrests
of the victims along with the perpetrators of violence when the women have
fought back. In many jurisdictions, law enforcement officers fail to differentiate
aggressor from victim at all (Walker 2000). So today there is an influx of women
arrested on domestic violence charges. And many of these women are incarcerated and/or mandated to batterer treatment programs that are designed for
violent men (Miller 2005).

Two contrasting explanations have been posed in the literature that attempt to
account for the phenomenon of dual arrest. Some researchers suggest that dual
arrests may be explained by gender symmetry in violent offending. Research from
the late 1970s based on self-reporting surveys by Murray Straus (1979) seemed to
show that women were as violent as men. The conflict tactic scales that were used
measured violence on a scale from slapping through life-threatening violence.
The survey did show that women admitted to doing a good deal of slapping of

their boyfriends and spouses. A major criticism was that the scale did not mea-sure the context of the violence, whether it was initiated or defensive, for exam-ple. Another possibility is that women who have used violence are more willing to accept responsibility for their actions than are men who typically minimize and deny their violent behavior (Miller and Meloy 2006). The study's conclu-sions that women are as violent as men in domestic relationships continue to be widely publicized in the media. Straus (2006) replicated this research using the same conflict tactic scales on respondents in 32 nations and got the same results, that women were as violent as men.

A more convincing hypothesis offered in the literature for the increasing inci-dence of dual arrest is that women are being arrested for the violence they com-mit as they try to defend themselves (Dasgupta 2002). We can find some support for this explanation in a unique piece of research that was designed by Muftic, Bouffard, and Bouffard (2007) to examine the contextual factors related to dual arrest. These researchers compared women who were arrested with their partner (i.e., dual arrestees) with women who were arrested alone (sole arrestees). They found that whereas women who were arrested alone for intimate partner violence may be similar to male offenders (i.e., using violence for power and con-trol), dual arrested women shared more similarities with typical victims of bat-tering (i.e., manifesting symptoms of fear and trauma). The incidence of dual arrest, we can conclude from this study, is more a reflection of pro-arrest law enforcement policy than of innate aggression in women. This conclusion is bolstered by Miller and Meloy's (2006) interviews with 95 female offenders in batterer treatment programs. Only five of the women exhibited preemptive, aggressive violence; the remaining 90 women used violence either to defend themselves or their children or out of frustration with an abusive situation that seemed beyond their control.

It is partly because of this rise in dual arrests nationwide that young women's arrest rates for assault have been on the rise. Consequently, as the arrest rates rise, responding to the perceived increase in female violence, the criminal justice sys-tem has been more willing to sentence the women to jail and to batterer interven-tion programs. One can well imagine what a dampening effect the dual-arrest policy has on victims who want to call the police for help. If there are any young children in the home, the mother typically will agree to plead guilty and even enter a batterer's intervention program in hopes of expediting her release and returning home. Since, as Susan Miller indicates, it is low-income and minority women who are most apt to call on the police rather than a private agency, or to be turned in by neighbors living in crowded quarters, dual-arrest policies may disproportionately affect poor and minority women. Moreover, the economic consequences of any arrest will be more devastating for lower-income households.

Eileen Abel (2000) provides some empirical research that helps validate what commentators have been saying about the problematic nature of the mandatory arrest and dual arrest practices. Using a sample that included 50 women enrolled in batterers' intervention programs and 50 women receiving victim services for domestic violence, all in Florida agencies, Abel found that more than three-fourths of women in batterer programs who had been arrested indicated they were arrested along with their partners. Arrested women were more likely than the nonarrested women to have been drunk or high on drugs at the time of their arrest. Further, compared to male batterers, from what we know in the literature, female "batterers" reported a high rate of past victimization and trauma, a history of having been the one to call the police, and fewer prior arrest experiences than their partners. In fact, the arrest histories of women in batterer programs were not significantly different from the women who were receiving domestic violence victim services. Abel's findings give support to the widespread claim that women who were charged with assault were probably victims who fought back in self-defense and not the perpetrators of violence.

The replication studies have failed to demonstrate convincingly that the arrest of batterers deters repeat offenses from occurring in sites other than Minneapolis; arrest may, in fact, as Miller (2005) suggests, make the situation worse. In their examination of data from FBI's *Uniform Crime Reports*, Dugan, Nagin, and Rosenfeld (2001) found that the homicide rate actually increased after mandatory arrest policies were implemented. Locking up aggressive men for short periods of time can antagonize them and lead to an escalation of the violence. Another factor increasing the level of danger is that mandatory arrest policies make some women, especially women from immigrant backgrounds, reluctant to call for help. In light of these facts, more research is needed on the effectiveness of the mandatory arrest and forced prosecution policies, and the findings should be publicized far and wide.

"No drop" policies may have the advantage of relieving a battered woman of having to decide whether or not to have her husband prosecuted for the crime of assault, but her lack of control over the situation can be disempowering to the woman at the same time. When a woman's choice is to have her husband arrested or not is taken away and when law enforcement practices place her at the risk of arrest as well, the impact on immigrant families can be pronounced. We learned from Hoan Bui (2007), who conducted interviews with 24 Vietnamese women who called the police for help, that the standard law enforcement procedures were counterproductive. The women who had made the emergency phone calls expressed concern over family shame and family breakups resulting from the criminal justice interventions. Some reported problematic relationships with extended family members on both sides of the family for making trouble. Their wish had only been to stop the violence at that moment, not to damage the family reputation or create more problems for themselves by causing the arrest of a family member.

One solution, consistent with feminist practice, might be to simply *listen* to the victim of the assault. In their study of gender differences in police officers' perceptions about violence cases, Stalans and Finn (2000) found that women officers working in situations of marital abuse consulted with the wife, and if she wished to settle the matter with the help of the police, the female officer gave consideration to the victim's preference and was more willing than male officers to make an arrest when the victim indicated an unwillingness to otherwise settle the matter.

Effective police responses with appropriate follow-up attention provide clear support for the family coupled with help in the form of providing safe alternatives for the victim. An excellent policy in New York State is the requirement that the police must inform all victims of crime of the availability of compensation for personal property, injury, medical expenses, lost wages, and even death benefits; restitution; notification; and all service programs available; most often victims are provided with an informational handout. Training is provided for state employees by the New York State Office for the prevention of domestic violence. Recently, the governor signed into law a historic "fair access to family court" bill that ensures protection to dating and same-sex as well as married couples (Office for the Prevention of Domestic Violence 2008).

Today, mandatory arrest policies are being reconsidered and revised in a number of quarters. The governor of Wisconsin, for example, has signed into law specific instructions for differentiating victim from aggressor; the officers are to consider if the aggression was an act of self-defense, the seriousness of the injuries inflicted, and to be attuned to the emotional state of fear (Office of Justice Assistance 2006). In her interviews with police officers in Delaware, Miller (2005) was impressed with the fact that the county police department frowned on dual arrests and trained its officers to believe that there is always an aggressor. Accordingly, the dual arrest pattern that is in evidence elsewhere did not materialize in that state.

EQUALITY IS NOT SAMENESS

Dasgupta (2002) examined the question of whether women are "just like men" in regard to family violence and found that there are contextual differences that affect men's and women's use of such violence. Such differences are influenced by sociohistorical factors including the historical use of violence to resolve conflict and power differentials based on gender, culture, economics, and physiology. If we agree with Dasgupta, as feminist criminologists increasingly do, we would expect the law to take the reality of gender difference into account, and we would also take into account the context of the situation.

In treating men and women exactly alike, dual arrest policies are a repudiation of the very reality of battering. Domestic violence, from this point of view, is construed as a fight between equal parties. The context of the violence is not taken into account, nor is the presence of the emotions of fear and terror by a beaten or threatened woman. This false equating of equality with sameness is further seen in family court in which child custody is an issue between divorcing parents.

CHILD CUSTODY DISPUTES IN CASES OF BATTERING

An unexpected consequence of women's bids for equal rights is seen daily in family court in battles over child custody. Ordinarily, in divorce cases, fathers do not contest the mother's right to custody. But of those who do, some are men with histories of wife abuse. And in such cases, the mother is at high risk of loss of custody now that the states (since the 1980s) have adopted a more or less gender-blind system for awarding custody of small children to fathers in those rare cases in which the father files a petition for custody. Keep in mind that he can more often afford to hire a lawyer than the mother. The father more often having a well-paying job, and a new wife or sometimes a mother who can care for the child, may appear to be in a better position to take responsibility than would the ex-wife as a single, working mother. And in domestic violence situations in which police have made dual arrests, the woman is in serious jeopardy of losing custody of her children (van Wormer and Bartollas 2007). Battering by the husband is often overlooked if the wife has flaws such as a drinking problem or a poor work history. It is common for courts to rule that the father's violence toward the mother has no effect on the children. As a result of these factors, fathers in contested cases are being awarded custody more often than their wives (Meir 2003). In Canada, because of a backlash against a rash of claims of father/child incest and the widespread belief that such claims may be false, some lawyers are advising the mothers in custody disputes to be silent about such abuse (S. Charlesworth, personal communication, March 16, 2000).

The fact that fathers have obtained much more clout in family and divorce court than they ever had previously can be viewed as part of an antifeminist backlash against the women's equality movement. Increasingly, fathers are fighting their ex-wives for custody of the children, and increasingly they are winning. For men who have a history of battering, one wonders if their decision to fight their ex-wives is a part of the overall pattern of wife abuse.

Lundy Bancroft (2002) discusses clever tactics used by abusers in custody and visitation disputes. Among these are asking for psychological evaluations of the mother (who may have developed psychological symptoms from years of abuse); playing the role of peacemaker and claiming to want to put all their fighting behind them; and accusing the ex-wife of turning the children against him. The reality is that a growing number of abusive men are succeeding in using claims of "parental alienation" to gain greater access to the children as well as to their ex-wives.

In response to these developments, a multiyear, four-phase study using qualitative and quantitative social science research methodologies by the Wellesley Centers for Women (2008) has documented a consistent pattern of human rights abuses by the family courts. Just as women who do not leave a battering situation can lose custody of their children to the state or be prosecuted for child neglect and negligence if the children are harmed by a violent husband or boyfriend, a woman who does leave can risk loss of custody for depriving her husband of his parenting role. In family court, as the Wellesley Centers for Women indicates, histories of abuse of mother and children are routinely ignored or discounted. These policies place battered women in danger as they are forced to either remain in the relationship or to continuously interact with a violent man without any protection from the court.

Fathers with a history of battering are twice as likely to seek the sole physical custody of their children as are nonviolent fathers (Meir 2003). In her survey of the case law in 2001, Meir identified 38 appellate state court decisions concerning custody and domestic violence. To her astonishment, 36 of the 38 trial courts had awarded joint or sole custody to alleged and *adjudicated* batterers. Two-thirds of these decisions were reversed on appeal.

Fathers' rights organizations vehemently contest these claims that fathers have the advantage in court as they aggressively fight for fathers' rights to joint custody and to sole custody of children in divorce cases (Miller 2005). Thanks to the Internet, this movement of divorced men and their second wives for new laws favorable to the father is sweeping the United States. That women are as violent as men and that they receive preferential treatment in court are major contentions of these groups. On The National Fathers' Resource Center, for example, at http://www.fathers4kids.com/html/DomesticViolence.htm is the following statement:

> The National Fathers' Resource Center and Fathers for Equal Rights demands that society acknowledge that false claims of Domestic Violence are used to gain unfair advantage in custody and divorce cases.

An Internet search reveals hundreds of such fathers' rights organizations nationwide. On a state-by-state basis under the guise of supporting more active roles for fathers in the lives of their children, these male consciousness-raising groups advocate for legislation to require that divorcing parents have joint custody of their children. Lawyers and judges generally oppose legislation for forced joint custody as conflict-invoking and harmful to children torn between fighting parents.

Because historically judges awarded custody to the mothers in contested cases unless the mother was proven to be unfit, we can surmise that the new gender neutrality standard is a factor working against mothers who can no longer assure that after divorce the children will remain with them. As Bancroft (2002, 268) passionately states, "The treatment that protective mothers so often receive at the hands of family courts is among the most shameful secrets of modern jurisprudence."

In the criminal justice system, similarly, when men are arrested for drug-related crimes, their wives and partners are often arrested along with them for conspiracy to commit a crime (van Wormer and Bartollas 2007). Many of these women have been threatened by their partners into participating in the illicit drug business, a fact that carries little weight in the women's defense. The evidence used against these defendants is generally provided by their partners as a means of reducing their own prison sentences.

Battered women caught up in legal situations are not always left to their own devices, however. The entry of women into the legal profession and therefore into the ranks of prosecutors and judges portends well for the future. Increasingly expert witnesses are being called to testify to help battered women in cases of child custody disputes, and even more seriously, in cases of homicide of the batterers.

EXPERT WITNESS TESTIMONY IN HOMICIDE CASES

In the defense of battered women who kill their batterers, expert witnesses are permitted to assist the court in understanding the dynamics of battering. More specifically, such testimony is allowed to describe the seemingly extreme behavioral responses of the battered victims including passivity (Smith and Rotondi 2007). Extensive legal research has examined the impact of such expert testimony; the results generally show this effort to have resulted in greater leniency toward battered women who killed their abusers.

It is important to note that despite occasional well-publicized cases of battered women who kill and are acquitted of murder or manslaughter, the law often shows greater leniency toward men who kill their wives than toward women who kill their husbands (Bannister 1993; Leonard 2003). The difference seems to be explained by the fact that battered women who have killed will cooperate with the police, making no attempt to cover up their crime. Men who kill their wives, on the other hand, can often afford a lawyer, and since they did not confess, they are in a position to enter a plea of guilty to a lesser charge. The plea of self-defense for a battered woman is often not believed, since she may kill her spouse while he is asleep or drunk or otherwise vulnerable. A woman who kills during a fight will still be convicted because she more likely will use a weapon while the man being more physically powerful is less likely to do so. It is hard for the jury in such cases of female homicide, as Bannister (1993) indicates, to appreciate the danger in which the woman may have been. The court system fails women, she concludes, because it is based on a male model of how to determine facts such as self-defense.

In a politicized battered woman's murder trial, expert witnesses often rely on a self-defense argument based on the concept of "battered woman syndrome." According to this argument—derived from Lenore Walker's (1979) theory of "learned helplessness"—repeatedly beaten women lose their faith in themselves and their judgment becomes impaired. They perceive use of force as their only means of escape. (Such a defense additionally may be used against battered mothers fighting for custody of their children; such women are often seen as incapable of protecting their children in their helplessness.) Donald Downs (1997) opposes this legal argument in that its success depends on portraying women as passive victims. Rothenberg (2003) concurs. Downs's recommendations regarding homicide cases are that the law be changed to help women argue realistically that danger need not be immediate to be present, that a woman beaten in her home has no duty to retreat when this is her home, and that what is seen as extreme force used by the victim may be proportionate to a man's long history of abuse.

Canadian law has been revised under a progressive Supreme Court decision. Judges must instruct jurors in battered women's cases that the woman is not required to leave the home. Formal consultations are being conducted with lawyers and women's groups on how the law can be brought into line with new thinking on abusive relationships (Geddes 1998). The justices were divided, however, over use of the battered woman syndrome concept. The fear is that the claims of self-defense by women who do not seem passive and helpless will not be fairly decided if the concept of "learned helplessness" is set as a standard for every case. Then it is hard to reconcile the contradiction between passivity and the committing of murder. We must keep in mind that many victims do not survive; they are murdered by their batterers. These are the true victims of a long period of domestic abuse. For the ones who kill their assailants, a more relevant and empowering defense than learned helplessness must be found.

To learn firsthand of effective strategies for defending battered women charged with homicide, van Wormer interviewed (on December 22, 2007) sociologist Ann Goetting. The author of *Homicide in Families* (1995) and *Getting Out: The Life Stories of Women Who Left Abusive Men* (2000), Goetting is an experienced expert witness who has provided court reports and/or expert testimony in over 20 situations in which women were on trial for murder of an abusive spouse or partner. One additional case in which the same format/strategy was used involved a mentally retarded man who killed his father who had victimized him.

As a member of a defense team that fights on behalf of battered women who killed their husbands or partners in self-defense, Goetting (2002, abstract) earlier, in a paper presentation articulated her theoretical framework as follows:

> As a feminist sociology professor and a researcher...I was able to read, teach, and research about domestic abuse—the politically motivated terrorism of women and children held hostage by batterers in our patriarchal social order—for only so long before I was compelled to act. I consider my expert witness work on battering and its effects as a form of feminist activism that follows naturally from the expertise I have gained as a researcher, teacher, and author of domestic violence. It is creative applied sociology.

Although van Wormer from a social worker's as well as a sociologist's perspective would have been tempted to use a normal-response-to-an-abnormal-situation defense, the strategy used here has the advantage of being empowering to the woman charged with the crime. Additionally, this strategy is directly related to the act of homicide itself.

Now we come to the recent interview. Goetting stated that her approach was grounded in social science research such as that summarized by Osthoff and Maguigan (2005). Osthoff and Maguigan's thesis in a nutshell is that while concepts such as battered woman syndrome and learned helplessness pathologize the battered woman, testimony on battering and its effects is useful in explaining why the woman did not leave the situation of abuse. However, the core of the defense that relates to the justification for the killing is that the woman's life was threatened—this is the classic self-defense claim. The focus is on the reasonableness of the woman's decision to use deadly force, not on an underlying pathology.

For the extensive reports that she writes for the woman's defense team, Goetting first peruses the legal documents in the case. The next step is the trip to the jail to interview the woman who is charged with murder. After she explains that she is on the woman's side and develops rapport, the first task is to determine if the accused is a battered woman, if she has the markers of abuse—for example, was she forced to live in isolation, controlled economically, and so on. Then comes a key question that is crucial to the case. This goes something like, "If you had not killed Joe where would you be in five years? Would you be working at Wal-Mart?"

The response typically is immediate: "I'd be dead." All but two of the women she has interviewed have responded this way. This response is significant in establishing evidence that can be used later in testimony to the jury to confirm the danger that the defendant was in; it is evidence of self-defense.

Regarding her role in the courtroom, Goetting says,

> For the battered woman, I become her voice. Battering is designed to confuse the woman; she has been in a relationship of captivity where she's confused. So she can't speak for herself in a way that would make sense to a jury. This is where the expert witness has an important role to play—in educating the jury in the dynamics of battering.

(For further details on preparing for expert testimony in homicide trials, see Stark 2002.)

In recognition of the need for expert testimony in murder trials of battered women, the state of California is allowing survivors of domestic violence who are serving time in prison to file a writ of habeas corpus to prove that prolonged violent abuse led them to commit their crime (Bevving-Ring 2007). Although all 50 states recognize the importance of expert testimony on battering and its effects, California law is the most advanced in providing for post-conviction habeas corpus relief when evidence of battering was present but not presented in court (Duley 2006).

Expert testimony is important, but a focus on providing safety for women in life-threatening situations is more important still to prevent situations such as those described above. An overreliance on the criminal legal system to prevent domestic violence has had unintended consequences as we have seen. We have talked about law enforcement responses as problematic at the first level of response. Now we consider alternatives to the adversary system itself, the impact of which is experienced by victims at the adjudication stage of justice, not to mention women on trial for crimes ranging from drug conspiracy to murder.

RESTORATIVE ALTERNATIVES FOR BATTERING SITUATIONS

The adversarial process dominates Anglo-Saxon justice today. This process has its roots in the Middle Ages in England when hired combatants fought duels on behalf of accused individuals (van Wormer 2004). It was a decidedly masculine system in its origins and continues in this competitive, ritualized vein today. In the atmosphere of warring forces that ensues, families and friends of the accused are torn apart from families and friends on the other side of the law. Such court processes and plea bargaining behind closed doors does little to enhance communication and healing among members of the community (Van Ness and Strong 2002).

The failure of the criminal justice system in meeting the needs of victims of crime and the failure to provide an atmosphere in which the offender is rewarded for expressing remorse are common themes in the literature (see Rozee and Koss 2001; van Wormer and Bartollas 2007; Zehr 2002). One alternative to the current legal process might include, as Duley (2006) suggests, a reframing of violence against women as a public health crisis, and one that needs more effective long-term responses. Today, globally, and especially in nations with Anglo-Saxon traditions—Britain, Canada, Northern Ireland, Australia, as well as the United States—alternative forms for preventing family violence have been introduced. These alternative, more informal methods stress reconciliation and arguably are consistent with women's ways of knowing and feminist theory (Gilligan 1982; Van Den Bergh 1995; van Wormer 2004). Unlike the standard legal model, restorative justice appreciates victim-survivor agency.

Choice is the hallmark of social work's strengths model, its aim to help clients find their own way, to carve out their own paths to wholeness (Rapp and Goscha 2006). Erez and Belknap (1998) found, in their study of battered women, that most of them had little faith in the criminal justice system and expressed a desire to retain choice and be treated as individuals in any attempt to stop the abuse. The shame and stigma associated with the criminal justice system, besides, may cause some women to feel the need to hide their involvement in an abusive relationship from friends and family (Grauwiler and Mills 2004).

The dilemma facing battered women's advocates for which there is no clearly correct solution is whether the process—giving the battered woman a choice as how to proceed—or whether the outcome—pursuing domestic violence cases to the full extent of the law, regardless of the victim's wishes—is more important. The coercion of victims that is engrained in the present system of prosecution is inconsistent with the feminist movement's goal of self-determination (Presser and Gaarder 2004). If the case comes to trial, and the victim is forced to testify, what she says against her partner may compromise her safety later. Moreover, child protective services may start investigating a mother for her failure to protect the children even if the children only witnessed the violence (Cheon and Regehr 2006). Perhaps for these reasons, only one quarter of all physical assaults, as indicated in the Violence against Women Survey, are reported to the police (Tjaden and Thoennes 2000).

A feminist view of justice has developed which, according to Presser and Gaarder (2004), has called into question the ideology of absolute justice—policies such as forcing the victim to testify in open court against her partner or spouse who assaulted her. Research in the 1990s, as these writers inform us, found that battering victims who have a say in legal or less formal proceedings may feel more empowered to get help, if not to terminate the abusive relationship. Women of color often see both the courts and social services as adversaries rather than allies, so an emphasis on judicial intervention may turn them away. Many women, moreover, are dependent on a man for financial support; others have drug problems or an undocumented immigration status that make them wary of pursuing criminal prosecution. It is important to note, as Presser and Gaarder emphasize, that restorative justice is not mediation; there is nothing to negotiate here; offender and victim are clearly differentiated from each other in this process.

Increased reliance on the police and mandatory processes to control violence against women reduces the exploration of more community-based long-term solutions (Duley 2006). Within the context of restorative justice, the recommended policy is to attempt to reduce domestic violence through an emphasis on rehabilitation, rather than prosecution, with the threat of prosecution serving as the incentive for participation in the programs.

Community conferencing is one way of effecting justice for victims of battering and is practiced in New Zealand with favorable results (Braithwaite and Daly 1998). Sentencing in such a system is handled by community groups that include the victim and her family, as well as the offender and individuals from his support system. Power imbalances are addressed in various ways, such as limiting the right of the offender to speak on his own behalf, and including community members in a sort of surveillance team to monitor the offender's compliance.

In Canada, similarly, community conferencing and healing circles are practiced even in cases of severe family violence through traditional native community ceremonies. In the case of an alcoholic, aboriginal man who had beaten his wife, for example, a sentencing circle was formed in the native tradition (Griffiths 1999). Seated in a circle, the victim and her family told of their distress, a young man spoke of the contributions the offender had made to the community. The offender was ordered into alcoholism treatment and the ceremony concluded with a prayer and a shared meal. After a period of time, the woman who had been victimized voiced her satisfaction with the process. This case, as Griffiths explains, was clearly linked to the criminal justice system. Others may be handled more quietly, by tribal members. Griffiths concludes on a note of caution: victims must play a key role throughout the process to ensure that their needs are met and that they are not revictimized.

Feminist researcher Mary Koss (2000) advocates what she terms *communitarian justice,* a victim-sensitive model derived from the community-based approaches of New Zealand's Maori people. Such methods are apt to be effective, notes Koss, because they draw on sanctions abusive men fear most: family stigma and broad social disapproval. Such conferencing, as Koss further indicates, is recommended for young offenders without extensive histories of violence.

The message to all concerned is that any form of family violence is unacceptable. Such conferencing can attend to the psychological as well as physical abuse a survivor has experienced and counter her sense of helplessness by involving her as an active participant in the process (Koss 2000). Measures can be taken, moreover, to reduce the survivor's vulnerability such as in providing access to an individual bank account or transportation, for example.

Rashmi Goel (2005) believes that restorative justice options are ill-suited to application among immigrant South Asian communities for domestic violence cases. Her reasoning is that women from South Asian culture might be placated by the familiar values of community, cooperation, and forgiveness into seeking restorative justice solutions and ultimately into staying in an abusive situation. The exact opposite argument is made by Grauwiler and Mills (2004). Their recommendation is for what they call Intimate Abuse Circles as a culturally sensitive alternative to the criminal justice system's response to domestic violence. Such circles are especially helpful, they suggest, to immigrant, minority, and religious families where it is more likely that the family will remain intact. This model acknowledges that many people seek to end the violence but not the relationship. Such restorative processes help partners as well who would like to separate in a more amicable fashion than through standard avenues.

The key point here is that women in battering situations need options so that they are in control of the situation. A victim needs to be advised of all options so that she can choose the one which most closely represents her needs. In the United States, there are laws that may prohibit justice-based intervention, due to No Contact Orders or by policy. A national group of victim-offender dialogue practitioners could be used in such cases while being careful to protect the victim from further harm.

CONCLUSION

Two major stumbling blocks to efforts to help save women's lives and to ensure their safety are (1) traditional attitudes linked to an antifeminist backlash, and (2) the political climate confusing achievement of gender equality with the enforcement of policies of gender neutrality. The denial of the realities of victimhood and motherhood are causing much misery to women in criminal court and in family court.

Fostering links between the criminal justice system and social service agencies might be especially helpful for women with limited resources; referrals to counseling programs for victims living with violence may provide such a link. A victim-oriented empowerment model would assume a less coercive atmosphere than is the case at present.

Empowerment, an important approach to help domestic violence survivors achieve self-determination and draw on their inner resources, is an essential component in any safety plan. Because all women are different—ethnically, racially, economically—it is important to broaden the goals of domestic violence interventions, to include strategies to end the violence without prosecution, and restorative justice approaches where feasible, as well as traditional prosecution with the woman's consent. Gender neutral policies such as dual arrests of both partners, child custody policies that favor the parent with the better job over the primary caretaker while ignoring reports of wife abuse, and prosecutions of battered women as conspirators in crimes initiated by their partners are not fair in that they do not take into account individual vulnerabilities and circumstances. The criminalization of intimate partner violence is essential, but the zero tolerance policies that have been enacted have led to the unintended consequences of an increase in the numbers of women arrested for intimate partner violence as well as a reluctance of some victims to call on the police for help when they need it. Moreover, mandatory arrest policies contribute to a sense of powerlessness that echoes the powerlessness they experience in a relationship with a batterer. Research suggests that expert testimony on battering and its effects may be especially helpful in legal situations such as those listed above in which the victim-survivor must explain her behavior and circumstances before a court of law.

There is no one solution to the complex systems of the law, a reliance on legal mandates, and the intimate partner violence that women are experiencing. There are standard prosecutions and sentencing of batterers to long prison terms, appropriate in many cases, and there are restorative justice initiatives that are meeting with some success elsewhere. Because the police are a battered woman's first line of defense when her life is threatened, we need greater resources there and laws that are of proven effectiveness in violence prevention. We have highlighted in this chapter the pressing need to engage in a process of gathering and analyzing data on the unintended consequences of certain criminal justice domestic violence practices. Women's advocates are right to work for reform in the system, and toward stringent policies against partner violence, and we call upon them to support empirical research on law enforcement policy and treatment effectiveness and to only continue to endorse programs that work.

To personalize the discussion of this chapter from the standpoint of battered women who took the law into their own hands and who are paying the price, we need to hear from the women themselves. And so we shall in the next chapter that follows.

REFERENCES

Abel, E.M. 2000. Seeking social justice for women in batterer intervention programs. Paper presented at the CSWE 46th Annual Program Meeting, New York City.
Bancroft, L. 2002. *Why does he do that?* New York: Putnam.

Bannister, S.A. 1993. Battered women who kill their abusers: Their courtroom battles. In *It's a crime: Women and justice,* ed. R. Muraskin and T. Alleman, 316–33. Englewood Cliffs, NJ: Prentice Hall.

Bevving-Ring, C. 2007. Freeing the survivors. *MS* 19, Fall.

Braithwaite, J., and K. Daly. 1998. Masculinity, violence and communitarian control. In *Crime control and women,* ed. S. Miller, 151—80. Thousand Oaks, CA: SAGE.

Bui, H. 2007. The limitations of current approaches to domestic violence. In *It's a crime: Women and justice,* 4th ed., ed. R. Muraskin, 261–76. Boston: Pearson.

Burns, R. 1979 (original 1785). "To a mouse," In *Oxford Dictionary of Quotations.* 3rd ed., 115. New York: Oxford University Press.

Cheon, A., and C. Regehr. 2006. Restorative justice models in cases of intimate partner violence: Reviewing the evidence. *Victims and Offenders* 1:369—94.

Chesney-Lind, M. 2002. Criminalizing victimization: The unintended consequences of proarrest policies for girls and women. *Criminology and Public Policy* 2:81–90.

Dasgupta, S.D. 2002. Framework for understanding women's use of nonlethal violence in intimate heterosexual relationships. *Violence Against Women* 8:1364–89.

Downs, D. 1997. *More than victims: Battered women, the syndrome society, and the law.* Chicago: University of Chicago Press.

Dugan, L., D. Nagin, and R. Rosenfeld. 2001. *Exposure reduction or backlash? The effects of domestic violence resources on partner homicide.* Washington, DC: U.S. Department of Justice.

Duley, K. 2006. Un-domesticating violence: Criminalizing survivors and U.S. mass incarceration. *Women & therapy* 29, no. 3/4: 75–96.

Erez, E., and J. Belknap. 1998. In their own words: Battered women's assessment of the criminal processing system's responses. *Violence and Victims* 13, no. 3: 251—68.

Family Violence Prevention Fund (FVPF). 2008. *Immigrant women.* FVPF. http://endabuse.org/programs/display.php3?DocID=116 (accessed August 2008).

Geddes, J. 1998. Victims who kill. *Maclean's,* February 23: 64.

Gilligan, C. 1982. *In a different voice: Psychological theory and women's development.* Cambridge, MA: Harvard University Press.

Goel, R. 2005. Sita's trousseau: Restorative justice, domestic violence, and South Asian Culture. *Violence Against Women* 5, no. 5: 639—65.

Goetting, A. 1995. *Homicide in families and other special populations.* New York: Springer.

Goetting, A. 2000. *Getting out: The life stories of women who left abusive men.* New York: Columbia University Press.

Goetting, A. 2002. Expert witness work on battering and its effects as feminist activism. Paper presentation, Family Violence Conference, San Diego.

Grauwiler, P., and L. Mills. 2004. Moving beyond the criminal justice paradigm: A radical restorative justice approach to intimate abuse. *Journal of Sociology and Social Welfare* 31, no. 1: 49–62.

Griffiths, C.T. 1999. The victims of crime and restorative justice: The Canadian experience. *International Review of Victimology* 6:279–94.

Hirschel D., and E. Buzawa. 2002. Understanding the context of dual arrest with directions for future research. *Violence Against Women* 8:1449–55.

Ingrassia, M., and M. Beck. 1994. Patterns of abuse. *Newsweek,* July 4: 26–33.

Koss, M. 2000. Blame, shame, and community: Justice responses to violence against women. *American Psychologist* 55, no. 11: 1332–43.

Kurst-Swanger, K., and J. Petcosky. 2003. *Violence in the home: Multidisciplinary perspectives.* New York: Oxford University Press.

Kurz, D. 1998. Old problems and new directions in the study of violence against women. In *Intimate violence,* ed. R.K. Bergen, 197–208. Thousand Oaks, CA: SAGE.

Leonard, E. D. 2003. Stages of gendered disadvantage in the lives of convicted battered women. In *Gendered justice: Addressing female offenders,* ed. B. Bloom, 97–139. Durham, NC: Carolina Academic Press.

Meir, J. 2003. Domestic violence, child custody, and child protection: Understanding judicial resistance and imagining the solutions. *Gender, Society, Policy & the Law* 11, no. 2: 657–731.

Miller, S. 2005. *Victims as offenders: The paradox of women's violence in relationships.* New Brunswick, NJ: Rutgers University Press.

Miller, S.L., and M. Meloy. 2006. Women's use of force: Voices of women arrested for domestic violence. *Violence Against Women* 12, no. 1: 89–115.

Miller, S.L., and E. Peterson. 2007. The impact of law enforcement policies on victims of intimate partner violence. In *It's a crime: Women and justice,* ed. R. Muraskin, 238–60. Boston: Pearson.

Muftic, L., J. Bouffard, and L. Bouffard. 2007. An exploratory study of women arrested for intimate partner violence: Violent women or violent resistance? *Journal of Interpersonal Violence* 22:753–74.

Office of Justice Assistance. 2006. Summary of changes to Wisconsin Mandatory arrest Law. January 5. AB436. http://oja.wi.gov/docview.asp?docid=6477&locid=97 (accessed February 2008).

Office for the Prevention of Domestic Violence (OPDV). 2008. New York. http://www.opdv.state.ny.us/ (accessed August 2008).

Osthoff, S., and H. Maguigan. 2005. In *Current controversies on family violence,* ed. D. Loseke, R. Gilles, and M.M. Cavanaugh. Thousand Oaks, CA: SAGE.

Presser, L., and E. Gaarder. 2004. Can restorative justice reduce battering? In *The criminal justice system and women: Offenders, prisoners, victims, and workers,* 3rd ed., ed. B. Price and N. Sokoloff, 403–18. New York: McGraw-Hill.

Rapp, C.A., and R.J. Goscha. 2006. *The strengths model: Case management with psychiatric disabilities.* New York: Oxford University Press.

Rennison, C.M. 2003. *Intimate partner violence 1993–2001.* Washington, DC: U.S. Department of Justice, Bureau of Justice Statistics.

Richey, W. 2005. Court sides with police in restraining order case. *Christian Science Monitor,* June 28: 25.

Rothenberg, B. 2003. We don't have time for social change: Cultural compromise and the battered woman syndrome. *Gender and Society* 17, no. 5: 771–87.

Rozee, P., and M. Koss. 2001. Rape: A century of resistance. *Psychology of Women Quarterly* 25:295–311.

Sherman, L. 1992. *Policing domestic violence: Experiments and dilemmas.* New York: Free Press.

Sherman, L.W., and E.G. Cohn. 1989. The impact of research on legal policy: The Minneapolis domestic violence experiment. *Law and Society Review* 23:117–44.

Smith, A., and R. Rotondi. 2007. When the victim recants: The impact of expert witness testimony in prosecution of battering cases. In *It's a crime: Women and justice,* 4th ed., ed. R. Muraskin, 277–89. Boston: Pearson.

Stalans, L., and M. Finn. 2000. Gender differences in officers' perceptions and decisions about domestic violence cases. *Women & Criminal Justice* 11, no. 3: 1–24.

Stark, E. 2002. Preparing for expert testimony in domestic violence cases. In *Handbook of domestic violence intervention strategies,* ed. A. Roberts, 216–52. New York: Oxford University Press.

Straus, M. 1979. Measuring intrafamily conflict and violence: The conflict tactics (CT) scales. *Journal of Marriage and the Family* 41:75–88.

Straus, M. A. 2006. *Dominance and symmetry in partner violence by male and female university students in 32 nations.* Presented at New York University, New York City, May 23. http://pubpages.unh.edu/~mas2/ID41H3a.pdf.

Tjaden, P., and N. Thoennes. 2000. *Extent, nature, and consequences of intimate partner violence.* Washington, DC: National Institute of Justice and the Centers for Disease Control and Prevention, July.

Van Den Bergh, N., ed. 1995. *Feminist practice in the 21st century.* Washington, DC: NASW Press.

Van Ness, D., and K. H. Strong. 2002. *Restoring justice.* 2nd ed. Cincinnati, OH: Anderson.

van Wormer, K. 2004.*Confronting oppression, restoring justice: From policy analysis to social action.* Alexandria, VA: Council on Social Work Education.

van Wormer, K., and C. Bartollas. 2007. *Women and the criminal justice system.* 2nd ed. Boston: Allyn & Bacon.

Walker, L. 1979. *The battered woman.* New York: Harper & Row.

Walker, L. 2000. *The battered woman syndrome.* New York: Springer.

Wellesley Centers for Women. 2008. Battered mothers fight to survive the family court system. http://www.wcwonline.org/o-rr25-1b.html (accessed February 2008).

Zehr, H. 2002. *The little book of restorative justice.* Intercourse, PA: Good Books.

9

Personal Narratives of Women in Prison for Partner Homicide

In about three-fourths of intimate murders in the United States, the woman is the victim (Rennison 2003). This still leaves a substantial number of cases, approximately 440, in which the woman killed her spouse or boyfriend. Since 1976, the number of male intimates killed was cut by around two-thirds while the decline in the number of female victims was cut only by about one-fourth. The increase in violence prevention programming and the availability of shelters or refuges is the generally stated explanation for the decrease in the numbers of women who kill their partners in self-defense.

Statistics Canada (1998, 2005) reveals a similar decline in the numbers of male domestic homicide victims but not of female victims of homicide.

Wells and DeLeon-Granados (2004) explain the striking decline in male homicides by their partners in terms of "exposure reduction theory" (p. 233). This theory holds that if a woman can escape from a dangerous battering situation, she will do so, and that if she resorts to using lethal partner violence, it is most likely a protective mechanism. In any case, it is a paradox, rarely realized that the proliferation of domestic violence prevention for which women and victims assistance advocates have fought so hard is saving the lives of battering men more than of female victims who are so often still stalked and killed in attempted breakup situations (van Wormer and Bartollas 2007).

In an extensive study conducted by Roberts (2007), over 500 battered women were interviewed about their relationships to their batterers. Interviews were gathered from four subsets of battered women in New Jersey. Samples were obtained from three police departments, three shelters for battered women, a convenience sample of battered women in the community, and, relevant to our purposes, a large sample of 105 women who had killed their partners and who were serving time in a state prison. From the total sample of women, Roberts developed a five-level continuum of severity of abuse. Level 1 involved short term abuse; women at level 2 had remained in a relationship of moderate to severe injury that lasted up to two years. In the third category were a smaller number of women who experienced intermittent abuse punctuated by long periods that were violence free. Women in the survey at these first three levels tended to be middle class and well educated. Level 4 included mainly less educated working class women who were subject to chronic and severe violence; many of these women reported that they engaged in mutual combat.

The 105 women who were classified at level 5, generally had endured a battering relationship for eight years or longer, although the range was 2 to 35 years. This relationship had resulted in the death of the abuser for which the women had been convicted and sentenced to prison. The majority of these women inmates had been in a common law relationship (cohabiting for 7 years or longer), a marital relationship, or had recently divorced. The overwhelming majority (59.2 percent) of these women lacked a high school education and the skills to earn a decent income on their own (Roberts 2002). Almost half (47.6 percent) of the inmate interviewees had been on public assistance for many years during the battering episodes.

The women in this category usually had begun at level 2 on the continuum, and then escalated to either level 4 or level 5 for several years, after which the death threats became more explicit and lethal. Also in a number of cases, the victim had finally left the abuser and obtained a restraining order, which he then violated. Many of the women in this category suffered from post traumatic stress disorder (PTSD), nightmares and insomnia, and some had attempted suicide. A smaller group of the convicted women indicated that at the time that they killed their batterer, they were delusional or hallucinating due to heavy use of LSD, methamphetamines, cocaine, or other drugs. The most significant finding related to these women is that the overwhelming majority (65.7 percent) had received specific lethal death threats in which the batterer specified the method, time, and/or location of their demise.

Although most perpetrators of domestic violence homicides are males, there is a considerable number of women who, following repeated acts of violence by their partner, lash out and kill him, sometimes accidentally or in self-defense. There has been much media coverage of battered women who were murdered by the batterer, with far less attention given to battered women who killed the abuser, were convicted, and are serving time in prison.

PERSONAL NARRATIVES FROM WOMEN IN PRISON

In this section of the chapter, we draw on personal narratives that were obtained in interviews with a large group of women, a subsample of a wider sample of formerly battered women who had been convicted of killing their husband, partner or ex-partner. All of the women who had killed the abuser and who were interviewed as part of this research project were incarcerated at a women's prison at the time of the interview. Convicted of murder or manslaughter and other charges, these women were sentenced to an average of 12 years in prison. Some of these women will likely be released on parole before serving their full sentence.

Often, a specific death threat was made against their lives by their abusive partners in the 24 hours prior to the homicide—and sometimes the death threat occurred just prior to the homicide. Some batterers were very specific about their threats, naming the time, lethal method and/or location of where they planned to kill their female partners. Some of the deaths of the abusive men seemed to be accidental, or in self-defense, as the man and woman were fighting over a weapon; other deaths were caused by impulsive, violent retaliatory acts on the part of the women.

Many of the women indicated that they were suffering from post-traumatic stress disorder (PTSD) symptoms which include nightmares, sleep disturbances, flashbacks, and intrusive thoughts. The overwhelming majority of the battered women in the lethal domestic violence group were more likely than the women in all of the other categories to have a history of substance abuse, and to have engaged in mutual combat in which they fought back physically rather than reacting passively to the man's brutal beatings. These women also were more likely to be high school dropouts, and to have erratic work histories in low paying jobs.

Of the 105 women in the study who killed their abusive husband or partner, this chapter features the experiences of three women—Alicia, Tamika, and Lucinda. They describe painful childhoods; abuse of alcohol and other drugs, often by *both* the woman and her partner; overwhelming anger; and mutual combat among both partners that resulted in lethal violence in which the woman who had been brutally victimized killed the abuser. Their interviews revealed frequent use of hallucinogenic drugs such as methamphetamine, LSD (acid), cocaine or crack, or PCP (angel dust), and a much higher occurrence of attempted suicide than the women in the other groups. The final commonality among this group of women is their incarceration at the same prison.

BACKGROUND INFORMATION

Alicia is a 28-year-old Caucasian woman who has shoulder length, dark brown hair and brown eyes. She is surprisingly attractive, considering that she has been incarcerated for six years at the state women's prison. She endured physical and emotional abuse from her mother and brother while growing up. Alicia, like many other abused women, blames alcohol and drugs for her husband's violent actions. But Alicia was also a substance abuser; it seems that her husband's violent rages, combined with the mutual volatility when both partners were taking drugs, led to her murdering him. Alicia stated that she killed her husband one month after their one year anniversary—and she admits that she had used a large amount of cocaine the night of the murder. In sharp contrast to the majority of the women in this category, Alicia had one year of college, but then dropped out and got married at age 20. Prior to the murder, she was working as a real estate agent.

Tamika is a 33-year-old African American woman, with short, curly black hair. She is rather heavyset, wears thin, black-framed glasses, and speaks softly. The front tooth is missing, the result of being punched in the mouth by the batterer. She also has a pronounced overbite, indicative of her family's not having had the money to pay for orthodontia when she was a teenager. Tamika's father was in and out of prison for most of her childhood and adolescence, and her mother was constantly sick. She is one of six children; her two older brothers molested her on separate occasions, and she was verbally abused by her grandfather and laughed at by her grandmother.

Lucinda is 36 years old and is of Latin descent. She wears her short auburn hair tucked behind her ears. She is a relatively small woman, but has a solid frame. As a child, her parents were always fighting, and the arguments were so loud and violent that the neighbors regularly called the police to their house. After Lucinda and her husband were married, his problems with alcohol became more apparent. He became an alcoholic, and his violent rages usually occurred whenever he had been drinking. At one point, he promised to stop drinking; he even joined Alcoholics Anonymous for a short time, but after a couple of months he stopped going to meetings and he resumed his old drinking habits.

As is common for many women in our study, these women typically endured physical, emotional and sexual abuse as children and/or adolescents. Family stressors include poor or neglectful parenting, substance abuse, illness, and family violence.

Unlike many of the other women in this group, Alicia reported having many fond memories from her childhood, particularly with her father, who taught her to ski, fish, and swim. She also reported positive memories of taking ballet classes and going to the ballet and symphony with her father. But Alicia also has some terrible memories of being abused by her mother and raped by a girlfriend's older brother:

> I was abused by my mother and it was on-going, physical, mental and emotional. I don't remember when it started, probably when I was very young. As a teenager, I was raped by my girlfriend's brother. We were at a party together, and I was involved with drugs by then. Lots of bad incidents with drugs. I never told anyone about the rape for a long time.

As an adolescent, Alicia rebelled with heavy-duty drug experimentation ranging from downers to speed—"everything except crack." When she drank, she did so excessively and she often blacked out. Her parents required her go to an addiction treatment program, but after leaving the program, she started using drugs again.

Tamika recounts a very traumatic childhood with repeated incidents of sexual abuse. She removes her glasses to rub her eyes as she tries to remember how old she was when her father went to prison:

> My father went to prison when I was seven. My mother and father used to argue all the time. My father was a thief. He used to rob people. I came across a lot of money one day—thousands of dollars that were hidden. A couple of days later, the police came and took him away. Right after my father was taken away, they put my mother away in a hospital. She had six kids.

Tamika also describes the sexual abuse she sustained from her brothers while she was young:

> I was sexually abused by my brothers. First, it was my one brother that was one year older than me. He only did it once. I was seven or eight. I don't think it was sex, but it was something...him and his friends did stupid things to me like that. Then my oldest brother sexually abused me and beat me for a long time. My grandmother saw him fondling me when I was 12. Then it stopped....I didn't really know what was going on—I knew it was wrong...there was no one to tell. For a while, I couldn't remember—you block it out.

Tamika found that alcohol could numb the pain of her tumultuous and violent childhood, and she began drinking heavily in junior high school. She then dropped out of school after she was assaulted by three men:

> I started drinking and having blackouts and not remembering things. In high school, I was assaulted by three men. They tried to rape me, but I got away. That's why I stopped going to school. I wanted to go to night school, so I did after I became pregnant by a boyfriend.

The emotional pain was so enormous that during her adolescence, Tamika tried to commit suicide three times.

> When I was 14, I took pills—sleeping pills, my grandmother's. My grandfather punished me because a guy came to the door. My grandfather called me a whore and punished me. He sent me to my room. I felt paranoid at the time. I told my grandmother I was going to kill myself. She said, "Go ahead," and laughed. I took the pills, about 21 of them, in my bedroom with a sip of wine. I remember going into the kitchen to the refrigerator's bottom shelf to eat a tomato and I fell. My brother told me later that he saw me and took me downstairs and stuck a toothbrush down my throat so I would throw up. He said he was holding me upside-down by my feet, and he was shaking me. I threw up. He saw the pills and then he called the ambulance. When I woke up, my grandmother, uncle, and the police were in the hospital. They had pumped my stomach and everything.

The second time, Tamika was at a party where everyone was doing a lot of drinking. When some of the guys tried to force themselves on her, she attempted suicide:

> Another time, I tried to cut my wrists at a party. All of the guys were trying to force me to do stuff against my will. I told them I would kill myself and I locked myself in the bathroom. They kicked the door in to get me out of the bathroom so I wouldn't hurt myself. I was about 17.

The third suicide attempt occurred when Tamika was 18 years old, and a former boyfriend, and father of her young daughter, took the little girl away:

> I was 18. My daughter's father took my daughter away from me. We were living together and I cheated on him. I was working and had a babysitter. He came while the babysitter was there and took my daughter and kept her. I stayed in a room for four months because I was so depressed. During those four months I tried to commit suicide. My grandmother was ill and had cancer. I was taking Percidans and all her medication. I was locked in the bathroom and took a few pills. She was outside the door. I told her I would kill myself if she didn't get my baby back.

EARLY INSTANCES OF ABUSE

The initial incidents of violence that were recounted by these women are very comparable to the first signs of abuse from the women in the other categories. There is nothing in these early recollections that would foreshadow the lethal violence that would ultimately take place.

Alicia recalls that the first violent incident occurred when her boyfriend was drunk.

> It happened before we got married. He was angry about something and threw a lamp against the wall. It didn't hit me, but it was frightening. Once he sobered up, he was very apologetic. Alcohol always triggered his violence.

Tamika explains the first time she was threatened—even though the abuse in this incident is verbal, the implications were frightening enough:

> He has a nasty mouth, and one time we were arguing and it got real nasty—it was when I caught him in a lie. He had taken our state income tax check and forged my name on it. I found it in his pocket. I was really mad and I told him I was thinking of going to Florida, and he said, "if you ever left the state with our daughter, I'll kill you."

Lucinda explains one of the first times her husband hit her:

> I was slapped, but why I can't remember. We were outside the 7-11 store...I always thought it was never his fault. He had an alcohol problem, and it happened after he

was drinking. He always made me think it was my fault. I did something to make it happen. I'd look at someone or the dinner burned, or I talked to a guy. I couldn't look at a man while I was talking to him. It would happen over anything.

ESCALATION OF THE BATTERER'S ASSAULTS, INCLUDING DEATH THREATS

Alicia speaks of her husband's drinking problem as a catalyst for the violent rages that occurred with increasing frequency—even though they were married for only a year prior to Alicia's killing him:

> Alcohol always triggered it. He was an alcoholic. If he didn't use me as a punching bag, he would destroy personal property. I had bruises all over my body, black eyes, and choke marks. Sometimes I would fight back, and it would only make it worse.

Alicia also suffered a miscarriage as a result of her falling down the stairs when her husband was chasing her to continue an assault. Her husband's violence was so extreme that she feared he was going to murder her:

> ...he tried to kill me. I was late coming home from work, and he called me a liar, this, that, and the other thing. He was drunk and drugged out. I was at a girlfriend's house, having dinner, and he pounded on the door. I came outside to see what he wanted, and he came after me and told me he was going to kill me, and when I saw the knife I ran. He was coming right at me, and he chased me down the street. My friends had already called the cops, and the cops came and he took off....I saw him the next day and he took off. I tried to talk to him and asked him why he tried to kill me. He has a history of calling me from time to time and leaving messages that he's gonna do this to me or that to me.

The injuries Alicia sustained were so severe that she needed to go to the emergency room on numerous occasions. Although it is likely that at least some of the ER staff suspected that Alicia had been beaten by her husband, she refused to discuss what had actually taken place.

> When I went to the emergency room, they would stitch me up and send me home. I would always make up a lie so they didn't know. My husband took me to the hospital a few times and was worried about me, so it looked good for him. One time a nurse questioned me about possible abuse, and I wouldn't answer any questions, so she stopped asking.

On one occasion, Alicia did get a temporary restraining order against her husband, but he ordered her to drop the restraining order with the threat that if she didn't, "they were going to find my body washed up on the beach." Alicia complied with his demands.

Tamika states that her husband was using drugs, which was the trigger for his violence. She also states that she wanted to leave him because he was so violent, but he didn't want her to leave—and, sadly, she never had the courage to take her children and flee to a shelter for battered women.

> We used to fight over drugs. Drugs triggered the abuse...I wanted to leave him, and he would always try to stop me from leaving. I was the type of person [who] wouldn't allow a man to hit me. I called the police on a lot of occasions. He was robbing money from me. I had my children. That's another reason why we used to fight. He used to want to have sex in front of the kids. I didn't want to. I thought it was wrong. The kids used to mimic us—it was terrible.

These are Lucinda's recollections of how her husband's assaults against her escalated as his problems with alcohol worsened:

> He was drinking more and more, and he was hitting me more often. I had black eyes...he hit or punched me. We were in the bathroom at his mother's at the time. I was pregnant and I ran down the street barefoot and called the police...they came an hour later. He insulted me and called me names—I was stupid or a bad mother. His mother did nothing.

Lucinda describes how she actually did leave her husband—for a while. She and her husband had been living in another state, and after a brutal assault, she asked her mother for the money to come back to live with her.

> One time after he beat me I called 911 and the police came and I said to arrest him. He told them I was nuts 'cause I was on pills from the doctor. The house was a mess, I had the baby. The police officer believed me and arrested him. One officer asked me if I had anywhere to go, so I said I was from New Jersey. He advised me to go back to New Jersey with the money I had. He said it would happen again. My daughter was just six months old. So I called my mother and told her, and she wired me some money. My girlfriend brought me to get the money and I bought a ticket and planned to leave the next morning. I had $450 and the ticket was $256. He called me and told me to drop the charges while I was packing to leave. I told him "no." He said, "I love you." He kept calling and finally I stopped answering, and I took my daughter and went back to live with my mother.

Lucinda's husband tracked her back to New Jersey from the West Coast, and she allowed him to live with her at her mother's home. This is an example of one of his death threats:

> He told me he'd kill me on the evening of our next anniversary. He said, "When we go out to celebrate our next anniversary, you'll be dead if you even look at anyone else." He always got that way—his jealousy got the best of him. But I was really scared, since our anniversary was less than one month away.

MEMORIES OF THE WORST INCIDENT

Each woman provided emotionally laden descriptions of the worst incident, which preceded her killing the batterer.

These are Alicia's recollections of her husband's most violent episode against her:

> We were drinking at a bar. The beating lasted about 25 minutes. He beat me with a barstool. I had bruises from head to toe. He also destroyed the house. We had a .22 caliber, which I took and threw into the bay because I was afraid he would kill me with it.

Immediately after this brutal assault, Alicia stayed with a girlfriend for four days. The friend begged her to not go back to her husband and cautioned her that, "*somebody is going to end up dead.*" But Alicia says she felt she had to return to her abusive husband because, "It was kind of an obsession. I wasn't really in love, but I didn't know that at the time." Although Alicia had gotten rid of one gun, there were two other guns in the house—a .357 caliber Magnum and a .44 handgun.

Tamika's tumultuous relationship with her husband was also characterized by some incidents in which *she* hit him back because he was beating her—as well as occasions on which Tamika started by hitting him and he retaliated with extreme violence. Because her husband was much bigger and stronger, she usually suffered injuries that were far more severe than his. Tamika recalls some instances in which she was the aggressor. On one occasion she was infuriated because he was smoking crack, and she grabbed a knife from the kitchen drawer. "I yelled at him, 'You want to die? I'll do it for you.' I had the knife and he tried to grab it, and I pulled it away and slashed his hands."

KILLING THE ABUSIVE PARTNER

Tamika's recollection of the worst incident is the argument that started when she became furious that her husband used their rent money to buy drugs, and ended when they were fighting over his gun, and she shot and killed him:

> It was over drugs, when he took the rent money to buy drugs. I hid the money and he took it. I started hitting him, and then he started beating me. He held me down to keep me from hitting him. When I hit him, he started hitting me and kicking and slapping me....He beat me bad as I was trying to leave. He was pounding my face like hamburger meat, screaming "F-you bitch." I think he was trying to stop me from going upstairs to call the police. Then he went for his gun and said he was going to kill me, but I got to it first.

As they were fighting for control of the gun, Tamika shot her husband and killed him.

Lucinda describes the incident that culminated in her accidentally killing her husband with a knife.

> I moved in with my mom. He came back to New Jersey after 10 months. I had another baby during this time. He moved into my mother's house and got a job. I told him to move out 'cause the arguments started again...he was physically abusive when my mom wasn't around. He was still drinking and we were fighting. I don't remember the exact details of the incident...a guy came over to visit my brother and my husband called me to the door and said, "Someone is here to see you," and the guy said he was looking for my brother. The guy left and we started arguing about it. He was drinking that day. I told him to get out and he wouldn't. Somehow or another I picked up a knife and he kept coming towards me and I hit him with the knife. I remember doing it once, but the police report said three times. He fell to the floor and there was blood all over. I tried to stop the bleeding and he was talking to me. So then I grabbed the phone and couldn't dial. I ran to the neighbor...they called the police. He went to the hospital and I went to the police station and I gave a statement to try to protect him. I don't know why. They charged me with murder one and a weapons charge.

Alicia describes how her despair after she realized that she had killed her abusive husband culminated in an attempt to kill herself:

> I have only vague recollections of what happened after I killed him. I went to my friend's house, and I locked myself in my friend's bathroom and cut myself real bad. I wanted to die. The paramedics came and took me to the hospital. I was in surgery for several hours and had over 70 stitches.

Alicia had fired a single shot at her husband, and that one shot killed him. She was charged with first degree murder, but the private attorney that her father hired negotiated a plea bargain in which Alicia pled guilty to a reduced charge of aggravated manslaughter. She was sentenced to seven years in prison. These are Alicia's concluding words showing how she has grown during her incarceration:

> The most difficult part about being in prison is the culture shock, mixing of personalities, overcrowding, and the loneliness. The noise level is unbearable. It is degrading and humiliating. The prison environment strips away one's self-esteem. You are given a lot of time to think and re-evaluate your life. There is nothing here—unless you're bright enough and lucky enough to look inside yourself and find something good.

Alicia has been clean (no alcohol or drugs) for the six years that she has been incarcerated. When she is released from prison, she plans to return to college to pursue a degree in psychology.

The jury found Tamika guilty of second degree murder. The public defender tried to have her acquitted, arguing that it was self-defense. He presented some graphic photos, taken by the hospital emergency room staff, showing the severe domestic violence injuries that Tamika had sustained during the course of their marriage. The prosecuting attorney pointed out that Tamika had aggravated the volatile situation by being physically combative with her husband on numerous occasions and sometimes causing him serious injury, such as the time she cut his hand with a knife. The jury weighed the aggravating factors against all of the mitigating factors; their verdict was that Tamika's husband was the primary aggressor more often and, on balance, he was responsible for the most serious injuries, including an occasion on which he had broken her jaw. The judge sentenced Tamika to serve 10 to 15 years in the women's prison.

Lucinda was initially charged with first degree murder and a weapons charge. The prosecutor then reduced the charge to aggravated manslaughter as part of a plea agreement. Lucinda was poor and did not have the benefit of a private attorney, and her public defender urged her to accept a plea bargain of a 20-year flat sentence, which she agreed to. As a result, the earliest time she can be released is after 18 years of incarceration.

The women in this category endured repeated violent assaults from the batterers who were usually alcoholics and/or drug abusers and who had repeatedly brutalized their wives and threatened to kill them. Many of these women also had their own history of abusing drugs and/or alcohol, and many had fought back in very violent ways. Some of the women had suffered terrifying nightmares and sleep disturbances, and many (44.7 percent) had attempted to commit suicide. An unexpected finding was the very high rates of depression for the chronically battered women and for the women who killed their partners (67.5 percent). In contrast to the community sample of battered women, the women in the prison sample frequently had a history of drug use. Other relevant factors that emerged in the interviews were reports of the batterer's extreme jealousy, emotional dependence, and drunken episodes. The women who had resorted to homicide had been traumatized by the emotional and physical violence and were angry at being repeatedly brutalized by the batterer. Traumatization plus anger seem to be have made for a volatile combination that spelled disaster for all of the women (and their families) in this category. Regretably, none of these women had sought help from a shelter for battered women. It seems that they did not want to allow themselves to be viewed as a "victim" of domestic violence who needed help from professionals to end the relationship in a safe manner.

RECIDIVISM RESEARCH

Roberts, Zgoba, and Shahidullah (2007) explored factors in recidivism rates in a random sample of 336 homicide offenders who were released between the years 1990 and 2000 from the New Jersey Department of Corrections. The released convicts were identified and followed for a minimum of five years. These offenders were tracked to determine if incarcerated homicide offenders who had no criminal histories prior to their homicide conviction recidivated less, and which specific variables correlated with recidivism. A four-fold typology of homicide offenders emerged from this analysis: (1) homicide that was precipitated by a general altercation or argument, (2) homicide during the commission of a felony, (3) domestic violence-related homicide, and (4) a homicide after an accident. Of the 336 instances of homicide, 84 were of the domestic violence-related variety. Examples on the men and women are

#22 "Shot victim. He believed she was unfaithful."
#44 "Shot wife after the she left him."
#64 "Stabbed his wife to death because he thought she was cheating on him."
#151 "Defendant used car to run over and kill husband who had beaten her badly in the car."
#214 "Shot and killed victim after years of emotional abuse."
#222 "Stabbed victim in back twice. Claimed unable to take abuse any longer. Defendant stabbed boyfriend in chest with kitchen knife after argument."

Most of the offenders in the Roberts et al. study above were female (65 percent), African American, and most of the victims were African American males. As we know from government statistics (Bureau of Justice Statistics [BJS] 2005), the rate of female-on-male intimate violence and homicide in the African American community is disproportionately high (Tjaden and Thoennes 2000). (Since 2004, however, there has been a significant decline in the numbers of black males who are so victimized.) Inconsistent with BJS reports, the weapon used in most of these killings was a sharp instrument rather than a gun. Consistent with national U.S. research, most of these acts were intraracial. About half of the perpetrators had alcohol or drug problems. Regarding recidivism rates, none of the homicide offenders committed another murder. The highest recidivism for new violent or drug crimes occurred in the felony homicide group (slightly over one-third), followed by the altercation-precipitated homicide offenders (27 percent), which was in sharp contrast to the domestic violence homicide offenders with less than 10 percent recidivism due to a new violent or drug offense.

CONCLUSION

The chapter takes us into the lives of the individual women who killed their partners. Several common themes emerge. Among these are the seeming inability of these women to find a way out of highly abusive and potentially dangerous situations, an inability where this applied, to document that the killings were in self-defense, situations of poverty, and the involvement of alcohol and other drugs in the violence. Also note that others in a study on recidivism showed in follow-up studies that they were not a danger to the community; in other words, they were not criminal types. Their acts could be construed as a normal response to abnormal and terrifying situations.

The tragedy is that so many of these homicides could have been prevented by appropriate outside help. To the subject of prevention, we now turn.

REFERENCES

Bureau of Justice Statistics (BJS). 2005. Homicide trends in the U.S.: Intimate homicide. Washington, DC: U.S. Department of Justice. http://www.ojp.usdoj.gov/bjs/homicide/intimates.htm (accessed February 2007).

Rennison, C.M. 2003. Intimate partner violence 1993–2001. Bureau of Justice Statistics. Washington, DC: U.S. Department of Justice.

Roberts, A.R. 2002. Duration and severity of woman battering: A conceptual model/continuum. In *Handbook of domestic violence intervention strategies,* ed. A. Roberts, 64–79. New York: Oxford University Press.

Roberts, A.R. 2007. Domestic violence continuum: Forensic assessment and crisis intervention. *Families in Society* 88, no. 1: 42–54.

Roberts, A.R., K. Zgoba, and S. Shahidullah. 2007. Recidivism among types of homicide offenders: An exploratory analysis of 336 from offenders in New Jersey. *Aggression and Violent Behavior* 12, no. 5: 493–507.

Statistics Canada. 1998. *Family violence in Canada: A statistical profile 1998.* Ottawa: Statistics Canada.

Statistics Canada. 2005. *Family violence in Canada: A statistical profile 2005.* Ottawa: Statistics Canada.

Tjaden, P., and N. Thoennes. 2000. *Extent, nature, and consequences of intimate partner violence: Findings from the National Violence Against Women Survey.* Washington, DC: National Institute of Justice, U.S. Department of Justice.

van Wormer, K., and C. Bartollas. 2007. *Women and the criminal justice system.* 2nd ed. Boston: Allyn & Bacon.

Wells, W., and W. DeLeon-Granados. 2004. The intimate partner homicide decline: Disaggregated trends: Theoretical explanations, and policy implications. *Criminal Justice Policy Review* 15, no. 2: 229–46.

Part III

Prevention

10

Safety Plans for the Prevention of Intimate Homicide

The public health or harm reduction approach to domestic violence requires the committed involvement of many sectors of the society and disciplines to prevent violence from occurring in the first place and to extend better care and safety planning to threatened individuals. The responsibility for overall community health resides in a number of systems—criminal justice, education, health, and social services working not separately but in tandem.

This chapter from a harm reduction/public health perspective begins with an examination of the steps of research gathering and dissemination of the facts. Then the strategies of primary, secondary, and tertiary prevention are described.

DEFINITION OF THE PROBLEM AND THE IDENTIFICATION OF RISKS

The public health formulation of the Centers for Disease Control (CDC) (2008) offers a framework that is useful to the social problem of domestic homicide. This model for data collection consists of the following key components:

- definition of the problem—developing surveillance systems;
- identification of risk and protective factors;
- developing and testing prevention strategies;
- assuring widespread adoption of these strategies.

Surveillance is the first step in violence prevention. This involves the collection and analyzing of data. Research on domestic homicide examines patterns of intimate partner homicide, the demographics of such violence, and attitude surveys on the problem. Take the findings as reported by the Family Violence Prevention Fund (2008) that pregnant and recently pregnant women are more likely to be victims of homicide than to die of any other cause. When this fact was revealed through research on the deaths of pregnant women, dissemination of the results took place through the popular media.

One logical prevention strategy that might be developed from this finding would be to urge gynecologists and obstetricians to provide information to all their patients concerning warning signs of impending danger and the telephone numbers of domestic violence crisis phone lines.

As described in Chapter 3 on murder-suicide, a recently developed surveillance system is being utilized to document the actual number of homicides that result in suicide. This documentation is crucial because the ability to predict which people are at greatest risk of committing injury or of being injured is key to our ability to provide effective interventions. The National Violent Death Reporting System (NVDRS) of the Centers for Disease Control and Prevention (2008) has recently begun to provide such crucial documentation. The potential is great for systematic analysis of the etiology and demographics of domestic violence and domestic murder-suicide from these data. As stated by the NVDRS, accurate, timely, and comprehensive surveillance data are necessary for the occurrence of violent deaths in the United States to be better understood and ultimately prevented.

NVDRS data can be used to track the occurrence of violence-related fatal injuries and assist public health authorities in the development, implementation, and evaluation of programs and policies to reduce and prevent violent deaths and injuries at the national, state, and local levels. In their analysis of data from this national data base, Bossarte, Simon, and Barker (2006) were able to determine, for example, that about one third of male-perpetrated homicides end in suicide. In the future, examination of the results should yield much more detailed information than we have at the present time on different varieties of domestic homicide.

Research on the identification of risk factors has further shown that heavy drinking is correlated with all forms of homicide including domestic homicide. According to a special report by the World Health Organization (WHO) (2006a), strategies for tackling intimate partner violence should also provide treatment for substance abuse. Recommended measures include the targeting of societal tolerance towards intimate partner violence, the acceptance of excessive drinking as a mitigating factor, and confronting the normative beliefs about masculinity and heavy drinking. Intimate partner violence may also be reduced, according to this report, through interventions to moderate alcohol consumption by reducing alcohol availability. In Australia, for example, a community intervention that included restricting the hours of the sale of alcohol within one town was found to have reduced the number of domestic violence victims presenting to a hospital.

It bears repeating as we learned from Campbell et al.'s (2003) delineation of risk factors contained in interviews with surviving family members of homicide (summarized in Chapter 2) that several factors emerged as closely associated with the murders. These were access to a gun and previous threats with a weapon, having a stepchild in the home, a pattern of estrangement and separations, and lack of police arrest for prior abuse. This last factor gives some indication of the deterrent factor of arrest at least in certain situations.

Now we turn to a look at the three major types of prevention strategies as defined by the Center for Diseases Control and Prevention (CDC). The concern of the CDC is with the prevention of disease and injury before they occur. Efforts are developed in response to actual and potential threats to public health.

PRIMARY PREVENTION STRATEGIES

Primary prevention focuses on mass educational campaigns such as in schools and in public health facilities. The first step toward ending the domestic homicide is to prevent the family violence—this includes, most especially, violence against children in the home. Legal remedies such as stringent gun control are relevant here. Primary prevention seeks to prevent the onset of violence and to change cultural attitudes conducive to gendered violence. Typical primary prevention strategies are mass education campaigns aimed at public school systems, community agencies, and publicity through the mass media.

The World Health Organization in 2005 conducted the first-ever study devoted exclusively to domestic violence globally. Consistent with the principles of primary prevention, the report recommends a range of vital interventions to change attitudes and challenge the inequities and social norms that perpetuate abuse. It further recommends integrating violence prevention programming into ongoing initiatives aimed at children, youth, HIV/AIDS, and sexual and reproductive health. Health service providers should be trained to identify women experiencing violence and to respond appropriately.

Child abuse is an area ripe for attention as around 1,000 children are killed by family members each year. Homicide, in fact, is one of the leading causes of death of children. In recent years, prevention efforts have been directed toward maternal infanticide. As a reaction to some high-profile cases of maternal infanticide, or mothers killing their infants shortly after giving birth, the Infant Homicide Prevention Act (House Bill 275) was enacted by the North Carolina General Assembly (North Carolina Department of Health and Human Services 2003). This law decriminalizes abandonment of an infant under certain circumstances and modifies some procedures involving abandoned newborns. Iowa passed a similar law following a sad case of a teenager who gave birth alone and then killed her newborn infant. These laws, commonly known as "safe haven" laws, are designed to provide a responsible alternative to infant abandonment. They give desperate mothers with limited resources an option for ensuring their babies' well-being without fear of criminal prosecution and without revealing their identity. Many infants' lives have been saved by these measures.

Not only infants but children aged 10–14 are also at risk. Most of the parents who kill do not set out to do so; the deaths are the end result of out-of-control violence against the infant or child. What could make a difference for infants and toddlers, researchers say, is education. Prenatal and parenting classes that cover anger management as well as child development are recommended. Parents also could use respite child care, advice and support from visiting nurses, and suicide hotline counseling. (For the facts, see the U.S. Department of Health and Human Services, 2007 report on child maltreatment.)

For children who have witnessed severe violence in the home or even a homicide, mental health counseling can be a tremendous help in normalizing responses and helping to put what happened in context. Children who have witnessed such situations need help in coming to terms with what took place and why, and to recognize that they were not responsible and could have done nothing to prevent such acts of violence. They may need to be encouraged to express their feelings about the violence. Such therapy when offered on a mass scale can be viewed as an effort to halt the cycle of intergenerational abuse.

Thanks to federal and local grant funding, interventions are being applied across the United States to teach students attitudes and behaviors to prevent violence in relationships and to end bullying practices on the playground. Experts in violence prevention deliver lectures to students about healthy boundaries in relationships, the warning signs of potential victimization, awareness of the dangers in signs of extreme jealousy and possessive behavior, and the importance of zero tolerance of violence and equality in decision making. For potential victimizers, work in the area of irrational thinking and "I can't live without you" motifs is provided.

Thanks in part to results of a much publicized teen and preteen dating survey conducted by the Theocratic Research Utilities, much attention has been paid lately to the risks of violence in early dating relationships. A major finding of the study was that one in three teens who had sex by age 14 said that they had been physically abused by an angry partner. For those who were not sexually active until later, the abuse rate was nine percent. Concern about the issue prompted the National Association of Attorneys General to pass a resolution encouraging school districts to implement teen dating violence education policies (*Washington Times* 2008). Academic research based on a focus group study of Mexican American youth, similarly, shows that the use of violence in dating relationships is widespread (Black and Weisz 2005).

Teen Dating Abuse: Warning Signs

Based on the literature on domestic violence, we have developed the following list of warning signs that a young woman should consider to determine if the relationship is likely to become violent. The warning signs are geared toward heterosexual female teens but can be adjusted to pertain to same-sex or male respondents.

____ 1. Does your date or boyfriend brag about beating up or intimidating people?
____ 2. Does he ever suggest that he knows how to kill, for example, by playfully putting his hands on your neck, then say he was only joking?

_____ 3. Does he own or have access to a gun, or show a fascination with weapons?

_____ 4. Has he ever forced you to kiss or have sex? Does he show an awareness of your wishes and feelings?

_____ 5. Does he use illegal drugs, especially amphetamines, speed, meth, or crack?

_____ 6. Does he get drunk on a regular basis or brag about his high tolerance for alcohol? Does he push you to drink alcoholic beverages or take illicit drugs?

_____ 7. When you are with him, does he control how you spend your time? Is he always the one to drive or criticize you severely if you take the wheel?

_____ 8. Is he constantly jealous? Does he control your friendships with other people and seem to want to have you all to himself?

_____ 9. Is he rapidly becoming emotionally dependent on you; for instance, does he say things like "I can't live without you"? Is his thinking of an all-or-nothing pattern (either you are his best friend or his worst enemy—often about past relationships)?

_____ 10. Do you have the feeling that only you understand him, that others do not or cannot?

_____ 11. Note the relationship between his parents. Is his mother very submissive to his father? Is there heavy drinking and/or lots of tension in his family?

_____ 12. Is there a history of past victimization by his father?

_____ 13. Is there a history of animal abuse in his background?

_____ 14. Has he ever struck you? Have you known him to lose control of his anger for certain periods of time?

_____ 15. Has he ever threatened or tried to commit suicide?

_____ 16. Does he get out of patience quickly with children or is he verbally abusive toward them?

_____ Total "Yes" answers.

If you have answered yes to two or more of these items, you should talk to a mature person before pursuing this relationship further. Before getting romantically involved with someone, consider what it would be like to break up with this person. Would you be able to cool the relationship and still remain friends or end the relationship if you wanted to? Consider how he would handle this. It is much easier to get out of a potentially dangerous relationship in the early stages than to wait and see how things turn out, or to see if you can change a person.

SECONDARY PREVENTION STRATEGIES

Secondary prevention, also called "screening," refers to measures that detect problems in need of treatment. This type of prevention focuses on halting the progression of the problem. Family violence screening may consist of using a danger assessment tool. Persons at high risk of injury are given a checklist of questions to determine their degree of risk. The asking of such questions has an educational function as well; these questions are designed to alert the individual to the fact that she (or sometimes he) may be in considerable danger. Individuals are asked about such matters as heavy drinking and illicit drug use and the availability of weapons in the house. Substance abuse assessment is essential since misuse of alcohol and other drugs may serve as a catalyst or excuse for violence.

Albert Roberts's Seven Stage Crisis Intervention Model offers a framework that can be applied by hospital staff, social workers, crisis intervention centers, or shelter workers. The model recommends that the following safety steps be taken (Roberts and Roberts 2005, 133):

1. Plan and conduct a thorough assessment (including a level of danger assessment); inquire about death, suicide threats, weapons present, etc., and immediate psychosocial needs.
2. Establish rapport and rapidly establish a relationship based on genuineness and respect.
3. Identify precipitating event that led the client to seek treatment; encourage the client to ventilate and describe the immediate situation.
4. Deal with feelings and emotions. Open-ended questions are recommended. Some examples: How are you feeling now? What are some of the options you're thinking about? What is the usual situation at home? Use verbal counseling skills such as reflection of feelings, reassurance, paraphrasing, and attentive silence.
5. Generate and explore alternatives. Helping the client find a safe place is essential.
6. Develop and formulate an action plan. Help the client face her fears and gain control as a self-empowering act. Whether the woman decides to leave the relationship or to stay, she needs assistance in making a shift from fatalistic thinking toward and attitude of hope and self-determination.
7. Follow up. Formal and informal arrangements need to be made to monitor the woman's progress and ensure her safety, and reinforce participation in self-help groups and/or community activities.

For cases of violence that are life threatening, a simple list of factors developed by Straus (1996) might be useful to practitioners. Key predictive factors singled out by Straus are three or more episodes of violence within the past year, police involvement, drug abuse, extreme male dominance, abuse of a child, violence outside the family (which shows the abuser is losing control), and a pattern of threats. Similarly, Bancroft (2002) stresses jealousy, possessiveness, and obsession as key danger signs.

Erin Marcus, MD (2008) advises screening for domestic abuse as a part of all medical examinations. Such screening for domestic violence is rare, however, as many doctors believe the risk of personal injury is a matter for the criminal justice system. Other health care professionals are afraid such questions would be taken the wrong way and considered offensive, and further that victims likely would deny the violence anyway. In a recent nationwide survey of 5,000 women cited by Marcus, only seven percent said a health professional had even asked about family violence. A major argument for including such a question is that just by asking, you may be planting a seed for change. Some women may confide in a nurse or doctor when directly queried, and then they can be referred to appropriate resources.

Mental health professionals, in conducting a biopsychological assessment to gauge the severity of the situation, need to realize the importance of imparting both empathy and hope. As we have seen in the research covered in much of this book, the sooner a woman extricates herself from a potentially lethal situation the better. In their interviews with the 501 New Jersey women who experienced violence in their dating and marital relationships, Roberts and Roberts (2005) found that one personality characteristic—self-reported psychological strength—was an important protective factor in ending the battering relationship at the earliest possible moment. The message here for mental health workers is the importance of helping boost a woman's self-efficacy or faith in herself to enable her to have the strength to take the measures she needs in order to protect herself.

Timing is of the essence because in an intimate relationship, emotional dependence strengthens over time, both on the part of the victim, breaking her resolve to leave, and more dangerously, of the man at risk for taking desperate measures if he fears or experiences rejection. Therefore, from the victim's standpoint, leaving at the first sign of a pathway to violence is a protective maneuver. This is why it is important to reach people who are on the path to victimization early in a relationship.

Giving information to the public, such as providing a list of warning signs or red flags of pending trouble, can open the eyes of many. Among the warning signs are abnormal levels of jealousy and possessiveness, intimidation, poor impulse control, violation of the woman's personal boundaries, and going to extremes in thought and deed.

Motivational enhancement techniques as formulated by Miller and Rollnick (2002) are of proven effectiveness in engaging a client and aiding in decision making. These are the same techniques that, as we will see in Chapter 11, have great potential in helping batterers make a decision to change. Motivational strategies are the practice component of harm reduction, the method that accompanies the model. This method, which emphasizes empathy and boosting the client's level of awareness, offers the client options. Through collaborative discussion, counselor and client consider the pros and cons (including risks) of the various options.

Stage 6 of Roberts's Seven Stage Crisis Intervention Model is the drawing up of a workable action plan. Central to this step is the client's sense of ownership of the plan. Stage 7 encompasses the details of the safety plan. If the client chooses to remain in the relationship, a backup plan can increase her security. Typically a backup plan would include having extra copies of key identification papers kept elsewhere, such as children's birth certificates, vaccination records, and the like; a source of money available for an emergency; memorizing emergency telephone numbers; having a cell phone for emergency calls; and having an extra set of car keys. But above all, the plan should include arrangements for a safe place to go. Since substance abuse by either party to violence enhances the risk that the violence will be deadly, the counselor is advised to explore options for discouraging heavy drinking and drug use. Getting rid of lethal weapons is of course a priority as well.

Social workers and victim assistance professionals must determine the level of danger in the familial environment before it escalates. Studies have also found that murder (or murder-suicide) may start out as escalating domestic violence in conjunction with severe depression and suicidal ideation among the abusers (Adams 2007; van Wormer and Bartollas 2007). One way to determine the extent of this danger is to do a lethality assessment (see Chapter 2, this book).

Expanding screening for returning combat veterans to determine if they need mental health counseling to help them readjust to society and to family life is another excellent prevention strategy.

TERTIARY PREVENTION STRATEGIES

Tertiary prevention is aimed at reducing the harm of activities that are already underway. The aim here is to minimize the damage and help free people from pathology. At this level, prevention efforts consist of interventions to help people alter their undesirable and destructive behavior. Relevant to domestic homicide, persons may be placed in batterers' education programs under the auspices of the criminal justice system or they may be sentenced to jail and prison terms for the protection of society. From the survivor's standpoint, nothing is more pathological than living on the edge of life-threatening violence. Harm reduction and safety plans as discussed throughout this book are examples of tertiary prevention. The strategy of motivational enhancement serves well to help people reach a decision about how to best ensure their personal safety and the safety of their families. In the aftermath of murder or escape from attempted murder, psychotherapy to help the survivors, including children, to heal is paramount. Work with children and youth may help break the intergenerational violence. Note that harm reduction attends to personal as well as structural factors in the prevention of family violence.

GLOBAL CAMPAIGNS

The Global Campaign for Violence Prevention was launched by the World Health Organization following the release of the World Report on Violence and Health in October 2002. The objectives of the campaign were to raise awareness about the problem of violence worldwide, to highlight the crucial role that public health can play in addressing its causes and consequences, and encourage action at every level of society. WHO urged all governments to take action to reduce violence against women. Major incentives were the realization that nearly half the women who die due to homicide are killed by their current or former husband or boyfriend and the awareness of the fact that violence accounts for approximately seven percent of all deaths among women aged 15–44 worldwide.

One of the principal contributions of the World Report on Violence and Health was to make a strong case that, with properly designed, adequately funded interventions, violence can be prevented and its impact reduced. This stemmed directly from its conceptual starting point: the public health approach to addressing public health issues (WHO 2008).

Data from a wide range of countries suggest that partner violence accounts for a significant number of deaths by murder among women. Studies from Australia, Canada, Israel, South Africa, and the United States show that 40–70 percent of female murder victims were killed by their husbands or boyfriends, frequently in the context of an ongoing abusive relationship (WHO 2002). These are among the findings of WHO's (2006b) extensive world report on violence and health. In addition to the hundreds of thousands of lives destroyed, the report shows that violence against women has been linked to a number of immediate and long-term conditions, including physical injury, chronic pain syndromes, depression, and suicidal behavior.

The recent WHO report proposes a set of principles to underpin prevention of gendered violence as follows. Such practices

- take place at both national and local levels;
- involve women in their development and implementation;
- reform the responses of institutions—including the police, health care workers, and the judicial system—and work to change cultural prescriptions for antiwoman violence.

These recommendations are geared to the eradication of the killings of girls and women worldwide—for example, dowry bride burnings in India and "honor killings" throughout the Middle East (see also Chapter 7). This formulation is useful in providing broad guidelines as a framework for the development of more specific policies to be applied at the local level.

For instance, some countries recently have passed laws criminalizing violence against women, and several have passed legislation outlawing female genital mutilation. As these laws are gradually implemented, they serve to protect girls and women who are at high risk of these dangers and also to promote their overall health.

LEGAL REMEDIES IN THE U.S.

Research studies have shown that, typically, when the batterer as male comes from a middle class background, is currently either in school or gainfully employed, and has a stake in preserving his position in society, the issuing of a protective restraining order or even an arrest generally puts a quick end to the violence (Roberts and Roberts 2005). Research also shows that such police activity is likely to be effective when the couple is not living together, and in the early stages of a dating relationship. Restraining orders, however, are less effective for men who are unemployed and have less to lose through criminal justice involvement.

Protective restraining orders have the advantages of clearly spelling out what the boundaries are and providing for documentation to others (for example, the children's school) in the victim's life that this situation is serious and that care must be taken to protect the individual. These restraining orders can be tailored to the needs and situations of individual victims. Such orders can restrict the abuser from

- having contact with the children;
- continuing to live in the home;
- sending threatening email messages or telephone calls;
- purchasing or possessing firearms.

Often it takes a full-blown crisis and a tragedy to produce the momentum to get key legislation passed. This is what happened in Chicago recently when a 22-year-old woman was shot by a former boyfriend, whom she had a restraining order against. The perpetrator was on parole and killed himself after killing his girlfriend. Legislation was then drafted to require parole violations to be issued in any case in which a parolee is charged with a domestic violence crime or sex crime (Kozlov 2008). Similar legislation to restrict gun ownership by batterers is also essential.

Thanks to advances in the technologies available, the courts can monitor offenders' movements, prove any violations of court orders, and move in quickly to protect a possible victim. Surveillance cameras also can be used. The mere fact of knowing these devices are present has a deterrent effect on at least some potential violators. A man bent on murder, however, is extremely dangerous, and if he is suicidal as well, all these attempts to provide protection will be to no avail. This is where the woman's advocate or mental health professional needs to consult a danger assessment tool to gauge the risks that she faces. If a man has nothing to lose and is highly impulsive with a history of life-threatening activities, a defensive approach must be taken. Some women in such circumstances have chosen to assume new identities and move far away from home. Whatever her decision, the fact that she receives help from victims' advocates and perhaps from the criminal justice system, the victim knows at least that her fears are taken seriously, and that she is not alone.

The World Health Organization (2002, 113) views the benefits of prevention globally in a vision of a future in which violence is not only prevented, but where health for all is achieved:

> Both policy makers and activists in this field must give greater priority to the admittedly immense task of creating a social environment that allows and promotes equitable and non-violent personal relationships. The foundation for such an environment must be the new generation of children, who should come of age with better skills than their parents generally had for managing their relationships and resolving the conflicts within them, with greater opportunities for their future, and with more appropriate notions on how men and women can relate to each other and share power.

CONCLUSION

As is the case with disease, where the health care system's resources are primarily directed toward cures rather than prevention, domestic violence services devote the most attention to providing help for victims. Moreover, society tends to wait for a major, well-publicized crisis to occur before adopting appropriate policies directed toward the causes of the problem. Consider this recent headline, for example, from the *Boston Globe* (Baxter 2008, 1): "Domestic Violence Deaths Prompt Action." We learn from the article,

> Declaring that "we have a public health emergency on our hands," Governor Deval Patrick yesterday unveiled plans to combat an alarming increase in deaths related to domestic violence.
>
> Patrick, in issuing the first-ever public health advisory on the issue, announced his plans to bolster police training and ordered a statewide review to determine the cause of the increase.

The following statement from the *Boston Globe* article is significant as well:

> Specific causes of the rise in domestic-violence-related deaths are difficult to pinpoint, but economic anxiety and a lack of coordination among state agencies, the police, and community organizations have contributed to the problem, Patrick said. Several state offices will review the past three years of data to see if any trends emerge, he said.

A major emphasis in the harm reduction model, as informed by an emphasis on public health safety, is the coordination of services. Hopefully, the state of Massachusetts will work toward remedying this problem as mentioned in the article, and other states will learn from this example.

In the following chapter, we consider psychoeducational strategies that are directed at the perpetrators themselves—the batterers—and even more importantly, strategies directed at the community to teach principles and attitudes on nonviolence.

REFERENCES

Adams, D. 2007. *Why do they kill? Men who murder their intimate partners.* Nashville, TN: Vanderbilt University Press.

Bancroft, L. 2002. *Why does he do that?* New York: Putnam.

Baxter, C. 2008. Domestic violence deaths prompt action. *The Boston Globe,* June 8. http://www.boston.com/news/local/articles/2008/06/06/domestic_violence_deaths_prompt_action (accessed June 2008).

Black, B., and A. Weisz. 2005. Dating violence: A qualitative analysis of Mexican American youths' views. *Journal of Ethnic and Cultural Diversity in Social Work* 13, no. 3: 69–90.

Bossarte, R.M., T.R. Simon, and L. Barker. 2006. Characteristics of homicide followed by suicide incidents in multiple states, 2003–2004. *Injury Prevention* 12:33–38.

Campbell, J.C., D. Webster, J. Koziol-McLain, C. Block, D. Campbell, M.A. Curry, F. Gary, N. Glass, J. McFarlane, C. Sachs, P. Sharps, Y. Ulrich, S.A. Wilt, J. Manganello, X. Xu, J. Schollenberger, V. Frye, and K. Laughon. 2003. Risk factors for femicide in abusive relationships: Results from a multisite case control study. *American Journal of Public Health* 93, no. 7: 1089–97. http://www.ajph.org/cgi/content/abstract/93/7/1089.

Centers for Disease Control and Prevention (CDC). 2008. Surveillance for violent deaths. National Violent Death Reporting System, April 11. http://www.cdc.gov/mmwr/preview/mmwrhtml/ss5703a1.htm (accessed June 2008).

Family Violence Prevention Fund. 2008. Domestic violence is a serious, widespread social problem in America. www.endabuse.org/resources/facts (accessed June 2008).

Kozlov, Dana. 2008. Murder-suicide prompts domestic violence measure. *cbs2chicago.com,* April 11. http://cbs2chicago.com/local/domestic.violence.legsilation.2.698142.html (accessed June 2008).

Marcus, E. 2008. Screening for abuse may be key to ending it. *The New York Times,* May 20. http://www.nytimes.com/2008/05/20/health/20abus.html (accessed June 2008).

Miller, W.R., and S. Rollnick. 2002. *Motivational interviewing: Preparing people for change.* New York: Guilford Press.

North Carolina Department of Health and Human Services (DHHS). 2003. January 3. http://www.dhhs.state.nc.us/dss//dcdl/childrenservices/2003/CS-01-2003.pdf (accessed June 2008).

Roberts, A.R., and B.S. Roberts. 2005. *Ending intimate violence: Political guidance and survival strategies.* New York: Oxford University Press.

Straus, M.A. 1996. Identifying offenders in criminal justice research on domestic assault. In *Do arrests and restraining orders work?* ed. E.S. Buzawa and C.G. Buzawa, 14–29. Thousand Oaks, CA: SAGE.

U.S. Department of Health and Human Services. 2007. *Child maltreatment 2005.* April 2. http://www.acf.hhs.gov/programs/cb/pubs/cm05/summary.htm (accessed June 2008).

van Wormer, K., and C. Bartollas. 2007. *Women and the criminal justice system.* Boston: Allyn & Bacon.

Washington Times. 2008. "Tweens" in sexual, abusive relationships. February 14. www.washingtontimes.com/news/2008/feb/14 (accessed August 2008).

World Health Organization (WHO). 2002. WHO urges governments to take action to reduce violence against women. Geneva: WHO, November 22.http://www.who.int/mediacentre/news/releases/pr89/en/index.html (accessed June 2008).

World Health Organization. 2005. Landmark study on domestic violence. Geneva: WHO, November 24. http://www.who.int/mediacentre/news/releases/2005/pr62/en/index.html (accessed June 2008).

World Health Organization. 2006a. Intimate partner violence and alcohol. Geneva: WHO. http://www.who.int/violence_injury_prevention/violence/world_report/factsheets/ (accessed June 2008).

World Health Organization. 2006b. Report of the United Nations Secretary-General. In-depth study on all forms of violence against women. Geneva: WHO. http://daccessdds.un.org/doc/UNDOC/GEN/N06/419/74/PDF/N0641974.pdf?OpenElement (accessed August 2008).

World Health Organization. 2008. *Preventing violence and reducing its impact: How development agencies can help.* Geneva: WHO. http://whqlibdoc.who.int/publications/2008/9789241596589_eng.pdf (accessed August 2008).

11

Work with Dangerous Battering Men

As we learned from research gathered for Chapter 2 on risks for homicide, the most dangerous batterers are impaired in their thinking and incapable of forming healthy relationships. When their possessive behavior and violence (including coercive sex) cause their partners to pull away from them, they use whatever means of power they can to maintain the sick relationship to the extent of threatening to kill the partner if she tries to leave. Some of these men are psychopathic, antisocial, and probably not amenable to change that is more than surface deep. If we agree with Dutton (2007) that batterers in general are striking out against their partners because of a variety of factors such as issues related to early childhood paternal rejection, continual exposure to family abuse, and a failure of attachment, we need to direct interventions accordingly. Moreover, we need to realize that even in the most macho of men, there is perhaps a legacy of victimization and suffering. We need to help men in trouble with their violence work toward a goal of developing and maintaining healthy relationships. The first step of course would be to help motivate them to work toward such a goal. Failure to address the issues that underlie the violence, while focusing on beliefs about "male privilege" in a patriarchal society, is a failure with life-threatening consequences. We are talking here of violence that potentially destroys the lives of every member of the family, of the children growing up, and of the partner who may eventually be killed and of the perpetrator who may spend the rest of his life in prison or who may kill himself. Never has it been more urgent to discover empirically based principles of treatment to put a stop to the violence before it escalates.

This chapter begins with a review of precepts of the dominant approach to batterer treatment—the model based on feminist ideology of the Duluth Intervention school. Then we consider alternative approaches that are also consistent with feminism but that are empirically based. Our attention turns to teachings from the science of motivational enhancement and innovations in restorative justice. This chapter is written in the belief that treatment effectiveness rather than ideology is primary.

THE ORIGINS OF THE DULUTH MODEL OF BATTERER INTERVENTION

The Duluth, Minnesota, Domestic Abuse Intervention Project (DAIP) is based on a feminist culturally based paradigm that makes sense from the point of view of the victim/survivor. It was designed to be used by paraprofessionals to be applied to men who had assaulted their partners and who were not going to receive jail time (Dutton 2007). The DAIP clearly has been a revolutionary force in its creation of a coordinated community response to domestic violence. Since its inception in the late 1970s, this Minnesota group has become nationally recognized for successfully coordinating the efforts of communities on behalf of battered women in an effort to end domestic violence (Shepard and Pence 1999; van Wormer and Bednar 2002). The underlying premise is that violence is used by men in order to control women's behavior and reinforce male dominance. Its focus is therefore on reducing batterers' power over their victims, and teaching these men new relationship skills (Pence 1999).

In her review of the project's evolution, Ellen Pence (1999) commented on the changing philosophy of the program. She describes an ideological shift that moved professionals from their early emphasis on psychological explanations for violence toward the notion that power and control were the underlying motivation for battering. According to Pence, the DAIP staff believed their analysis to be based on neutral observation, while in fact they remained blind to the discrepancy between their theory and the actual experiences of the men and women with whom they worked. While staff persisted in explaining the underlying power motive, few men seemed to identify with the explanation. Male batterers in treatment, who so often see themselves as victims rather than victimizers—victims of the system, of the mass media, and of their partners—could be expected to resist many of the precepts of this model. In addition, attempts to explain the violence of men who were appalled by their own actions, the unilateral violence by women against men, and the existence of lesbian violence further undermined the theory that violence was solely a tool of male control. Pence expressed her hope that the DAIP in the future would come to adopt a more multidimensional framework.

Another, more recent historical reminiscence is provided by Daniel Sonkin (2006). As a pioneer in providing treatment to men in trouble for assaulting their partners, Sonkin experienced the development of batterer education from the ground up. In the early days, as he informs us, shelters for women were not concerned with treatment for men; their focus was solely on services for women. Sonkin himself during the late 1970s took the initiative of having crisis calls by battering men referred to him and eventually offering first couples counseling and then specialized treatment groups for batterers. As Sonkin recalls, the 1980s brought counseling services for battering men at mental health centers and on military bases. Gradually, it was realized that partner abuse would never end through counseling the victim alone and helping her to leave the situation. Work also had to be directed at the source of the problem—the perpetrators—and to help change their behavior. Otherwise, the men would just be free to enter into another violent relationship. But the question remained: What would the focus of the treatment be? Treatment advocates were divided into various camps— family systems therapists, mental health professionals who took a cognitive-behavioral approach, and feminist peer counselors—each one as dogmatic as the other. Debates and infighting ensued; the disputes that went on were uninformed by empirical research to support any group's claim to superiority.

Two additional developments of the 1980s were federal legislation to provide funding for treatment programming on the local level and involvement of the criminal justice system to aggressively pursue domestic violence cases. The feminist forces rather than the mental health professionals played a major role in rewriting the laws. In California, in the 1990s, for example, a law was passed spelling out the type and length of treatment perpetrators must complete if they are to avoid serving a jail term. Only programs offering group counseling can be certified by local probation departments; couples and family counseling is forbidden; and providers can be peer counselors as well as professionally trained therapists. The dominant theoretical framework that guides certification is that domestic violence stems from sexist and patriarchal beliefs in the society; violence against women is seen as tacitly accepted by the culture. This acceptance of male-on-female violence is indeed true in many parts of the world (see Chapter 7) but United States' national surveys indicate otherwise (Simon et al. 2001). In fact, there is more acceptance of women hitting men than vice versa. The problem of battering from this perspective is male socialization in the patriarchal society, an exclusively sociopolitical explanation. Sonkin finds the passing of such legislation worrisome in that it inhibits treatment providers from developing new and innovative approaches. The problem of battering is too complex, as he suggests, for simplistic, restrictive solutions.

In a telephone conference of February 21, 2006, between the Duluth model training coordinators Michelle Johnson and her associate and van Wormer, the coordinators described their philosophy regarding use of the Wheel. It is not sanctioned by DAIP, they stated, to adapt the Wheel for gender-neutral treatment; some were doing this by removing the term *male privilege*. But the Wheel refers specifically to male-generated violence; it therefore is not to be used in gay/lesbian situations, for example. Permission can be granted for publication of the Power and Control Wheel only if the author's writing reflected the mission of the DAIP so the writing on domestic violence would have to be submitted in advance. "We believe," as Johnson stated, "that the cause of domestic violence is the patriarchy." To summarize the rest of the conversation in a nutshell: The DAIP spokespersons said that permission to use the Wheel would not be given for a book that used a holistic approach to domestic violence because there was only one reason for such violence that could be considered.

Let us clarify at this point that we endorse a feminist, gender-based treatment model, not just one geared toward batterers and their victims but as a strengths-based empowerment model as used by many therapists. Further, we whole-heartedly agree with writers such as Jackson Katz (2006), author of *The Macho Paradox,* that the mistreatment of women is a pervasive characteristic of our patriarchal society and that we need a far-reaching cultural revolution to keep men from hurting women. We are pleased to learn that, as of this writing the U.S. Senate voted to increase funding for programs under the Violence Against Women Act (VAWA) as reported by the *Feminist Daily News* (2008). This amendment that was introduced by Senator Joseph Biden is to increase funding by $100 million, funding that would have been seriously cut by the Bush administration. Our hope would be in the future that VAWA, unlike in the past, would not be guided by a single model of batterer programming in recognition of the fact that this model may not relate to everyone or even to the majority of batterers. Violence in intimate relationships has many complex causes and varies by the individual case.

DULUTH MODEL EDUCATIONAL GROUPS FOR MEN WHO BATTER

There are many strong points of the standard Duluth intervention model. The community intervention projects as described by Pence and Shepard (1999, 16) are organized around eight key components:

1. Creating a coherent philosophical approach centralizing victim safety.
2. Developing "best practice" policies and protocols for intervention agencies that are part of an integrated response.
3. Enhancing networking among service providers.
4. Building monitoring and tracking into the system.
5. Ensuring a supportive community infrastructure for battered women.
6. Providing sanctions and rehabilitation opportunities for abusers.
7. Undoing the harm violence to women does to children.
8. Evaluating the coordinated community response from the standpoint of victim safety.

Many of the skills that are taught by adherents to the Duluth intervention model are the same as those taught to group members in other programs, such as at substance abuse treatment centers. These are cognitive approaches to handling irrational thoughts, communication skills, and assertiveness training. One failing of this approach, as Dutton (2007) suggests, is in its neglect of the therapeutic relationship, a vital requisite to treatment effectiveness. The building of rapport with group members is impeded by the use of shaming strategies to get the offenders to acknowledge their use of male privilege and power games in interaction with their partners.

The standard Duluth curriculum for batterer education is built around the basic concepts as revealed in the Power and Control Wheel (see Chapter 5, Figure 5.1). This teaching aid, which was created with the input of 200 battered women, illustrates their perceptions of the dynamics of abuse in their relationships (van Wormer and Bednar 2002). The cogs of the wheel describe methods used by abusive men, in addition to or instead of physical violence, to maintain power and control in the relationship. These methods are coercion and threats, intimidation, emotional abuse, isolation, minimizing, denying and blaming, using children, using male privilege, and economic abuse. Over the course of a 26-week program, participants are challenged to identify their controlling behaviors from the Wheel, replacing them with more respectful behaviors taken from a complementary teaching aid, the Equality Wheel. The cogs of the Equality Wheel describe methods of negotiation and fairness, nonthreatening behavior, respect, trust and support, honesty and accountability, responsible parenting, shared responsibility, and economic partnership (Pence and Paymar 1993). Using techniques such as control logs, action plans, videos, role playing, and group exercises, the Duluth model focuses on the use of violence by a batterer to establish power and control over his partner (Miller, Gregory, and Iovanni 2005). Even though the diversity in the offenders' backgrounds is acknowledged, facilitators are advised to avoid getting sidetracked by discussion of personal problems and to maintain a continuous focus on power and control tactics, and methods for changing them. The intent to control is presumed to be present in all participants, and denial and minimization are expected behaviors. The facilitators, therefore, must be prepared to engage in frequent and possibly almost continuous confrontation (Pence and Paymar 1993). Miller et al., however, report that as men reject some of the required topics outright—for example, sexism and homophobia—facilitators observed by these researchers glossed over them and focused on more tangible problems such as substance abuse. These authors curiously would like to see more rather than less confrontation of the men as required by the model.

State standards and requirements for government grant funding typically follow the teachings of the Duluth model. The below sidebar includes an excerpt from a talk given by Kenneth Hudson, a co-facilitator of the Waterloo (Iowa) Batterers Educational Project, in which he describes a typical Iowa intervention that was being conducted during the spring of 2008.

CO-FACILITATING A BATTERERS' EDUCATION GROUP

Kenneth Hudson

When an individual is found guilty of domestic abuse, the Code of Iowa requires the presiding judge to sentence the offender to the Batterers' Education Program (BEP). The Department of Correctional Services is solely responsible for the BEP program throughout Iowa. In most areas of Iowa, BEP consists of 24 weekly sessions. Each session is two hours long. The abuser is required to pay for the program and attend every BEP group session until completion. If the abuser violates the rules of the program, the judge may sentence him to jail.

The Batterer's Education Program's main objective is to teach offenders how to have fulfilling relationships without the use of coercion, manipulation, intimidation, and violence. The success or failure of each offender rests squarely upon the shoulders of that individual. Some offenders are receptive to the program and have a sincere desire to change their abusive behavior. Regrettably, some are not, and they may discontinue being physically violent but will augment their intimidating, manipulating, and threatening behavior. And then, there are others, who have no intention of stopping their violent and abusive behavior, and simply try to "skate" through the program to avoid incarceration.

For an abuser with a habitual history of abusive and violent behavior, long-term change is a continuous process that usually occurs over a number of years. BEP is just the initial step on an abuser's journey towards nonviolence. The batterer must be vigilantly committed to change and fervently willing to do the necessary work to achieve that goal.

I teach the Batterer's Education Program in northeast Iowa. My background is in law enforcement. I'm presently working toward a degree in social work and a certificate in substance abuse counseling. We have seven classes designated for male offenders and two designated for female offenders. Each session is co-facilitated by two people—one female and one male. This is highly necessary to give abusers a balanced and dual-gendered perspective on the frequently life-ending results of domestic violence, and the overall debilitating effect it has on victims and families.

In our group, we try to stress open dialogue, to encourage the men to speak freely so they can work on their issues and learn that violence is wrong. If they don't realize violence is wrong, we are not doing our job. We discuss male stereotypes; how boys are not allowed to cry. We talk about name calling and negative labels such as sissy. The men first come in and refuse to participate, but they have to or it's a violation. My style is confrontation. I'm not here to pamper them. We do not allow jokes about women or gays. They can be kicked out for not cooperating. On the flip side, I let them know I'm here to help them.

We have BEP participants of all ages and from various socioeconomic levels. Our classes are normally composed of individuals from various racial, ethnic, and cultural groups. Occasionally, interpreters are utilized to translate the curriculum to non-English speaking participants.

Initially, most offenders are very angry during their first several sessions in BEP. Recently, an abuser in class threatened two facilitators. Police immediately arrested that individual. Offenders must adhere to BEP policy and openly state what they did to get them into BEP, and their statement must corroborate with the court record. Occasionally, we have to employ corrective measures to maintain control of group sessions. This could include a verbal admonishment, issuance of a "violation" into their file, or expulsion from the class entirely.

Either way, their behavior in class is documented and the presiding judge is privy to said behavior at their next court appearance.

In BEP, we focus on the abuser's actions and behavior only. We are not concerned with the actions of their victim(s), or the details that lead them to their decision to be abusive. It is our responsibility as facilitators to disseminate the BEP curriculum in an effective, thought-provoking manner. One of our goals is to challenge abusers' belief systems and give them various methods and strategies to peacefully resolve disagreements and confrontations without becoming abusive.

During class, we use role reversal scenarios and focus on peaceful alternatives to resolving disputes. We also utilize various training videos and exercises to promote positive interactions. We discuss male privilege in depth, and the Power and Control Wheel extensively. We encourage thoughtful, reflective discussion. The Equality Wheel is utilized and referred to copiously. Adherence to a belief system of honesty and accountability is meticulously interwoven throughout class discussions. Oftentimes, abusers will challenge one another's statements and belief systems during class. This encourages participants to get feedback from their classmates, and it precipitates a more focused "open" dialogue. It also serves as a catalyst to "real talk"—a time during group discussion in which there is a combined consensus on the qualities of nonviolence and the merits of living one's life honorably, equitably, and peacefully.

Overall, I enjoy facilitating BEP classes. It has given me an opportunity to proactively combat domestic violence. It has been instrumental in my professional and personal growth. It has also given me an opportunity to hone my social work skills, and hopefully, encourage other men to take a stand against domestic violence.

(Unpublished paper. Printed with permission of Kenneth Hudson, August 6, 2008.)

PERSONAL TESTIMONIALS FROM TREATMENT PROVIDERS

Both firsthand testimonials by people who have used the Duluth intervention formulation and empirically based studies, some using control groups, raise questions about the efficacy of the one-size-fits-all model. Ellen Pence (1999, 29), for example, one of the founders and leading advocates of this approach, now acknowledges its limitations:

> By determining that the need or desire for power was the motivating force behind battering, we created a conceptual framework that, in fact, did not fit the lived experience of many of the men and women we were working with...I found that many of the men I interviewed did not seem to articulate a desire for power over their partners.

Susan Bednar (2001), a professional social worker who was the sole facilitator of a court-mandated group for batterers, faced numerous problems in establishing rapport. The men in the group viewed themselves as victims and were resistant to treatment as focused on the Power and Control Wheel. Bednar (2001) discovered the drawbacks from the standard feminist-based intervention model the hard way:

> The men felt victimized in a multitude of ways. From their perspective: Their partners had been violent or emotionally abusive; the police had been brutal and the system corrupt; being arrested and jailed was humiliating and the label of "batterer" a personal affront. These men didn't see themselves as dominating others, but wanted to be able to control their own lives. Everything and everybody around them seemed determined to take that control away from them. Often this process seemed to start in their own childhoods, when they themselves were abused, or when they witnessed their fathers abuse their mothers. No one protected them then, and they learned to protect themselves. The only feeling stated they described besides "angry" were things like "kind of OK," or "all right, I guess." Nearly all had a history of substance abuse, and many perceived this as part of their problem.

In her efforts to reach the men, Bednar (2001, 174-75), as a professional social worker, found herself relying more and more on a positive, strengths-based approach:

> Help arrived in the form of another paradigm. Initially an exercise in applying social constructionist theory to a problem which was familiar to me, I blundered through how I might view this situation from a perspective that views reality itself as negotiated. Terrifying at first, it required me to leave any preconceived notions behind. I could not decide ahead of time what "reality" was. I would have to work it out with my clients.
>
> I started by joining the men in writing their individualized action plans. My own action plan consisted of brainstorming about how I might use the Duluth Model while still permitting multiple perspectives, validating the other person's point of view, encouraging collaboration and moral deliberation, and encouraging the generation of alternatives that were not my own or those of the model. The model was one voice at the negotiating table. Now there would be others as well.

Bednar's shift to a more flexible approach paid off, and she was able to move the treatment forward once she developed rapport with the men. Although obtaining power and control may appear to be the intent of the batterer, it is unlikely that he himself defines the situation in this manner. By disregarding, or failing to take into account the batterer's own view of reality which may differ from ours and include a multitude of contributing factors, we may actually be creating the resistance that is generally seen as endemic to this population, thereby lowering our probability of success. Sensitivity to, and understanding of, the perceptions of batterers is badly needed if we are to effectively reach these potentially dangerous men.

STUDIES OF TREATMENT EFFECTIVENESS

A recent article in the *Journal of the American Medical Association* (JAMA) by Stuart, Temple, and Moore (2007) on the research effectiveness of batterer education programming states that the treatment results are discouraging. Their recommendation is for further development of the model based on empirical research. Unlike other areas of counseling and therapy, which have developed and improved over time as new strategies and approaches have been tried, the batterers' educational programming has remained fairly static since the beginning. Contrast this with the substance abuse field, for example, where there has been a gradual movement away from use of a cult-like, confrontational style geared to break client denial to a more individualized, motivational approach. A major impetus for change, admittedly, was the requirement from third party payers that treatment be professionalized and of proven effectiveness.

A male leader of a batterers' education group for parolees, who was interviewed anonymously for this book by van Wormer, describes his approach as follows:

> Our goal is to help the men change their way of thinking about women and violence. When they first come, they check in. The individual states what he did, such as choking his partner or burning her with cigarettes. I receive the paperwork and read the arrest report. Then I see if the man's statement about his offense jibes with the report. If he says it was all a mistake, we pounce on him. Also if the men blame their wives, such as saying, "she pushed my buttons," we don't want to hear that, not what she did.
>
> All cases don't involve wives or partners. One is in the program for threatening his mother; he was convicted of this. We have had brother against brother, one father and son in the same batterers' education class.
>
> Some facilitators of the other groups only do the curriculum. They avoid any counseling or real work at a deep level. They don't get the men to work on their thinking and feelings related to their violence.
>
> In our group, I have seen some real changes in people. One man told us of his abusive childhood, how he became violent and stabbed a guy 18 times who had laughed at him. He served 10 years in prison. Today he is on medication, and it appears he is making progress. Another man, a biker type and unemployed, was in his 22nd session. He went to Kroger's (grocery store) and another man bumped into him with a cart. He later told me, "If I wasn't in your class, I would have ripped the guy apart."

One can expect that the funding sources for batterer intervention programs will likewise stress accountability, especially since public funding is involved. As long as the programs fail to get impressive results, they are vulnerable to budget cutbacks; pressures for evidence of success, therefore, can be expected to intensify.

Research on treatment effectiveness generally relies on a comparison of modalities that are easily distinguishable from each other. Ideally, there is a control group which receives no treatment. In the field of domestic violence services, an experimental design would have to be set up with group facilitators providing relatively pure forms of the modalities for which they were trained to deliver. In actual practice, there is considerable overlap, for example, between the cognitive-behavioral treatment (CBT) approach and the feminist focus on male privilege. Most programs use blended theoretical techniques. A second complicating factor in measuring treatment success concerns program completion. Since on average, 50 percent of the batterer group participants never complete the program, one gets inflated figures when only the program completers are considered for evaluation (Bennett 2008). When you calculate recidivism rates based on the minority of men who complete the program, you get an artificially low rate of recidivism.

Based on the available research literature on batterer treatment, let us consider the findings concerning what works. Lest our expectations be too high to be realistic, there are certain factors we need to take into account in working with court ordered battering men. First, as we know, battering men are resistant to treatment. The fact that they are mandated to intervention, often, as they believe, unfairly because of "lies" told to the police by their partners or because the violence was mutual, makes it difficult to engage them in the counseling process (Stuart et al. 2007). Other reasons we should anticipate only modest effects from batterer interventions include the frequency in this population of social factors such as poverty and unemployment, untreated substance abuse and mental disorders, and a cultural mismatch between client and group facilitators (see Bennett et al. 2007).

Melanie Shepard (1993) reported on a DAIP evaluation study that measured changes in abusive behavior both during participation in the program and at one-year follow-up. As reported by the women during both these time periods, the results were highly encouraging. In a later follow-up examination of police and court records, however, a different picture emerges: Of the 100 men studied, 40 percent had been arrested for domestic assault, or had been subject to an order of protection because of domestic assault. Although the program appears to have a short-term impact on the rates of abuse, the long-term recidivism rate is disturbing. The significance of this study is in warning us against forming conclusions about a program's success within too short a period of time. Tineke Ritmeister (1993) reported on an impact survey of 76 shelters for battered women. Although 55 percent of shelters responding to the survey reported noticing a decrease in violence as a result of the batterers' groups, a staggering 88 percent of the shelters perceived that the batterers' programs either had no decrease in emotional violence or discovered ways to control the woman through use of more sophisticated psychological techniques. This apparent transition from physical to emotional abuse is disturbing.

We now will consider two larger-scale and more recent examples from the developing literature on batterer intervention, one more encouraging than the other. In the first research study that we have chosen, Babcock, Green, and Robie (2004) conducted a meta-analysis of 22 batterer intervention studies that included both CBT and feminist-oriented formats. They found that the effectiveness as measured by rearrests of the men was low regardless of the theoretical framework used. They concluded that the recidivism of men who were arrested and not sentenced to treatment was about the same as for men who were arrested and referred to treatment. When treatment fails so consistently, not only is batterers' programming a waste of time and resources, but the impact on victims may be profound. Because of such programming, many of the victims decide to remain with their husbands in the belief that the treatment will end the violence. In fact, according to Bennett (2008), having a batterer placed in counseling is one of the strongest predictors that a woman will leave a domestic violence shelter to give him a second chance. For this reason, some victim advocates and policy makers are justifiably concerned that the court mandates to counseling might hold out a false promise of safety under high-risk circumstances.

Bennett et al. (2007) found more favorable results in their large-scale study of a sample of 899 men who were assigned to a community-based intervention for battering. The 30 programs in the study had similar treatment modalities. The purpose of the study was to compare those who completed the program with those who dropped out. They found that men who completed batterers' intervention programs were less than half as likely to be arrested for later domestic violence as men who did not complete the program. At 2.4 years following intake, only around 14 percent of those who completed the program and 35 percent of non-completers were rearrested for domestic violence. The results are encouraging. The researchers concluded that around 20 percent or one in five of the men was deterred from committing another act of reported violence due to participation in a batterer education program. Factors that were correlated with program completion were motivation to change, employment, being married, and interestingly, Latino ethnicity. Improvements in batterer programming, according to Bennett et al., such as working to enhance participants' motivation to change should keep men in the program longer, thus having positive effects on their recidivism as well.

Stuart et al. call for systematic, theoretically based, empirical research to determine what works with batterers sentenced to treatment. They suggest that conjoint couples counseling be considered in cases where the violence is mutual rather than one-sided. They strongly endorse that motivational techniques, which are of proven effectiveness with other involuntary clients, be employed here. Treatment interventions, as they further suggest, should be tailored to types of violent men, and substance abuse treatment included where needed. One study by Jones and Gondolf (2001) showed that the probability of violence recidivism could be reduced significantly—by 30–40 percent—if the individual obtained treatment for substance abuse problems. We agree with Bennett et al. (2007), Dutton (2007), and Stuart et al. (2007) that batterer intervention can be improved. A model that is monolithic and overly prescriptive and proscriptive lends itself to criticism. We believe that it could be significantly improved with an incorporation of techniques and strategies that are of proven effectiveness. The first step, therefore, would be to get such proof.

ALTERNATIVE TREATMENT APPROACHES

The best predictive factor for a successful outcome from therapy is the strength of the relationship that can be established between the group leader or therapist and the client. As a change agent, the therapist must first start where the client or group member is. This is a principle of any effective group leadership; an outsider cannot take over with ideas that conflict with the group culture. So in working with violent and potentially dangerous men who are likely to view themselves not as abusers of women but as victims and to even feel hostility toward women, the starting point is to reach them where they are. Common sense would tell us that a focus on male privilege and power in the society or in the home would be met with resistance. Only when the men become motivated to work on their problems and to change will they be ready to let go of some of their rigid, controlling attitudes and behavior. With the risk of homicide a major concern in battering relationships, we need to look to science rather than ideology and adopt practices of proven effectiveness. Admittedly, research on the effectiveness of batterer intervention programs is still in the early stages. To best determine what works, therefore, we must be open to innovation.

Various treatment intervention types other than the Duluth-inspired model have been developed. At the individual level, pharmaceutical and cognitive approaches have been applied. At the macro or societal level, prevention efforts are proliferating in schools and universities; the focus is on training men to be mentors on the campus. Workshops are provided with the aim of preventing violence against women through teaching men what it means to be a "real man."

Treatment interventions need to be aimed at all these levels for widespread change in a violence-prone society. To understand the dynamics of male-on-female violence, we need to consider biological as well as cognitive and social-psychological influences. A holistic approach to battering, such as the one recommended here, links intrapsychic deficits—a hypersensitivity to abandonment, inability to control negative emotions, and poor impulse control—with biological conditions such as low serotonin levels in the brain, high testosterone production, and brain damage from head injury. We also recognize cultural contributions such as traditional gender-role and machismo attitudes.

Biologically Based Interventions

Biologically, the tendency toward antisocial, risk-taking, and impulsive behavior may play a role in the development of both substance abuse and violence. Studies link low serotonin in the brain to both aggression and addiction, as well as to a host of other behaviors, such as obsession, depression, hyper-reactivity, and pathological anxiety (Dutton, 2007; van Wormer and Bartollas 2007). Also keep in mind, as was discussed in Chapters 2 and 4, that illicit drugs and alcohol are closely associated with violent outbursts in violence-prone men. Bennett et. al (2007) have found, in fact, that for battering men, the best predictor of re-assault in any follow-up period was drunkenness. For this reason, substance abuse treatment is essential right from the start. We agree with Bennett and his colleagues who recommend an integrated substance abuse/batterer intervention program; such programming has been found to be more successful than traditional serial or parallel interventions for engaging offenders in treatment and in reducing rearrest at follow-up.

Further, the intervention modality that we favor—motivational interviewing—is of proven effectiveness with clients who are angry and who have substance abuse problems (Roffman et al. 2008).

Cognitive Modalities Including Motivational Enhancement

This brings us to a consideration of cognitive treatment modalities, such as motivational interviewing, which is widely recognized as an approach that is directed at the client's cognitions in order to elicit change. Other models direct their attention to the client mind-set and work to replace unhealthy thinking patterns with more functional ones.

But before we discuss the specifics of cognitive-based intervention, let us consider the psychology of battering and review research that was described in Chapter 2.

Research summarized by Marano (1993) and Dutton (2007) gives us some insight into how irrational responses to their partners' relationships with other people can breed violent outbursts. A research design presented a series of scenarios of potentially jealousy-provoking situations to two groups of men—men with a history of violence and men without such a history. The difference in responses was pronounced: the batterers tended to misinterpret the wives' motives in the scenario as intentionally hostile. The other men in the comparison group did not feel personally threatened by the scenarios. This experiment confirms what psychologists tell us about abusive men and their underlying insecurities, their intense dependence on their partners, and their tendency to "fly off the handle" when the women in their lives begin to pursue new interests or make new friends. Their own overdependence on their spouses may cause these men to resent, hate, and sometimes even kill them. If substance abuse is involved, of course, thinking becomes even more clouded; drunks are notoriously irrational. Treatment for such men, once they have obtained sobriety, may involve helping them to see that as long as they give their spouses undue power over their emotions and behavior, the abuse is likely to continue.

The treatment challenge is to help clients develop some insight into the thinking-feeling nexus and to develop healthier ways of regarding themselves and of relating to the world. Hopefully, in gaining insight, they ultimately might come to realize that as long as they give their partners such undue power over their emotions, their resentment and anger will continue to fester. The teaching of empathy is another treatment task that is important so the men can appreciate how their controlling behavior is experienced by the other person.

Changing the thinking to change the feelings to change the behavior is a major theme that transcends diverse approaches. Because the effectiveness of cognitive approaches is widely recognized by the mental health professions, whenever mental health professionals are involved in facilitating batterer intervention groups or in providing individual therapy to men with a history of domestic violence, they will closely attend to the client's explanations and mind-set. Even the standard batterer intervention model in the United States, according to Bennett (2008), has incorporated cognitive techniques into its psycho-educational program. Motivational interviewing places even more emphasis on attending to the client's thought processes. This approach is built on basic principles from the teachings of social psychology in the art and science of persuasion—influencing people to do things they would not do ordinarily. These same truths have now been adapted to the treatment milieu and are being used to reinforce people in their giving up of practices that are self-destructive. The scientific basis of this treatment modality distinguishes it from others that have gone before, and from programming in which the politics takes precedence over science.

The basic rules of motivational enhancement therapy, as spelled out by Miller and Rollnick (2002), are as follows:

1. Express empathy.
2. Develop discrepancy between one's statements (for example, "I want to get closer to my wife") and one's behavior.
3. Avoid argumentation. The more a person states his or her position, the more he or she is committed to believing it.
4. Roll with resistance. Emphasize the client's decision to change is a choice.
5. Support self-efficacy and hope that the client has the ability to take the desired steps toward change.

As the reader undoubtedly will note, these principles are in sharp contrast to those that inform the Duluth batterer intervention program. The Duluth program proponents rely on argumentation and group pressure to convince batterers that their use of violence is an expression of male privilege that has been learned in a patriarchal society (Pence 1999). The starting point of the motivational approach, in contrast, is in establishing rapport with the client.

One major advantage of motivational treatment is that it specifies strategies of demonstrated effectiveness when geared toward the client's readiness to change—whether this is the precontemplation stage (strong resistance to change), contemplation stage, or action stage. Central to this whole treatment strategy is the belief that clients are amenable to change and that timing is crucial in persuading clients to take the steps that will free them from harm. (For details on this modality, see Miller and Rollnick 2002, and van Wormer and Davis 2008.)

In her research on the use of the motivational or "transtheoretical" model, Scott (2004) categorized battering men in treatment into precontemplators, contemplators, and participants at the action stage. She found, not surprisingly, that the precontemplators were 2.3 times as likely as contemplators to drop out and almost 9 times as likely as those at the action stage to drop out. This finding is important because program completion is positively associated with a low-rearrest rate for violence. Thus, as Scott concludes, interventions aimed at increasing client motivation can be highly effective.

Roffman et al. (2008) have come up with an excellent idea for enhancing motivation and preventing violence. In addition to working with men after they have been court ordered into treatment, these researchers have devised a strategy that is directed at people with violent tendencies who might be reached through a media campaign to provide "checkups" to see if they need treatment. The checkup is a variant of motivational enhancement therapy that is tailored for the nontreatment seeker, with the intention of eliciting voluntary participation in a "taking stock" experience. Checkups can be provided after screening for risk factors, according to Roffman et al., or can be freestanding with participants invited through public announcements. The results are not in yet, but a federally funded telephone-delivered intervention designed to motivate substance abusing male batterers into action—to self-refer into domestic violence and/or substance abuse treatment—shows some promise. Predictions are that such early voluntary enrollment is likely to be the prevention of injury and abuse that otherwise would continue until arrest and adjudication followed.

SOME ADDITIONAL ALTERNATIVE INTERVENTION DESIGNS
Restorative Justice

Chapter 8 discussed restorative justice as a nonadversarial approach to justice, influenced by indigenous methods of settling disputes. This approach is widely used in New Zealand and Canada, especially in work with juveniles, but it is also applied to family members in situations of domestic violence. Restorative justice stresses the involvement of three parties: the victim, the offender, and the community that have been affected by the crime (Zehr 2002). Ideally, through direct participation by each of these parties in the resolution process, the needs of all may be addressed. The purpose of the conferencing that takes place is to enforce cultural norms against violence and to indicate to the batterer that the community is there to help but also to make it clear that the violence must end. In the Intimate Abuse Circles for restorative justice, the offender apologizes to the victim and the community (Dutton 2007). The aim of such conferencing is to right the wrong that has been committed, and to restore the balance in a relationship or in society. The ultimate focus is on restoring the offender to the community rather than on simple punishment. A growing interest in restorative justice has been sparked, in part, by the crime victims' movement and, in part, by the growth of community conflict resolution programs (Viano 2000).

Feminist researcher Mary Koss (2000) advocates what she terms "communitarian justice," a promising new model in its victim-sensitive orientation. Such methods are apt to be effective, notes Koss, because they draw on sanctions abusive men fear most: family stigma and broad social disapproval. Such conferencing, as Koss further indicates, is recommended for young offenders without extensive histories of violence. Offenders who have a personality disorder such as antisocial personality would be screened from participation in such a process. More commonly, restorative justice relevant to domestic violence often takes the form of teaching empathy by having a crime victims' panel—a group of survivors of domestic violence who tell their stories and relate what it feels like to be violently victimized by one's spouse or partner. In hearing the stories of pain and suffering that the crimes of violence engendered, those offenders who can be reached will not only feel for the victims as people who were hurt by the careless or cruel behavior of others, but often they will get in tune with their own past victimization. Getting in touch with their own feelings may help prepare them for greater sensitivity to the feelings of others. In short, two themes—offender accountability and the empowerment of crime victims—ideally come together in the victim/offender initiatives. Just as offenders, in these encounters, see the human face of victims, so the survivors come to see the human face of offenders.

A Spiritually Based Restorative Approach

Excellent results are reported by Ronel and Tim (2003), who applied a restorative approach with a strong spiritual component to treatment of violent men referred from the Israeli courts. A major treatment goal was to increase the batterers' motivation to shift from an egocentric outlook to an empathic view of others. In contrast to a group process in which male batterers are seen as the "enemy," the emphasis here is on caring relationships to draw men closer to the prevailing society rather than alienating them from it. The goal of this program is abstinence from situations such as irrational thinking and arguing that might lead to violence, ultimately resulting in recovery and regaining of self-respect. According to the authors, hundreds of abusive men have gone through this spiritually based program. A remarkable aspect is the defusing of client resistance through the offering of unconditional love. Unfortunately, reports of success with this method are anecdotal; no experimental research of treatment effectiveness has been provided.

OUR HARM REDUCTION PREVENTION MODEL

Harm reduction employs a public health perspective to social problems and employs a wide variety of methods and intervention strategies to reduce and prevent harm. Since domestic violence including domestic homicide is a public health problem, a harm reduction model is not only relevant but essential to its prevention. Such a model is first and foremost pragmatic; it has individual as well as societal components.

In their essay on the concept of public health, Hammond et al. (2006) make a number of points that we can apply to the prevention of domestic homicide. Central to this model is a commitment to the identification of policies and programs aimed at the total society. To reduce violence, for example, the focus is placed on the social, behavioral, and environmental factors that are known to lead to violence. Second, the development of policies and programs for preventing violence must be grounded in science, and this must be a multidisciplinary, empirically based effort. The third and related principle of the public health perspective is that it provides a means for looking at violence that seeks to transcend existing bureaucratic or disciplinary boundaries that have impeded progress toward finding effective solutions in the past. This approach is in contrast to traditional responses to violence that have been fragmented along disciplinary lines and narrowly focused on the criminal justice sector.

Hammond et al. emphasize the importance of primary prevention, or of preventing a problem before it starts. Instead of focusing on healing individuals who have been injured, primary prevention takes place at the societal level and is proactive rather than reactive. The focus is two-pronged: as an educational campaign, it is aimed at both potential perpetrators and at everyone else—potential victims who need to be taught to recognize the signs. Consider dating violence among United States' high school students, for example. One in five teenage girls experiences such violence (Heisterkamp 2008). From a harm reduction perspective, the need is for educational programming, starting at the junior high or middle school levels, to help youths learn the qualities of a healthy relationship and an awareness of traits such as jealousy and possessiveness that might be warning signs of pending violence.

Fortunately, violence prevention programming has begun to make headway in schools across the United States. Funded through grants from the Waitt Institute for Violence Project, the "Mentors in Violence Prevention" is described by one of its spokespersons, Alan Heisterkamp. A former high school principal in Iowa and a well-known proponent of the school-based violence prevention curriculum, Heisterkamp believes that much can be done to end gender violence through peer group training in the schools. Parent education is also important. Speaking before a college student and faculty audience in Iowa, Heisterkamp (2008) articulated the idea behind his program: "We can prepare women to avoid unhealthy relationships," he said, "but we need to have a conversation with boys and men about being 'real men.'" Empowering student leaders and athletes to mentor and educate younger students, older boys working with younger boys and girls with girls, the school mentoring program operates campuswide. The heart of the training consists of role playing intended to allow students to constructively respond to incidents of harassment, abuse, or violence before, during, or after the fact. School leaders are taught to be aware of media sex stereotypes, of the sexism involved in the use of negative terms to refer to girls and women, and of other instances of sexual harassment. Training is given in taking the role of an active bystander and defusing potentially violent situations. In middle school the emphasis from the school's perspective is on bully-proofing the school.

Harm reduction at the secondary level is aimed at high-risk populations such as battered women who come to the emergency room for treatment and men who have alcohol and other drug problems (especially cocaine and methamphetamine) such as are associated with violence. Screening for violence-related problems should be routine in substance abuse work. Families that come to the attention of the Department of Human Services for child abuse fit under this category and should be screened for wife-partner violence as well.

Tertiary level prevention consists of treatment that takes place after the problem (such as a disease or problematic behavior) has been identified. The goal here is to prevent a reoccurrence of the problem, which is the violence, and to prevent the violence from escalating further. Most of the current funding and efforts to combat intimate partner violence focus on reducing victims' risk for future violence or ameliorating the effects of past abuse (Hammond et al. 2006). We need to invest an equal amount of money and other resources on the men who are causing the problem.

To summarize the major arguments of this chapter, interventions with battering men, to be effective, need to be holistic, directed at each aspect of the biopsychosocial model of human behavior. Interventions aimed at the biological level may include a referral to a substance abuse treatment center, to a self-help group such as Alcoholics Anonymous or Narcotics Anonymous, or to a mental health center for a psychiatric evaluation. An integrated treatment design shaped by motivational strategies would be relevant both to substance abuse problems and domestic violence.

Psychologically, the cornerstone of treatment is an understanding of the roots of violence in battering men in general and of each individual person who communicates through the use of such violence. Proven psychological strategies are employed to enhance the batterer's motivation for working on issues that he has probably never addressed. In hopes of changing his behavior, therapeutic attention is directed toward the replacement of irrational beliefs (such as "I can't live without her") with healthier thinking patterns (for example, "I am an independent person; my wife is an independent person").

Court-certified programming should allow for a variety of approaches tailored to individual need and after screening for readiness to change. Approaches might include anger management, substance abuse and mental health treatments, individual therapy focused on early childhood victimization issues, and possibly some interventions at the family and community levels. A typical goal might be to help men abandon their egocentric world view as they learn to tap into their own inner strengths and to acknowledge the strengths of others. Men with a history of violence, once they are motivated for treatment, can be helped to monitor themselves for warning signs in their thinking ("stinking thinking") that might lead them down the road to trouble. Learning to empathize with others can be regarded as the culmination of the treatment effort, because once a person can put himself or herself in another's shoes, abusive behavior levels off. (Conversely, combat soldiers, for success in battle, are taught to dehumanize the enemy.) In the treatment group, men who are capable of empathy can successfully address relationship issues and learn fighting-fair strategies of assertive but not aggressive communication. In so doing, they will have successfully moved from work in the psychological to the social realm. The social realm involves interaction and relationships—problematic areas for men with a habit of communicating through using threats and violence to get their way.

At the societal or macrolevel, an original idea from New Zealand is to drastically increase spending on support services for battering men (Gibson 2007). Members of a group called the Tairawhiti Men against Violence are calling for a safe house or drop-in center for men. Then when men are banned from their homes or feel they are out of control, there would be a place for them to go for shelter and counseling.

Another intervention at the macrolevel involves tightening gun control laws and restricting the access to firearms by convicted batterers. This is a serious step in reducing rates of lethal violence. States that carefully limit access to guns by individuals under a restraining order have significantly lower rates of intimate partner homicide than do states without these laws. Karen Slovak (2008) in her survey of mental health social workers, found that they rarely asked about owning firearms when they were assessing clients for risk factors for suicide, accidents, homicide, and so on. Her recommendation is for specialized training for mental health professionals on the hazards of gun ownership. Since the overwhelming majority of murder-suicides involve a firearm, as do a majority of domestic homicides, stronger state laws are required to reinforce federal laws requiring that such weapons be removed from homes of domestic abusers.

CONCLUSION

In order to prevent homicides of both men and women in dangerous relationships, we need to take a realistic and balanced view of the true dynamics of woman battering. We also need to do more to place our change efforts onto the source of the problem which rests with the perpetrators of the abuse. As seen in the government data and systematic research on persons serving prison terms for killing their spouse or partner, the homicides were rooted in the violence itself. In most of these cases, a battered woman was killed, but in many other cases, it was the batterer himself.

The major part of the funding for domestic violence services is for victim protection, safe spaces, and counseling. Certainly, our sympathies are with the victim, and this support is vitally needed. But therapy for the victim alone may mean that one woman will achieve independence from her abuser for a time, but she still may not be safe. He, the former batterer, may still have visitation rights to the children following divorce. Some will use this power to intimidate and threaten their former wives. Still others will enter into new, abusive relationships. In the effort to save lives, therefore, batterer intervention is essential.

Admittedly, batterer treatment is not easy, especially when done in a group setting due to the preponderance of such clients who are decidedly unmotivated for treatment. Since the large majority of them are at the precontemplation stage of change, group facilitators will have a great deal of defensiveness and minimization to overcome. Treatment for batterers begins, as does all treatment, with establishing a relationship and motivating the offenders to work on issues related to the violence. Ideally, these batterer groups will be led by a male and female team so that both gender perspectives can be presented to the group. Treatment goals are to help the men unlearn violence and, if at all possible, to learn empathy and trust. To achieve these ends, confrontational or shaming techniques that further undermine the batterer's already precarious self-esteem must be avoided. The theoretical framework on which standard batterer intervention is based, as we have seen, is alien to the very participants the model was designed to serve. Instead of an approach based on ideology, we need an approach based on sound empirical research. We already know from such research on evidence-based practices that we must build a working relationship and meet individuals where they are before we can help them move from that point and beyond. The pioneers of the Duluth intervention model have gotten us off to a good start; the movers and shakers of this massive project, which includes much more than batterers' education, have brought victims, service providers, and law enforcement professionals together; sponsored national training; and enriched our knowledge concerning the dynamics of intimate partner violence. There is no need to discard the Duluth model, only to reconceptualize it based on the limited but worthwhile evidence that we now have about what works and what does not. It is time for a paradigm shift toward a more motivational, harm reduction approach that is tailored to individual problems and needs. Such a paradigm shift might entail broadening our perspectives about appropriate treatment while suspending our feminist belief systems (or at least removing them from the forefront of the treatment process) in favor of a paradigm built on a pragmatic, harm reduction approach geared toward reducing the harm to all parties.

This chapter has focused primarily on prevention of domestic homicide, mainly at the psychological level, through a focus on direct intervention with perpetrators of violence, who are also potential perpetrators of death by domestic violence. Since research tells us that most men who commit partner homicide have a pattern of escalating violence and use verbal threats, prevention at this earlier level of violence is apt to be highly effective. But we also recognize that simultaneously, we need to endorse programming throughout the school system to teach our children nonviolent ways of resolving conflict. Principles of restorative justice may be applied here and at the community level as well, to reinforce community standards of behavior.

Harm Reduction, Prevention Model

We conclude this book with our scheme for prevention of death by domestic violence, a multifaceted harm reduction model:

At the Biological Level

- Screen all clients for substance abuse and provide integrated treatment.
- Screen all clients for mental disorders and provide appropriate treatment for both substance and mental disorders simultaneously; refer for medication where appropriate.

At the Psychological Level

- Use motivational enhancement strategies to help batterers change and victims to adopt a safety plan.
- Screen for depression and suicidal ideation.
- Take a cognitive approach directed at irrational thinking associated with violence.
- Provide anger management and assertiveness training.
- Offer individual counseling for early childhood victimization and trauma from other causes.
- Help clients refrain from blaming victims—teach empathy.
- Help battered women from a stages-of-change model to protect themselves and their children.

At the Societal Level

- Establish school antiviolence programming with an emphasis on male mentoring.
- Develop school programs to teach principles of healthy relationships.
- Endorse media campaigns against intimate partner violence.
- During medical checkups, screen for firearms in the home, and emphasize the dangers in having firearms available, especially in households characterized by chronic conflict and/or heavy substance use.
- Screen for high-risk situations in hospitals, substance abuse treatment centers, and child welfare departments.
- Rely on criminal justice sanctions where appropriate.

- Draw on restorative justice practices for resolving conflict and protecting and healing victims.
- Establish safety structures for victims of violence, potential victims, and safe houses for men at risk of committing violence.

REFERENCES

Babcock, J., C. Green, and C. Robie. 2004. Does batterers' treatment work? A meta-analytic review of domestic violence treatment. *Clinical Psychology Review* 23, no. 8: 1023–53.

Bednar, S. 2001. Recovering strengths in batterers. Sidebar in *Counseling female offenders and victims: A strengths-restorative approach,* K. van Wormer, 174–76. New York: Springer.

Bennett, L.W. (2008). Batterer treatment approaches and effectiveness. In *Encyclopedia of interpersonal violence,* ed. C.M. Renzetti and J.L. Edleson. Thousand Oaks, CA: SAGE.

Bennett, L.W., C. Stoops, C. Call, and H. Flett. 2007. Program completion and re-arrest in a batterer intervention system.*Research on Social Work Practice* 17, no. 1: 42–54.

Dutton, D. 2007.*Rethinking domestic violence.* Vancouver, Canada: University of British Columbia Press.

Feminist Daily News. 2008. US Senate votes to increase funding for programs under Violence Against Women Act (VAWA). *Feminist Daily News Wire,* March 18. http://www.feminist.org/news/newsbyte/uswirestory.asp?id=10881 (accessed March 2008).

Gibson, M. 2007. Violent men need a safe house too. *Gisborne Herald,* November 23. http://www.gisborneherald.co.nz (accessed March 2008).

Hammond, W.R., D.J. Whitaker, J.R. Lutzker, J. Mercy, and P.M. Chin. 2006. Setting a violence prevention agenda at the Centers for Disease Control and Prevention. *Aggression and Violent Behavior* 11:112–19.

Heisterkamp, A. 2008. *Coaching boys into men.* Presentation at the University of Northern Iowa, Cedar Falls, January 28.

Jones, A.S., and E. Gondolf. 2001. Time-varying risk factors for reassault among batterer program participants.*Journal of Family Violence* 16, no. 4: 345–59.

Katz, J. 2006.*The macho paradox: Why some men hurt women and how all men can help.* Naperville, IL: Sourcebooks Trade.

Koss, M. 2000. Blame, shame, and community: Justice responses to violence against women. *American Psychologist* 55, no. 11: 1332–43.

Marano, H. 1993. Inside the heart of marital violence. *Psychology Today,* November/December: 50–53, 76–78, 91.

Miller, S.L., C. Gregory, and L.A. Iovanni. 2005. One size fits all? A gender-neutral approach to a gender-specific problem: Contrasting batterer treatment programs for male and female offenders.*Criminal Justice Policy Review* 16, no. 3: 336–59.

Miller, W.R., and S. Rollnick. 2002. *Motivational interviewing: Preparing people for change.* 2nd ed. New York: Guilford Press.

Pence, E. 1999. Some thoughts on philosophy. In *Coordinating community responses to domestic violence: Lessons from Duluth and beyond,* ed. M. Shepard and E. Pence, 25–40. Thousand Oaks, CA: SAGE.

Pence, E., and M. Paymar. 1993. *Education groups for men who batter: The Duluth model.* New York: Springer.

Pence, E., and M. Shepard. 1999. An introduction: Developing a coordinated community response. In *Coordinating Community response to domestic violence: Lessons from Duluth and beyond,* ed. M. Shepard and E. Pence, 3–23. Thousand Oaks, CA: SAGE.

Ritmeister, T. 1993. Batterers' programs, battered women's movement, and issues of accountability. In *Education groups for men who batter: The Duluth model,* ed. E. Pence and M. Paymar, 169–78. New York: Springer.

Roffman, R., J. Edleson, C. Neighbors, L. Mbilinyi, and D. Walker. 2008. The men's domestic abuse check-up: A protocol for reaching the nonadjudicated and untreated man who batters and who abuses substances. *Violence Against Women* 14:589–605.

Ronel, N., and R. Tim. 2003. Grace therapy: Meeting the challenge of group therapy for male batterers. *Clinical Social Work Journal* 31, no. 1: 63–80.

Scott, K. 2004. Stage of change as a predictor of attrition in a men's batterer program. *Journal of Family Violence* 19, no. 1: 37–47.

Shepard, M. 1993. Evaluation of domestic abuse intervention programs. In *Education groups for men who batter: The Duluth model,* ed. E. Pence and M. Paymar, 163–68. New York: Springer.

Shepard, M., and E. Pence, eds. 1999. *Coordinating community responses to domestic violence: Lessons from Duluth and beyond.* Thousand Oaks, CA: SAGE.

Simon, T.R., M. Anderson, M.P. Thompson, A.E. Crosby, G. Shelley, and J.J. Sacks. 2001. Attitudinal acceptance of intimate partner violence among U.S. adults. *Violence and Victims* 16, no. 2: 115–26.

Slovak, K. 2008. The "F" word: Is social work overlooking the topic of firearms? Slide presentation at the National Conference of Baccalaureate Program Directors. Destin, FL, March 5–8.

Sonkin, D.J. 2006. The male batterer: A twenty-year retrospective. The White Ribbon Campaign Europe. Unpublished paper. http://www.eurowrc.org/06.contributions/1.contrib_en/17.contrib.en.htm (accessed August 2008).

Stuart, G., J. Temple, and T.M. Moore. 2007. Improving batterer intervention programs through theory-based research. *Journal of the American Medical Association* 298, no. 5: 560–63.

van Wormer, K., and C. Bartollas. 2007. *Women and the criminal justice system.* 2nd ed. Boston: Allyn & Bacon.

van Wormer, K., and S. Bednar. 2002. Working with male batterers. *Families in Society: The Journal of Contemporary Human Services* 83:557–565.

van Wormer, K., and D.R. Davis. 2008. *Addiction treatment: A strengths perspective.* Belmont, CA: Cengage.

Viano, E.C. 2000. Restorative justice for victims offenders. *Corrections Today,* July: 132.

Zehr, H. 2002. *The little book of restorative justice.* Intercourse, PA: Good Books.

Index

About the Authors and Contributors

Katherine van Wormer, MSSW, Ph.D., a native of New Orleans, was active in the civil rights movements in the South and in Northern Ireland. From the late 1970s she has been actively involved in the women's movement and in promoting services for battered women. Today Dr. van Wormer is Professor of Social Work at the University of Northern Iowa. She has authored and co-authored 13 books, most recently *Women and the Criminal Justice System, Addiction Treatment: A Strengths Perspective,* and *Working with Female Offenders: A Gender-Sensitive Approach* (in press).

Albert R. Roberts, Ph.D., who died just as this book was being completed, was at the time of the writing a Professor of Social Work and Criminal Justice at Rutgers University, New Brunswick, New Jersey. Dr. Roberts conducted seminars and taught research methods, crisis intervention and brief treatment, program evaluation, family violence intervention, and juvenile justice. He was the founding editor of the Springer Series on Family Violence. He authored and edited over 30 books, including *The Social Worker's Desk Reference and Crisis Intervention Handbook* and *Battered Women and Their Families.*

Marilyn Peterson Armour, MSW, Ph.D., is Associate Professor, School of Social Work, at the University of Texas, Austin.

Carolyn A. Bradley, Ph.D., LCSW, LCADC, is Assistant Professor of Social Work at Monmouth University, West Long Branch, New Jersey.

Alissa Mallow, DSW, LCSW, is Assistant Professor, Department of Sociology and Social Work, at Lehman College, Bronx, New York.

Woochan S. Shim, MSW, Ph.D., is Assistant Professor, Department of Social Welfare, Daejeon University, South Korea.

Kelly Ward, Ph.D., LCSW, LCADC, is Associate Professor and BSW Program Director at Monmouth University, Long Branch, New Jersey.